BUILDING A PROFITABLE BUSINESS

The Proven, Step-by-step Guide to Starting and Running Your Own Business

2nd EDITION

Charles Chickadel & Greg Straughn

ADAMS MEDIA CORPORATION
Holbrook, Massachusetts

Acknowledgments: We would like to thank the many entrepreneurs and small business people whose experience and knowledge have made significant contributions to this publication. Special thanks to the Small Business Administration and the Bank of America, whose publications have informed and encouraged thousands of new business owners.

Published by
Adams Media Corporation
260 Center Street, Holbrook, MA 02343

ISBN: 1-55850-272-6

Printed in the United States of America

D E F G H I J

Library of Congress Cataloging-in-Publication Data
Chickadel, Charles
Building a profitable business : the proven, step-by-step guide to starting and running your own business / Charles Chickadel & Greg Straughn. — 2nd ed.
p.   cm.
Includes index.
ISBN: 1-55850-272-6
1. New business enterprises—Handbooks, manuals, etc. 2. Small business—Handbooks, manuals, etc. I. Straughn, Greg, 1957– . II. Title
HD62.5.C45   1994
658.1'1—dc20   93-45484
                                                                                               CIP

This publication is designed to provide accurate and authoritative information with regard to the subject matter covered. It is sold with the understanding that the publisher is not engaged in rendering legal, accounting, or other professional advice. If legal advice or other expert assistance is required, the services of a competent professional person should be sought.
— From a *Declaration of Principles* jointly adopted by a Committee of the American Bar Association and a Committee of Publishers and Associations

This book is available at quantity discounts for bulk purchases.
For information, call 1-800-872-5627
(in Massachusetts 617-767-8100).

Visit our home page at http://www.adamsmedia.com

CONTENTS

Marketing (continued)

Operations

Administration

Administration (continued)

Finance

Resources

List of Forms, Worksheets, and Checklists

Forms followed by (BP) are designed for use in creating your business plan.

Foreword

I truly believe small business drives the American Dream. But, too many new business owners get behind the wheel without knowing where they are going.

Now, more than ever, business owners need all the help they can get. The tough economy is forcing marginal businesses under in record numbers. Even in good times, about 80% of the U.S. small businesses don't make it to their fifth year.

But you don't have to become a statistic. Based on interviews with thousands of business owners and consultants, I am convinced more businesses fail due to a lack of information than a lack of money.

This is where *Building a Profitable Business* comes in. This easy-to-use package of business information can help you transform your dreams into a profitable small business.

Just knowing how to make something or sell something is not enough in today's complex business climate. Running a business requires a myriad of skills that most people don't learn on the job. Just knowing all the things you need to know is a major challenge for most small business owners.

Although there are thousands of business books out there (including my own), you would need scores of them to obtain all the information contained in this one. The authors save you time and money by distilling the most pertinent and critical information. There are checklists, tips, suggestions and forms to fill out. Dozens of handy worksheets provide a step-by-step path to solving the most common small business problems.The system is even fun to work with.

Running your own business is hard enough in today's world. But if you really want to succeed, the first secret of success is to admit you need help and get it as fast as you can.

Building A Profitable Business is an affordable, practical guide to setting up and running your business. Soon, these pages will become your most trusted advisor.

Here's to your success.

Jane Applegate

Nationally syndicated columnist and author of *Succeeding in Small Business: The 101 Toughest Problems and How to Solve Them.* (New American Library)

GETTING STARTED

START-UP ROADMAP

PASSPORT TO
SUCCESS

START-UP ROADMAP

How It Works

Congratulations on your decision to use **Building A Profitable Business.** Designed to help you plan, start, and operate your business, it is intended for all service, retail, consulting, professional and manufacturing businesses.

Here's how it works. **Building A Profitable Business** consists of three major components: this binder, containing the most comprehensive and usable information on starting and succeeding in a small business currently available, Expree Business Plan software, and an optional recordkeeping system that includes a file box, file folders, and labels.

This discussion is about how to get the most benefit from the information and tools in this binder (the *Filing & Recordkeeping* section discusses how to use the optional file box and folders).

Start-Up Roadmap

On the next two pages, you'll find the *Start-Up Roadmap* which guides you visually through the text, giving you an overview of small business: developing a plan, getting off to a good start, and operating a business successfully.

Following the *Roadmap* is the "Going Into Business Checklist," a guide to establishing your business legally and launching it successfully.

The Major Topics

The main text of **Building A Profitable Business** is divided into five major topics. These topics are

> *"Every venture is a new beginning."*
> T.S. Eliot

divided into five sections, each devoted to a key element of that topic. The sections contain the information you need to make sound business decisions, as well as examples to help you understand small business.

Forms, Worksheets, and Checklists

Among the most helpful elements of **Building A Profitable Business** are the worksheets, forms, and checklists at the end of each section for you to copy for your own use. Some of them help you gather information, others help you run your business on a daily basis, while still others help prevent costly errors. Preceding each form, worksheet, or checklist is an full explanation along with tips on how to get the most out of it. Many of these forms and worksheets can be used to create a business plan. This process is explained completely in the "Business Plan Guide."

Resource Directory Plus

Also in **Building A Profitable Business** is a *Directory of Small Business Resources* containing sources of free consulting, capital, tax advice, market research, and much more. It also contains a publications section with other valuable resources to help you succeed in your business.

Start-Up Roadmap

WHAT NEEDS TO BE DONE? (Find out about the rewards and demands of business, and whether your business can be successful)

Getting an Overview

Gain an overview of owning a business → Read *Passport To Success* (B-1)

Determine if the idea or the business is workable → Read the *Business Assessment* section and complete the forms (1-1)

Find out what you need to know to start the business → Read the *Business Plan* section for an overview of the most important aspects of the business of business (2-1)

WHERE IT IS IN BUILDING A PROFITABLE BUSINESS
(Page numbers shown in parentheses)

Developing Your Plan (Obtain the information necessary to document your decisions and plans)

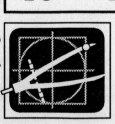

Determine legal structure and capitalization needed
(How the business will be organized and funded)
→ Read the remaining sections in **Business Development,** starting with *Business Organization* and complete the worksheets marked (BP) (3-1)

Develop a marketing plan
(How the business will make money)
→ Read the sections in **Marketing,** starting with *Marketing Plan,* and complete the worksheets marked (BP) (6-1)

Work out operational issues
(How the work will be done)
→ Read the sections in **Operations,** starting anywhere, and complete the worksheets marked (BP) (11-1)

Develop administrative practices
(How the business will be run)
→ Read the sections in **Administration,** starting anywhere, and complete the worksheets marked (BP) (16-1)

Develop financial systems
(How the money will be handled)
→ Read the sections in **Finance,** starting anywhere, and complete the worksheets marked (BP) (21-1)

Starting Out (Plan your business on paper, line up your capital sources, and take the necessary steps to launch your business)

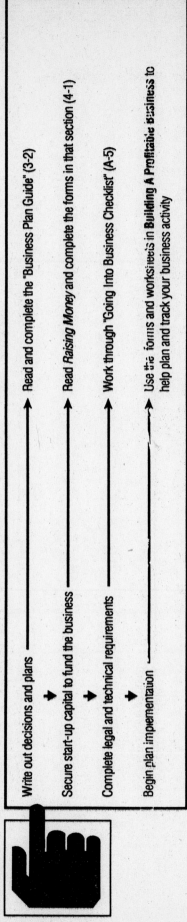

Write out decisions and plans → Read and complete the "Business Plan Guide" (3-2)

Secure start-up capital to fund the business → Read *Raising Money* and complete the forms in that section (4-1)

Complete legal and technical requirements → Work through "Going Into Business Checklist" (A-5)

Begin plan implementation → Use the forms and worksheets in **Building A Profitable Business** to help plan and track your business activity

Operating Your Business (Stay organized, focused on your business plan, and out of trouble as you build your business)

Maintain accurate and organized business records → Use **Building A Profitable Business** filing and organization system to maintain your business records

→ Use **Building A Profitable Business** forms to gather and store key information about your business

Continue to review and evaluate business activities → Re-read the *Promotion* section and use the forms in it to plan and implement your marketing, advertising, and publicity activities (9-1)

→ Re-read the *Accounting* section and use its forms to control your finances (21-1)

→ Re-read the *Taxes* section and use the forms in it to ensure compliance with tax and regulatory requirements (23-1)

→ Re-read the *Cash Management* and *Budgeting* sections and use the forms in them to manage your cash flow (24-1 & 25-1)

Get help when needed → Review **Resources** section for sources of assistance (26-1 & 27-1)

Tips for using the following form:

Note: You are encouraged to copy this form for your own use. Keep the unmarked original in a safe place and make copies of it to work from.

Going Into Business Checklist – The first part of this checklist shows the major legal and regulatory requirements applying to all businesses, and those applying specifically to businesses hiring employees and to corporations. The second part shows which activities, in addition to those mandated by law, are necessary for starting a new business. After each item is a reference in parentheses to the section containing more information on that topic. Use both parts of this checklist to ensure that you get your business started off right.

Use this checklist as a quick step-by-step guide for getting your business <u>officially</u> started. It is designed to help keep you out of trouble by alerting you to the various legal and regulatory responsibilities faced by new business owners. Some of the items below have section references in parentheses which indicate where to find further information on those subjects.

All Businesses

❏ If you are going to do business under a name other than your own, register this name by filing a Fictitious Business Name Statement with your County Clerk (*Business Organization*).

❏ If you are going to engage in business outside your county or form a corporation, check with the Secretary of State's office to determine if your business name is available.

❏ Call the City Tax Collector to see if you must register your business. If so, register it.

❏ Check with City and State Licensing Divisions to see if a license or permit is needed to conduct your business. Obtain any required licenses.

❏ Check with the local Zoning Department to determine if you can legally operate your business at your intended location. You'll need to know if the area you've selected is zoned to permit the kind of activity you plan to engage in.

❏ Apply for building permits if you plan to make structural improvements to your facility.

❏ Check with the State Tax Board to see if you need a Seller's Permit. Obtain a Seller's Permit, if required. If your state has a sales tax, and you resell merchandise, or sell your own products or services to end users, you will probably be required to charge and collect state sales taxes (*Taxes*).

❏ Apply for a Taxpayer's Identification Number (FEIN – Federal Employers Identification Number) from the IRS and check to see which tax forms you'll need ("Tax and Key Regulatory Requirements" in *Taxes*).

If Hiring Employees

❏ If you intend to hire employees, register with the State Employment Development Department (*Personnel*).

❏ If you become an employer, obtain and display state and federally mandated employee information (*Personnel*).

❏ Obtain Worker's Compensation Insurance if you hire employees (*Insurance*).

For Corporations Only

❏ If your business is going to operate as a corporation, prepare and file incorporation papers with the State Department of Corporations. You will also have to draw up Articles of Incorporation and Corporate By-laws as part of the incorporation process (*Business Organization*).

See other side for specific activities neccessary for starting a business.

This checklist contains the activities, in addition to those mandated by law, necessary for starting a new business. Cross off any not applicable to your business. Because every business is different, no attempt has been made to prioritize these items, many of which can be done simultaneously. They are presented in the order in which they are addressed in **Building A Profitable Business**. For best results, use this checklist in conjunction with the start-up schedule you develop for inclusion in your business plan. Simply assign dates for each of the items below. Together these forms will help keep your new business moving forward. Following each item is the section that contains information on that subject.

❑ Determine whether you're ready to start this business (*Business Assessment*).

❑ Do a feasibility study to assess the viability of this particular business (*Business Assessment*).

❑ Decide whether to operate as a sole proprietorship, partnership, or corporation (*Business Organization*).

❑ Begin writing out your business idea in the form of a business plan. You don't have to worry about what to write because as you complete each form, worksheet, and checklist in this system, you'll be creating the contents of your business plan – painlessly and automatically (*Business Plan*).

❑ Begin lining up sources to finance your venture (*Raising Money*).

❑ Set long-term and short-term goals for your business (*Goals, Motivation, & Training*).

❑ Develop a marketing strategy to achieve your business goals (*Marketing Plan*).

❑ Determine who your customers and competitors are (*Market Research*).

❑ Design and order stationery and business cards (*Promotion*).

❑ Plan your sales and distribution strategy (*Sales & Distribution*).

❑ Plan your advertising, sales promotion, and publicity activities (*Promotion*).

❑ Develop price strategies and compute your break-even point (*Product Development*).

❑ Develop customer service policies (*Customer Service*).

❑ Line up suppliers and order start-up inventory and supplies (*Purchasing*).

❑ Develop operating procedures (*Procedures*).

❑ Acquire the necessary equipment and machinery (*Equipment*).

❑ Choose a business location and negotiate and execute the lease (*Facilities*).

❑ Develop security measures to protect your business assets (*Facilities*).

❑ Determine the appropriate insurance coverage needed to cover the risks inherent in your business and select an insurance agent or broker (*Insurance*).

❑ Apply for the necessary copyrights, trademarks, or patents necessary to protect your intellectual property (*Legal*).

❑ Plan your staffing requirements and hire the necessary employees (*Personnel*).

❑ Set up files and other recordkeeping systems (*Filing & Recordkeeping*).

❑ Set up accounting and bookkeeping procedures (*Accounting*).

❑ Familiarize yourself with financial statements and their use (*Accounting*).

❑ Choose a bank and open a business account (*Banking*).

❑ Familiarize yourself with local, state, and federal tax requirements and submit the required documents (*Taxes*).

❑ Set up cash management procedures for conserving cash (*Cash Management*).

❑ Set up expense and income forecasts (*Budgeting*).

PASSPORT TO SUCCESS

What is Success?

Success has been defined as "the progressive attainment of a worthy goal." While this is a good general definition, each one of us has our own specific idea about what success means to us.

What does success mean to you? For some people it means status, prestige, and respect; for others it means fame and celebrity; and for others it means power – the ability to influence and command others. But regardless of whatever else it entails, for most people their definition of success includes financial independence.

Just what is financial independence? Like success, financial independence means something different to each of us. A better question might be: "What amount of income would make you feel financially independent?"

For some people that might be $25,000 per year, for others it might take $250,000, while for others it might take $2,500,000. The important thing isn't the amount of money itself. What really matters is making enough money for you to feel financially independent.

The Superhighway to Success

There are a number of ways to become financially independent. When you try to visualize financially successful people, images of big business tycoons, corporate lawyers, entertainers, sports stars, and super salespeople may come to mind.

But in reality, 75% of all self-made millionaires became wealthy through owning their own businesses. And so can you. Today there are over one million millionaires in America. Business ownership is truly the superhighway to success.

The Roadblock to Success

Because the vast majority of financially independent people have achieved their success through owning their own businesses, it isn't surprising that so many people have started down the superhighway to business ownership and financial security.

But this superhighway has a huge roadblock on it. As a result, most of the one million new businesses started each year don't survive long enough to make their owners financially independent.

According to the U.S. Department of Commerce, over 80% of all new businesses fail within the first five years — and about half of them don't even make it through the first year.

The U.S. Small Business Administration (SBA) says that the reason for 92% of these failures is lack of business experience and expertise. That's the chief roadblock to the success of any business.

Most people who go into business for themselves are usually pretty good at what they do. And they think that if they provide a good product or service, their business will flourish.

That's not necessarily the case. Contrary to this "better mousetrap" myth, providing a good product or service isn't guaranteed to bring a hoard of eager buyers beating a path to your door.

Doing a good job is the hallmark of a good employee. A successful business owner, on the other hand, has to provide a good product or service _and_ understand how the business works.

A clear example of the importance of business expertise is this quote from an SBA brochure on Venture Capital:

> "Most venture capital firms concentrate primarily on the... firm's management. They feel that even mediocre products can be successfully manufactured, promoted, and distributed by an experienced, energetic management group."

How to Get Around the Roadblock

As you can see from the quote above, the two important keys to business success are experience and energy. The reason experience is so important is that it teaches so many valuable lessons. Once these lessons are learned, a business owner is far less likely to make the kinds of serious business errors that lead to the failure of so many new businesses.

Understanding how business works is one way to make sure your business doesn't become just another statistic. In order to succeed in business, you have to do what the failures didn't do: acquire the knowledge that successful business people have discovered for themselves through trial and error.

But you don't have to go through the costly, painful process of trial and error learning. You can prepare yourself for business success by learning all the activities that go into making a business successful, and by making sure each of them is handled properly.

The other key that determines business success is energy. Energy for business comes from self-motivation. Highly motivated people are successful because their enthusiasm for what they're doing has a positive influence on everyone around them. A high level of motivation also creates excitement, giving a person huge reserves of physical energy, enabling them to accomplish even more.

From rags to riches in one's own business is a popular version of the American Dream.

You'll Be Wearing Many Hats

The first thing to realize about the importance of business experience is that regardless of the type of business, the owner is usually going to have to perform a wide variety of functions in addition to being the boss.

A new business owner is often the only employee. This means the owner may have to act as a salesperson, bookkeeper, production worker, secretary, purchasing agent, and customer service representative from time to time.

In order to be successful in business you'll have to know which activities are necessary for your particular business and make sure each of these tasks is being handled competently.

Not all the hats you'll be wearing are going to fit well. So don't neglect a business task because you can't or don't want to handle it. You can either learn to do it yourself, or you can hire someone to do it for you. If you're not good at math, hire a part-time bookkeeper.

The Importance of the Right Attitude

While knowing the business of business is necessary for success, it isn't the only thing you need. The right attitude is equally important – some experts say that it's even more important.

Each of us is somewhat different. We each have our own opinions, beliefs, likes, and dislikes. Yet one thing that all successful business people have in common is their attitude. They're highly motivated. They know they can get the job done. They know they'll succeed. That makes them very positive about themselves and their businesses.

Courage isn't the absence of fear, but rather acting in spite of it.

How You Can Get the Right Attitude

The right attitude is the winner's attitude. It's a can-do attitude. We all start life with this attitude. Just think about how many times a baby falls down, then gets up, falls down again, then gets up, again and again until it finally learns to walk.

When we were small children, we had this attitude, but over the years our parents and teachers, who in trying to protect us, continually told us "No" and "You can't do that." They meant well, but in trying to keep us out of harm's way, they didn't realize these admonishments were also causing us to doubt ourselves and as a result, lose self-confidence.

Now as adults, we need to regain that self-confidence. We need to feel positive about ourselves and our chances once again. Fortunately it's not that hard if you're willing to take on a few new habits. As an added benefit, these new habits will not only help you become successful, but they'll also help you feel better about yourself.

In order to get the winner's attitude, here's what you have to do:

■ **Expect success.** Experts in motivation say that 85% of success is based on mental attitudes, so keep yours positive. Look for the opportunity in every situation. View setbacks as stepping stones rather than obstacles. Keep your eye on your goal. Don't be sidetracked by circumstances; keep working your plan.

■ **See yourself as successful.** Form a clear mental picture of yourself attaining your goals. Pictures are far more powerful than words, so create a mental picture of yourself as already successful. See yourself enjoying the kind of success you want. And try to experience the feelings you'll have when you meet your business and personal goals.

■ **Prepare yourself for success.** Keep informed about your field and about business in general. Read positive books and magazines. Listen to success-oriented tapes at home and in your car. Attend seminars and workshops.

■ **Associate with positive people.** Your reference group determines your success. So spend your time with winners and get rid of the losers in your life. There are a number of organizations where you can find success-oriented people: Chambers of Commerce, Toastmaster groups, trade associations, and many other organizations attract dynamic people. Choose at least one that suits you, join it, and get active in it.

■ **Act like a winner.** Positive thinking and positive talk (to yourself as well as to others) are the ways to stay mentally healthy, just as positive health habits are the way to stay physically healthy. Use your body and mind to build the energy needed for the efforts required for success. Get motivated and stay motivated.

Habits Are the Key to Success

Everyone has habits. The difference between someone who succeeds and someone who fails is the kind of habits they have. Bad habits are easy to form, but hard to live with. Good habits are hard to form, but easy to live with – and they lead to success.

Failures generally find it difficult to sacrifice the immediate pleasure bad habits may offer. That's why they don't accomplish much. Successful people, on the other hand, realize that success depends on them. They're willing to put their long-term goals ahead of short term pleasures by cultivating the habits that lead to success.

The fact is that no white knight is going to come to your rescue and make your life just the way you want it to be. If you're going to become successful, you're going to have to do it yourself. This means developing the self-discipline to replace your bad habits with good habits.

Fortunately that's easier than it sounds. You don't have to change overnight. It's mostly a matter of gradual improvements. Each day that you do something toward your goals, you're building better habits. And each time you say "No" to some waste of your time or money, you're building better habits too. Remember that winners are in control of their habits, while losers are controlled by theirs.

Even though there's a vast difference between the rewards of winners and losers, the actual difference in performance is often very small. Sometimes only a few hundredths of a second is the difference between the glory of an Olympic victory and the obscurity of an also-ran.

The major difference between winners and losers is consistency. Winners are consistently just a little bit better. They keep at it and they keep trying to improve.

So aim to become a little better each day – do something toward your goals. And in a short amount of time, you'll be amazed at how much you've accomplished and how "lucky" you've become. Keep at it; don't be discouraged by set-backs. Persistence is self-discipline in action. It's also the measure of your belief in yourself.

The Superhighway to Success leads to financial independence and self-satisfaction.

You Can Do It

Millions of people have already started successful businesses. Many of them overcame severe hardships and handicaps. Are you too old? Col. Sanders was collecting Social Security when he started his fried chicken empire. Do you have money problems? H.L. Hunt was a bankrupt cotton farmer before becoming a billionaire in the oil business.

No time? Not enough education? Handicapped? You're not alone. Successful businesses have been started by people with all these problems – and worse!

It all boils down to your motivation and your business savvy. You can measure your motivation by your commitment to your business.

If you're committed to making your business successful and you make the effort to prepare yourself with the necessary business skills, you're bound to succeed – provided you stay at it.

So get yourself ready for business success. Be clear about your goals and get motivated to accomplish them. Learn as much as you can about business. Use **Building A Profitable Business** to help you keep yourself and your business organized. And do something every day toward making your dream come true. Millions have already done it. So can you. Start now.

BUSINESS DEVELOPMENT

BUSINESS ASSESSMENT

BUSINESS PLAN

BUSINESS
ORGANIZATION

RAISING MONEY

GOALS, MOTIVATION &
TRAINING

BUSINESS ASSESSMENT

Why Are You Starting Your Business?

In *The Small Business Bible*, Paul Resnik calls the ability to make honest assessments about oneself and one's business one of the "make-or-break" factors that determines whether a small business succeeds or fails. The first thing to assess is yourself: why are you starting the business, what strengths do you bring to it, and what do you hope to get out of it?

There are many reasons for starting a business, but some of them are more likely to lead to success than others. The desire for accomplishment is much more likely to result in business success than a desire to escape a currently unpleasant situation. Here are some of the most common reasons given for starting a business along with a brief discussion of each:

"I want to be my own boss." This can be an excellent reason if you want to be able to show what you can do without someone else holding you back. It's important to remember that when you're your own boss, you have to motivate and manage yourself – there won't be anyone else around to tell you what to do, how to do it, or when to do it. Before starting a business, you have to determine whether you have the necessary discipline for self-management.

"I want financial independence." Since most self-made millionaires become wealthy through ownership of their own businesses, this may seem like a good reason. But the other side of the coin is that it often takes a considerable amount of time for a business to become profitable, and many businesses never do. So, while business ownership may be a good vehicle for creating financial independence, if

you're hoping to "get rich quick," you could be setting yourself up for disappointment.

"I want to use my skills and knowledge more fully." Owning your business gives you a great opportunity to focus your efforts on the things that you're best at, so you have a chance to really shine. At the same time, in order to keep the business going, new business owners usually have to do many things they'd prefer not to do. This often makes it difficult for them to spend as much time as they'd like doing the things they enjoy most, unless they have someone else doing the things they'd rather not do.

"I want total creative freedom." When you're in business for yourself, you will have total creative freedom. But how long you stay in business will depend on the degree that what you do finds a market. No matter how creative you are, unless you give your customers what they want, they'll go elsewhere. Successful business owners find a way to express their creativity within the demands of the marketplace.

"I don't like policy and procedure." Dislike of paperwork and rules is a common trait, and the wise business person keeps busywork to a minimum. Business success depends to a large degree, however, on doing thing in a consistent way. Franchises, the businesses with the highest success rate, have the most highly developed systems and the most written policies and procedures designed to save them time and money. Successful independent businesses follow their lead.

"I don't work well with others." Most business activity involves working with other people. There are many situations in business that require you to interact with people under stressful conditions: dealing with irate customers, negotiating with suppliers, and hiring and training employees are just a few of the most common. If you have a hard time getting along with people on the job, you may have difficulty building the necessary team to make your business successful.

What Kind of Business Person Are You?

Every successful business owner plays at least three roles: technician, manager, and entrepreneur. The technician is an expert in the particular business and how it operates. The manager is responsible for the crucial elements necessary to make any business viable: marketing, finance, administration, and personnel management. The entrepreneur is an innovator for whom the business is a way to realize a vision.

Because it's rare for one person to be able to play all these roles equally well, a person going into business must know which parts of the business they can handle themselves and which parts they're going to need help with. If your technical knowledge is incomplete, you'll need to either acquire the necessary skills, bring on a knowledgeable partner, hire a key employee, or engage an experienced consultant.

Even though you can find others to compensate for any technical or managerial shortcomings you may have, the one role you ought to assume yourself is that of entrepreneur. An entrepreneur is a goal setter, a risk taker, and a decision maker. Entrepreneurs take charge of situations rather than hoping that things will somehow work out. They are constantly asking themselves how they can use their current circumstances to achieve their goals.

Does this sound like you? If it does, you're likely to have what it takes to make your business successful; if not, ask yourself what strengths you bring to the business. Even if you're excellent at what you do, unless you possess some entrepreneurial traits, like enthusiasm and persistence, you're apt to find running your own business more troublesome than rewarding.

The following questionnaire can help you decide if you have what it takes to be successful in your own business.

Self-Assessment
Take an Objective Look at Yourself

The most important factor for success or failure in a small business is you, the business owner. While you can't always control what happens to your business, you are responsible for how you respond to it. That's why it's so important for you to take a close look at yourself. The following questions will help you learn whether or not you're cut out for business ownership.

Do You Have What It Takes to Make Your Business Successful?

Business experts have identified a number of traits that indicate if a person is likely to become successful in their own business. The more "Yes" answers you have to the questions below, the more likely you have what it takes to make your business successful. Each question is followed by a discussion of why that particular trait is important.

Yes No

❑ ❑ **Are you a self-starter?** Successful business owners are always trying to make things happen, they don't wait around for the phone to ring, or to be told what to do next.

❑ ❑ **Do you get along with different kinds of people?** Even the smallest business brings you into contact with different kinds of people: customers, employees, suppliers, and bureaucrats. The larger your business gets, the more people you'll have to deal with.

❑ ❑ **Do you have a positive attitude?** With all the ups and downs in the business world, an optimistic outlook is a necessity. You have to be able to view each setback as a stepping stone to your eventual success.

❑ ❑ **Do you like to make your own decisions?** One of the major reasons for business failure is poor decisions. And procrastination is the main obstacle to good decision-making. In a successful business, important decisions are made on a daily basis, not put off.

Yes No

☐ ☐ **Do you enjoy competition?** The business world is highly competitive and it's getting even more so. Tomorrow's winners will be those who don't mind going up against the competition to prove who's the best.

☐ ☐ **Do you have willpower and self-discipline?** When you're your own boss, it's vital that you be able to motivate yourself. You won't have someone else looking over your shoulder to urge you along.

☐ ☐ **Do you plan ahead?** Probably the most important ability necessary for business success is planning. Going into business with detailed plans increases the likelihood of business success.

☐ ☐ **Do you get things done on time?** If you don't, it means you're probably disorganized. Good organizational skills and time management are crucial to business success.

☐ ☐ **Can you take advice from others?** Nobody knows it all and nobody has the time or money to make every mistake on their own. Being open to the wisdom and experience of others is the hallmark of a leader. People who listen spend more time doing what works, and less time doing what doesn't.

☐ ☐ **Are you adaptable to changing conditions?** Constant change is the only certainty in today's business world. Successful business people view change as an opportunity, not as a threat.

☐ ☐ **Are you prepared to work 12 to 16 hours a day, six days a week, and holidays, if necessary?** Overnight successes in business are few and far between. In the beginning, you'll have to do whatever is necessary to get your business launched successfully. After you've been in business for a while, you may find yourself fondly recalling your old "9 to 5 grind."

To get where you want to go, you have to know where you're starting from.

Yes No

☐ ☐ **Do you have the physical and emotional energy to run a business?** Operating your own business can be much more draining than working for someone else because you have to handle all the pressures and solve all the problems. Everything is up to you.

☐ ☐ **Are you prepared to lower your standard of living for months or years?** It takes months, sometimes years, for a business to start making a profit. Can you arrange your life so that you can live without a steady salary for as long as it takes to launch your business successfully.

☐ ☐ **Are you prepared to lose your savings?** If you're not willing to risk your own money in your venture, you should probably begin questioning your confidence in the venture and your commitment to it.

☐ ☐ **Would you decide against starting this business if you knew your chances of staying in business for two years were less than 50-50?** These are the actual odds for success and failure in a new business. But not every business starts with the same odds. Those businesses started by people with business experience and expertise have a far greater chance of success, while those started by owners with little or no experience or expertise have a far greater chance of failing.

☐ ☐ **Will you have the support of your family and/or spouse?** Without support at home, running a business can become like fighting a war on two fronts at once.

The Old Pro Says:

"Starting your own business is more than just creating a job for yourself."

What's in It for You

Everyone starting a business begins with certain expectations. Being clear about those expectations in the beginning helps you see if that business can provide what you want.

Some of the things you want out of your business will be intangible – like a feeling of accomplishment or the sense of independence that comes from being your own boss.

In addition to these intangibles, most new business owners also expect financial rewards. In many cases these expectations are realistic, but in others they're not. It's amazing the number of people who believe they are going to become independently wealthy just by having an idea. In order to make money, ideas have to be turned into products, which must be sold. Success doesn't just happen, it takes hard work.

The following questions will help you clarify the financial considerations related to starting a new business. Use this information to evaluate each of your business ideas to see how the financial return on your time and money compares to the return you'd get investing your money and working for someone else.

If the total amount in the last question is greater than what you can realistically expect from your business, are you willing to do without the additional income just to be your own boss, knowing that it could take years for your business investment to pay off – if it ever does? For many people, being a business owner means more than just the financial return. They'd willingly take a pay cut to be self-employed. Others, however, need to know that their investment in a business will pay off at least as well as an investment made elsewhere.

Another thing to keep in mind is that when you make an investment in your business, you're also making an investment in yourself. While it's hard to put a dollar value on character development and the business experience you'll gain, these important results of business ownership shouldn't be ignored as you decide what's in it for you.

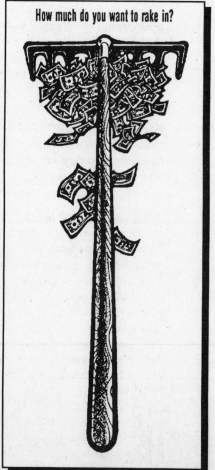

How much do you want to rake in?

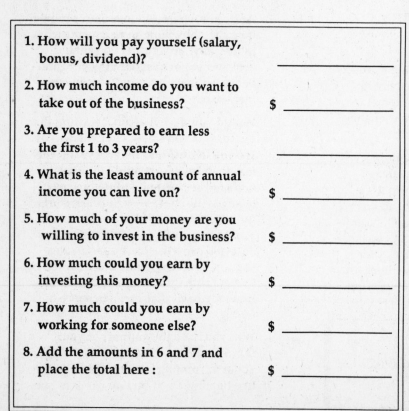

1. How will you pay yourself (salary, bonus, dividend)? _____

2. How much income do you want to take out of the business? $ _____

3. Are you prepared to earn less the first 1 to 3 years? _____

4. What is the least amount of annual income you can live on? $ _____

5. How much of your money are you willing to invest in the business? $ _____

6. How much could you earn by investing this money? $ _____

7. How much could you earn by working for someone else? $ _____

8. Add the amounts in 6 and 7 and place the total here : $ _____

Business Assessment

Along with assessing your own suitability to go into business, you should also make an objective assessment of the business itself. Ideas for a new business can come from a number of sources. Many new businesses are started by people who worked in the same field for someone else. Other businesses are started by owners who did detailed analyses to determine what business was particularly "hot." And some business ideas just seem to come "out of the blue."

But regardless of where the business idea came from, you should assess its strengths and weaknesses. The time to get answers to all your questions is <u>before</u> you have invested your time and money. Gathering all the information you need before you invest a lot of money or quit your job to start the business will help guard against costly disappointments.

Once you've determined you have what it takes to start and succeed in your own business, you still need to take an objective look at your business idea.

Is This Business Right for You?

Even highly motivated entrepreneurs with business experience need to answer to this question. The more "yes" answers you have to the questions below, the more likely this business is right for you.

<u>Yes</u> <u>No</u>

❏ ❏ **Are you truly interested in this particular business?** If you're not really interested in the business, but think it would be a great way to make some quick money, forget it. Without a real commitment to your business, you probably won't have the perseverance to stick with it until it succeeds.

❏ ❏ **How much time do you have to run the business?** Generally, launching a business is a time consuming job. If you can't run it yourself, you'll have to hire someone to do it for you. Or you may be able to start out working part-time from your home.

<u>Yes</u> <u>No</u>

❏ ❏ **Do you know which skills are critical to the success of your kind of business?** Knowing this is essential. If you don't know, it's better to hold off starting the business until you do. Interview people who are already successful in this kind of business.

❏ ❏ **Do you have these skills?** If not, you can get them by working for someone else in a similar business until you do. Classes may be available at your local community college for some types of business.

❏ ❏ **Does this business use your skills and abilities effectively?** If you're not spending most of your time doing what you're good at and what you like to do, you probably won't be satisfied for long.

❏ ❏ **Can you find employees and/or consultants that have the expertise you lack?** If not, you will have to obtain the needed expertise yourself.

❏ ❏ **Does this business meet your career goals?** Is this business your life's work, a stepping stone, or a detour? The closer it comes to matching your career objectives, the better you're likely to do in it.

❏ ❏ **How will the business affect your family?** Running a business without your spouse's support is a prescription for failure. Let your family know what kind of changes the business may have in your family life and find out how they feel about it.

❏ ❏ **Are you willing and able to obtain the necessary information about this business, either by getting it yourself or by paying someone to get it for you?** This involves getting the answers to the questions in this section and in the *Market Research* section. Even if you feel you don't have the time to answer all these questions, answer them anyway so you can discover potential problems before putting your money at risk. If you're not willing to get this information yourself and can't afford to hire someone to get it for you, you'll be entering the business blindly.

Can Your Business Succeed?

Now it's time to find out how likely your business is to succeed. You'll need to answer "yes" to at least one of the following three questions for your business to have any chance of success.

<u>Yes</u> <u>No</u>

❏ ❏ **Does this business serve a presently unmet need or want?** The surest way to business success is discovering a latent want and satisfying it. As Henry Kaiser said, "Find a need and fill it."

❏ ❏ **Does this business serve an existing market where demand exceeds supply?** When existing businesses can't keep up with the demand for a particular product or service, a new business in this area should meet with success, if operated properly.

❏ ❏ **Can this business compete successfully with existing businesses because of an "advantageous situation," such as better price, location, etc.?** These days competition is so intense that a "me too" business isn't going to make it for long. There has to be a definite reason why customers would buy from you instead of your competitors.

Does Your Business Idea Have Any Fatal Flaws?

So far your business idea has proven to be sound. Now it's time to look closer to uncover any hidden problems looming on the horizon, to discover any "fatal flaws" or potential problems that could sabotage your business. A "yes" answer to one or more of the following questions indicates your business has little chance of success.

<u>Yes</u> <u>No</u>

❏ ❏ **Are there any factors, such as restrictions, monopolies, or shortages, that make the materials or employees you need for your business unavailable ?** You can't assume what you need for your business will always be available at affordable prices. Make sure you can get everything you need <u>before</u> you start your business.

> *"You look at any giant corporation, and I mean the biggies, and they all started with a guy with an idea, doing it well."*
>
> Irv Robbins, Co-Founder
> Baskin-Robbins Ice Cream

<u>Yes</u> <u>No</u>

❏ ❏ **Does your business create any potentially damaging environmental effects?** Any business that threatens the environment is going to run into opposition. Government regulations, negative publicity, court injunctions, and class action lawsuits are just some of the many difficulties such a business could face.

❏ ❏ **Are there any major risks, such as health hazards, patent or trademark infringements, or potential illegalities, associated with this business?** Lawsuits are expensive to defend against and generally take years to settle even when you're in the right. So make sure your business idea doesn't start with regulatory or legal liabilities.

❏ ❏ **Are any of these risks beyond your control?** Risks that can't be controlled are going to end up controlling the business. So if you can't control the risks, forget about this particular business idea and look for another one with fewer perils.

If your business idea has survived the assessments so far, congratulations. You'll find information in the following sections that you need to help make your business the success you want it to be.

But if your business idea didn't make it through the tests above, be grateful that you've saved yourself a lot of time and money. And now you can begin the process again with another business idea — one with more chance of success.

BUSINESS PLAN

The Critical Difference

Business success often seems a matter of luck, or even magical, to many inexperienced business owners. They don't realize that there is usually a critical difference between those businesses that succeed and those that fail. Often that make-or-break difference is a business plan. Without a plan, a business can easily flounder and fall victim to poor business decisions resulting from a lack of planning. A well prepared business plan serves at least three critical functions:

■ **Getting the business started off right.** A business plan serves as the foundation for any new business. It helps a business get off to the right start and helps it stay on track. Putting together a business plan forces you to think strategically about your business. It allows you to plan your business on paper before you've committed your time and money to it. Having to consider each of the practical matters that goes into starting and operating the business may reveal crucial details that you might not have considered. Unless you know how each part of the business is going to function before you begin operations, you're taking a chance that some unforeseen detail could sabotage your entire effort. Besides being useful for anticipating and avoiding problems, a business plan is also useful for uncovering unanticipated opportunities.

■ **A blueprint for success.** A business plan is as essential to building a business as a blueprint is for building a house. In fact a business plan is the blueprint for your

business's operations and growth. It details your business objectives and how you intend to accomplish them. Setting down in writing what you are going to achieve shows you clearly where you need to focus your time, energy, and capital. Once your business is in operation, the business plan serves as a monitor to help you gauge your success by giving you a convenient way to compare your actual results to your plans.

■ **Raising Money.** A business plan is essential for raising money. One of the most common reasons for business failure is under-capitalization. Businesses need financing to take them from the initial business idea to success in the marketplace. Often the amount needed is beyond the resources of the business owner. Without a business plan it is virtually impossible to raise capital for the business from outside sources. Lenders and investors are more interested in the management team than in the product or marketing opportunity. They'll want to know if you have the knowledge and ability to make the plan work, and what makes you and your business unique — what you have that no one else does.

A business plan should be written specifically to the audience for whom it is intended. When a business is in the formative stages, the business plan should be written to aid you in making sound decisions for getting the business up and running. This kind of plan is designed to help you put the business together piece by piece.

Once the business is operating, the business plan should be written to convey your vision to employees and others who are helping you achieve your dream. It should provide a step by step recipe for what is going to be done and who will do it.

Any time a plan is needed to raise capital, it should be written with the lender or investor in mind. It needs to convey your enthusiasm and optimism about the anticipated success of your business without making unwarranted claims. And it also has to explain how and when the lenders or investors will be paid off.

The Old Pro says:

"When you fail to plan, you plan to fail."

Your Business Plan

Writing a business plan may seem like a lot of work. Which may explain why so few business people actually develop one — and why so few new businesses succeed.

To make it easier for the new business owner, we've developed a simple way to put together a business plan. Using the "Business Plan Guide" below, you can create a business plan the same way you might eat an elephant – one bite at a time.

While there's no one "right way" to prepare a business plan, the following business plan outline is suitable for any business. For each necessary element of the plan, you'll find a reference to a worksheet or form that helps you to assemble the necessary information. The worksheets whose information is intended for use in your business plan are indicated by the symbol (BP) to the right of the worksheet's title.

You won't have to waste time figuring out what to write under each heading. All you do is take the appropriate information from the worksheet shown in parentheses following each heading and

place it in the proper order in your plan. Then you merely have to write out the information in your own words. Since you'll know exactly what information to put under each heading, you'll have the plan finished before you know it.

Using this guide you can create a business plan for either of two purposes:

1. **Internal or personal uses**. If you intend to use your plan as a guide for your personal activities in the business or to communicate your plans to a limited number of employees, all you need to do is complete the forms marked with the (BP). By gathering these documents in one place you will have a outline of the critical elements needed to start and manage your business. You can skip the first five sections of the following outline.

2. **External Uses**. If you intend to use your business plan to raise equity capital or get loans you will need to do a few, simple additional steps. In addition to gathering these documents you will need to add some introductory information and have the document typed. If you intend to use your plan for raising money follow the complete outline starting on page 2-4 and is illustrated on page 2-6.

Planning your business in advance helps you prevent problems and discover opportunities.

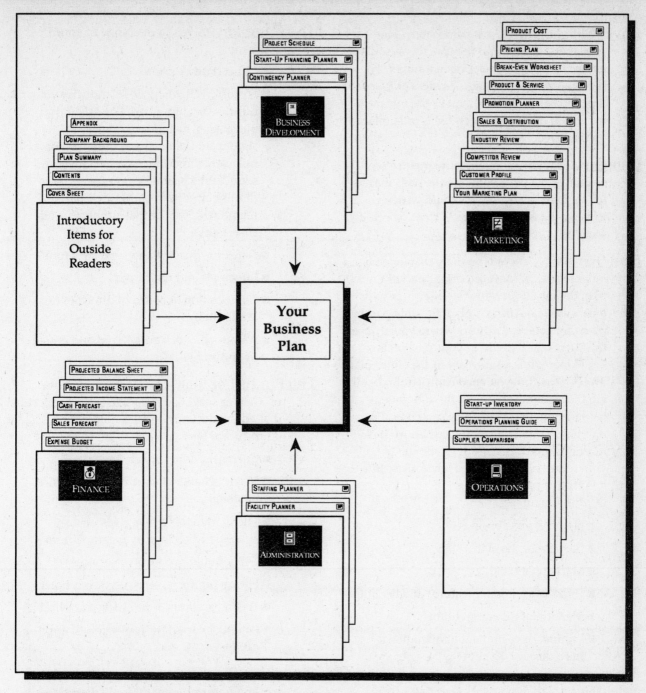

The illustration above gives a visual representation of how the elements for your business plan come together from the various sections of this manual.

This "Business Plan Guide" on the next three pages follows the organization of most business plans. The underlined bold headings indicate the major sections of the plan, while the bold-faced headings represent subsections. The bulleted items represent important information that should be included in that section or subsection and the appropriate worksheet for each item is shown in parentheses.

To start putting your business plan together, complete the information required by each worksheet. As you complete the worksheets, use a loose-leaf binder to keep them organized. Once you've competed and organized all the worksheets, convert the information from them into prose form and write the necessary transitions. Plans intended for external audiences should be neatly typed. Using a computer-based word processing program makes it much easier to put together and revise your business plan.

<u>Cover Sheet.</u> Include the business name, the principals' names, and the contact person's name, address, and telephone number. To personalize plans going to lenders or investors, the name of the person or organization for whom the plan is intended is often placed on this page.

<u>Contents.</u> Provide a conveniently organized outline of the plan, showing the page numbers for each major section. It should be designed to make it easy for readers to locate specific sections. Avoid excessive detail.

<u>Plan Summary.</u> Though no more than one page long, this is the most important part of the plan because it presents the essence of your business idea. And it is often the only part of a plan that gets read. This is where you arouse the interest and desire of your recipients to know more. It is a summary of the entire plan. The information you need comes from distilling the contents of each of the subsequent sections into one or two key sentences. Preparing this section helps you focus on what is most important because it forces you to boil your entire plan down to a few concise but descriptive paragraphs.
<u>Do this section last.</u>

- Name of your business
- Purpose of the plan
- Market potential
- Significant product features and benefits
- Mention of the competition
- Product development or operational milestones
- Management qualifications of the principals
- Summary of financial projections
- Amount of financial assistance requested
- Earnings projections and potential returns to investors (showing how any borrowed or invested money will be paid back)

<u>The Company.</u> Gives an overview of your company.

- General description
- History. Tell when, how, and why your business was founded. For existing businesses, include a summary of significant financial and organizational milestones and the major products and services the business has offered. Also discuss important employees, banking relationships, principal suppliers, and customers
- Date of formation and legal structure
- Principals and their roles
- Composition of board of directors (if applicable)
- Amount of stock authorized and issued (if applicable)

<u>The Product or Service.</u> In presenting your product or service, emphasize the major factors that will make your business successful. ("Product or Service Worksheet")

- Current product or service
- Major benefits of your product, service, or store
- The unique thing that gives you a strategic advantage over competitors
- Other initial products or services
- Future products, services, or locations
- Technical status of product (if applicable)
- Patent or copyright protection (if applicable)

<u>Marketing Plan.</u> Describes who your customers are, and how you intend to sell, distribute, and promote your product, service, or business.

Marketing Research
- Industry description ("Industry Review Worksheet")
- Target market size and composition ("Customer Profile Worksheet")
- Competition ("Competitor Review Worksheet")

Sales & Distribution ("Sales & Distribution Planning Guide")
- Type and number of salespeople
- Distribution channels

Promotion
- Marketing strategy ("Your Marketing Plan")
- Marketing activities and expected results ("Promotion Planner")

Pricing
- Pricing policies ("Pricing Plan Worksheet")
- Cost breakdown for components ("Product Cost Worksheet")
- Break-even analysis ("Break-Even Worksheet")

Projections ("Sales Forecast")
- Annual sales forecasts by month

Production / Operating Plan.
Describe how your business will operate, how the work will flow, and what you'll do to ensure the work will be done efficiently, cost-effectively and on time.

Schedule
- A development schedule that outlines what needs to be done and when it will be completed. Identify all critical activities and how they will be handled.

Ordinary Operations ("Operations Planning Guide")
- Days and hours of operation
- Field service and support
- Describe how the product is produced

Equipment ("Equipment & Supplies Needed Worksheet")
- Equipment and supplies needed

Suppliers ("Supplier Comparison Form")
- Sources of necessary materials, merchandise, or supplies

Inventory ("Operations Planning Guide")
- How inventory will be maintained

Contingencies ("Contingency Planner")
- Provide "Plan B" approaches for any problems that could develop. This is the place to discuss how unexpected events could adversely affect the business.

Administrative Plan.
Describe how the business will be managed.

Management Team
- Describe the management team and how each contributes to the business's success. Tell why each of the owners and key employees are qualified for their duties, including both their experience and education. Investors are most interested in the management team, so use this section to impress them with all the credentials you have for the venture.

Staffing
- Personnel requirement ("Staffing Planner")

Facilities
- Describe the office, store, or facility your business needs ("Facility Planner")
- Explain where the business is or will be located and why

Financial Plan.
If your business is a start-up, this section will contain your financial projections for the next three years. For existing businesses, also include current financial statements and those for the past two years.

Pro forma financial statements
- An income statement ("Projected Income Statement"), also called a profit and loss statement, is a summary of earnings and expenses over a month, quarter, or year. The income statement shows the profit or loss during that time period. Income statement projections should be prepared for each of the next three years.
- A balance sheet ("Projected Balance Sheet") shows the assets, liabilities, and capital on a particular date, indicating the financial condition of the company. One is prepared at the beginning of operations and others are prepared as projections covering each quarter for the next three years.

Quit worrying, make a plan.

Financial Plan (continued)

Cash needs

- A cash forecast ("Cash Forecast") should be prepared before starting the business. It shows the cash flow in and out of the business over time. This is important to know because even a profitable business can have a negative cash flow. The cash forecast shows the amount of money needed for the business and how the money will be used. Lenders and investors pay special attention to this section because cash is the life blood of business.

- The Expense Budget ("Projected Expense Budget & Capital Expenditures") indicates where funds are being spent. It also includes a section on Capital Expenditures, which are long term, "hard" assets such as buildings, equipment, vehicles, furniture, and fixtures.

Financing

- Sources of funding ("Start-Up Financing Planner")

What-if scenarios

- What If's ("Projected Income Statement" and "Cash Forecast") You may want to include an analysis showing the affect of other levels of revenues on financial performance. For these "what if" scenarios, prepare three forecasts – a best case, a most likely case, and a worst case. If you're using a computer spreadsheet program, this is a fairly simple task, though it may be grueling if done by hand.

Appendix

- Resumes of owners and key employees
- Pictures of the product
- Floor plan and location map for retail establishments (or if otherwise applicable)
- Names and addresses of:
  - ☐ Auditor or accountant
  - ☐ Lawyer
  - ☐ Banker
  - ☐ Debt or equity holders

Once you complete your plan according to this guide your Contents page should look something like this:

Contents

Plan Summary
The Company
Product or Service
Marketing Plan
  Market Research
  Sales & Distribution
  Promotion
  Pricing
  Sales Projections
Operating Plan
  Scheduling
  Equipment
  Suppliers
  Inventory
Administrative Plan
  Management Team
  Staffing
  Facilities
Financial Plan
  Financial Statements
  Cash Needs
  Financing Plans
Appendix
  Resumes
  Product
  Floor Plans
  Key Professional Contacts

Get a Second Opinion

Once your plan is completed to your satisfaction, have a knowledgeable business associate review it. Or take it to your local SCORE office (see listing in **Resources**). The business department at a local college may also be able to provide someone to review your plan. Make any necessary revisions, then have someone, whose business judgement you respect, review and discuss it with you before showing it to a banker or investor.

Your business plan is a working document and it will continue to change as your business grows. Prepared and used properly, your business plan can put you on the road to business success, and keep you there.

Contingency Planning

Benjamin Franklin once said that there's nothing certain except death and taxes, but in business there's at least one other certainty – the unexpected. According to Murphy's law, "Everything that can go wrong, will go wrong, usually at the worst possible time." There is so much of the unexpected in business that some business owners consider Murphy an optimist.

While it's important for you to maintain a positive attitude about your business, you also need to be aware of any conditions that could sabotage your success That way you can plan a course of action to neutralize or overcome them. Planning for the unexpected means including contingency funds in your budget estimates. Use the "Contingency Planner" to help anticipate potential problems.

Tips for Using the Following Form:

Note: You are encouraged to copy this form for your own use. Keep the unmarked original in a safe place and make copies of it to work from.

Contingency Planner – By answering each of the questions posed on this form, you are preparing your business to deal with the kinds of events that often have catastrophic consequences for small businesses. Thinking about these contingencies in advance can help you to handle them should they ever occur.

Meridian Learning Systems also offers Express Business Plan, a software-based business planning tool. With it all the information discussed in this chapter can be developed into a professional business plan. It even automates the financials. For more information call 510-669-9000.

The following "what if" questions will help you get the contingency planning process started. What effect would each of the conditions below have on your business and how would you respond?

1. What if your business received no revenues for six months? _____

_____

_____

_____

2. What if sales were only 50% (30% or 20%) of forecasts? _____

_____

_____

_____

3. What if a key person departs? _____

_____

_____

_____

4. What if your major source of supply was no longer available? _____

_____

_____

_____

5. What if your competitors react differently than you forecasted? _____

_____

_____

_____

6. Are there any pending or potential government regulations that could affect your business? _____

_____

_____

_____

BUSINESS ORGANIZATION

Comparing Legal Structures

One of the most important decisions you will make when starting your business is which legal structure to choose. The legal structure you select will determine how your business will be taxed, how it can raise money, whether you will be personally liable for its debts, and how much paperwork you'll have to do.

Some of the considerations that should go into this decision are:

- How soon you want to start your business

- The possibilities for business growth

- The ability to attract investment capital or loans

- The continuity of the business should something unexpectedly happen to you

- How much personal risk you're willing to accept for the liabilities of the business

- Your personal tax situation.

Listed below are the major types of legal structure available, along with a brief discussion of each:

A **Sole Proprietorship** is owned and operated by one person, though it may have employees. For all practical purposes, though, the owner is the business. Since only the appropriate licenses are needed to begin operations, sole proprietorships are the least costly and most common form of business, comprising 70% of American business entities.

Sole proprietorships have the option of operating either under the owner's own name or under a "fictitious business name," such as "Bottom Line Consulting." The words "incorporated" or "corporation," however, cannot be included in the fictitious name. A sole proprietorship is not taxed as a separate entity; instead all business income is reported on a Schedule C filed with the owner's tax return.

Although only a few larger companies are owned by one person, sole proprietorship is the preferred form for most small enterprises. Stores, shops, restaurants, and service businesses ordinarily do business as sole proprietorships. A business can be started as a sole proprietorship and later can be easily changed to another legal form.

A **Partnership** is a form of business owned by two or more people. Also called a General Partnership, a partnership pools the skills and capital of the partners. Like a sole proprietorship, a partnership can operate under a "fictitious business name." It too, can have employees in addition to the partners. Only about 10% of the nation's businesses are partnerships. Though partnerships must file tax returns for informational purposes, they are not taxable entities. Instead, the partners each report their individual share of the income and deductions on their personal tax returns.

If one partner needs income and another needs to shelter income from other sources, the partnership's income and expenses can be divided, within certain limits, by a different percentage than the ownership of the firm if this provision is part of the partnership agreement.

While not legally required, a written and notarized partnership agreement, outlining the roles and responsibilities of each partner, is a practical necessity. Written partnership agreements help prevent misunderstandings and disagreements that can lead to lawsuits. Additionally, a partnership agreement provides a working guideline to the business relationship.

Partnerships are declining in use due to the partners' personal liability exposure. Many professionals, such as doctors and lawyers, who formerly practiced as partnerships, are now incorporating to shield themselves from personal liability.

A **Corporation** is a distinct legal entity that has an existence apart from the people who own it. Corporations are formed by the authority of a state government. Though not required by law, the process of incorporation is often handled by attorneys because of the volume and complexity of the paperwork involved. However, many self-help books are now available to help you set up a corporation without a lawyer.

About 20% of American businesses are corporations. There are several features that make incorporation attractive as a legal structure. The first is that its owners, the shareholders, generally have no personal liability for debts or lawsuits against the corporation. The shareholders' losses are limited to their investment in the corporation. The ability to issue common stock and other kinds of securities gives a corporation considerably more options for growth and fund raising than the other types of business organization.

A corporation is a separate taxable entity and its income may be taxed twice: once as the corporation earns it, and then again when dividends are paid to the shareholders. This double taxation can be minimized by paying the corporation's earnings out as personal income to those of the shareholders who are also employees of the corporation.

The three main legal structures for a business:

Sole Proprietor   **Partnership**   **Corporation**

The state of incorporation is normally the one in which the corporation will conduct its principal business, but many corporations are being formed in states like Delaware, with favorable corporate laws. A corporation must qualify as a "foreign" corporation in each state in which it does business.

Virtually all large companies are corporations, so if your goals include growing your business into a huge national or international concern, incorporation is probably the preferred way to organize your business. Even businesses with modest growth plans may also choose incorporation as a way to gain the advantages the corporate structure can provide, particularly the limitation on personal liability.

Operating as a corporation requires a fair amount of recordkeeping. If corporate records aren't kept properly, the business can lose the benefits of operating as a corporation.

In addition to the three most common forms of business organization, there are two variations that may be beneficial for certain kinds of businesses:

S corporations receive most of the advantages of a corporation, while permitting the profits to be taxed as a sole proprietorship. Though this type of business organization is highly regulated, with the number of stockholders currently limited to thirty-five, it often offers the new business owner the best of both worlds. Your accountant or attorney can tell you if the advantages of an S Corporation make it the preferred legal form for your business.

A **Limited Partnership** is a more regulated kind of partnership, requiring a certificate of limited partnership. The limited partners can't actively participate in the business and they have no additional liability for claims against the partnership arising from debts or lawsuits. The most they can lose is their original investment. The limited partnership is fully controlled by the general partner who has a fiduciary responsibility to all the limited partners. Because of its complexity, a limited partnership should be formed only with the assistance of an attorney.

Choosing the Legal Structure That's Best for Your Business

If you're not sure about which type of business structure is best for your business, it may help you to consider:

- The amount of money you need to raise to start your business
- How much control you want to maintain over the business
- The degree of personal responsibility you can afford to take for business debts
- How you want the earnings from the business to be taxed.

Use the accompanying "Legal Structure Comparison" to get a more detailed look at how these legal structures compare with each other regarding the questions above and other considerations. If you're still in doubt about which legal form is best for your business, consult an attorney who is knowledgeable about the various types business organization.

Notes:

Decision Criteria	Sole Proprietorship	Partnership	C Corporation	S Corporation
Control	One person controls all aspects of the business	Each partner (2+) may participate in decision making	Each shareholder exercises control according to their share	Each shareholder exercises control according to their share
Ownership	One owner	Each partner owns a percentage	Each shareholder	Each shareholder (35 or less)
Transfer of Ownership	Entire company is sold	Depends on partnership agreement, can be difficult	Each shareholder may sell their shares	Each shareholder may sell their shares
Management	Owner or delegated manager	Partners or delegated to managers	Delegated to managers who may also be shareholders	Delegated to managers who may also be shareholders
Profits	Direct to owner	Direct to partners as agreed	Held by the corporation, paid as dividends to owners	Flows through to owners
Losses	Can be deducted from other income on individual tax return	Can be deducted from other income on individual tax return	Losses can only be offset against corporate income (current or future)	Can be deducted from other income on individual tax return
Taxes	Taxed at individual rates to owner	Taxed at individual rates to partners	Profits taxed at corporate level, dividends taxed to shareholders	Taxed at individual rates to owner(s)
Regulation	Little	Little	Significant	Very high
Liability	Unlimited to owner	Unlimited to general partner(s)	Limited to corporate assets	Limited to corporate assets
Raising Money	Depends on owner, generally most difficult among options	Expanded resources, with additional individuals involved	Expanded credibility, makes process somewhat easier	Expanded credibility, makes process somewhat easier
Continuity	None, terminates with death of owner	None, unless provided for in partnership agreement	Permanant existence	Permanant existence
Ease of Starting	Very easy	Easy to start; should develop partnership agreement	Time-consuming, requires multiple state filings	Time-consuming, requires multiple state filings
Cost of Starting	Very inexpensive	Inexpensive	Costly	Costly
Flexibility	Very flexible, owner makes all decisions	Flexible, partners consult on major decisions	Limited by charter and government regulation (although charter can be broadly written)	Limited by charter and government regulation (although charter can be broadly written)
Changing Form	Simple to change to other forms, difficult to change back	Simple to change to other forms, difficult to change back from corporate forms	Relatively simple to change to this form, difficult to change back to non-corporate forms	Relatively simple to change to this form, difficult to change back to non-corporate forms
Owner's Salary	Not deductible	Not deductible	Deductible by corporation if owner is actively employed	Deductible by corporation if owner is actively employed

RAISING MONEY

Every Business Needs Money

Every business needs money to get started. And just about every business needs money at some point to finance growth or get through a difficult period. Additional capital may also be needed to cope with seasonal peaks or to purchase new facilities and equipment.

Many businesses have failed because the owners didn't know how to predict their cash needs, didn't know what sources of funds were available, and didn't know the most effective ways for obtaining funding. Often these failures were attributed to insufficient financing.

But lack of money isn't really what makes most businesses fail. Pouring more and more money into an ill-advised venture, or one run by an owner lacking good management skills, won't make it successful. Money isn't a substitute for a sound business idea, a well-prepared business plan, and careful execution of that plan.

Smart business owners acquire a basic understanding of financial matters and financial planning in order to avoid becoming victims of financial disaster. Some of the financial pitfalls inexperienced business owners fall into when raising money are not requesting enough financing, asking for too much, not matching the incoming funds with actual business needs, and not considering the real cost of money.

Determining Your Financial Needs

Before raising any money for your business, carefully review your financial needs. The first thing to determine is exactly what you want the money for: start-up costs, increased working capital to meet expenses due to expansion, or equipment purchases, for instance. Be clear about what the money is intended for and how it will help make your business successful.

Once you know how you're going to use the money, you'll know how much money you're going to need. Then determine how you'll pay it back. And finally, ask yourself if you can afford the cost of the money, whether that cost is in the form of interest on a loan or having to give up a share of the ownership in the business.

The best time to ask these questions is before you actually have financial problems. This is one of the main reasons for preparing the "Cash Forecast" (see *Budgeting*). Any projected cash deficits (negative cash flow) could be a warning that financing is needed. Not all projected deficits require additional funding because you may be able to find ways to reduce expenses or convince suppliers to extend credit terms to prevent projected deficits from occurring.

Though cash flow projections are helpful, they're not the only way a business plan can help you raise money. In fact, your business plan is your primary tool for raising capital. Investors and lenders both want to see in writing what they're being asked to put up money for and how they'll be repaid. Trying to get loans or investments without a business plan is almost certainly a waste of time.

Sources of Funds

All sources of new business financing can be reduced to three basic types:

■ **Bootstrapping**. The first place to look for business financing is yourself. If you're not willing to risk your own money to capitalize your business, other people probably won't either. Here are some of the ways you can generate money to fund your business:

   Savings. Since savings don't have to be paid back and you don't have to give up ownership, using savings is a preferred way of financing a new business.

   Home Equity. A great many homeowners have tens or eve hundreds of thousands of dollars in equity in their homes that could be made available for financing a business. Since home equity loans are actually a second mortgage, defaulting on the loan can mean losing the house.

   Life Insurance. Those who have "cash value" life insurance may be able to borrow against the built up value of the policy.

   Credit Cards. Since credit card interest rates are high, this isn't often a wise option, though some entrepreneurs have used it in emergency situations. This is a fairly high-cost form of debt.

   Internal Measures. An established company can generate capital internally to avoid both debt and dilution of ownership. Some of the ways are getting extended credit from suppliers, asking for prepayments from customers, and instituting cost cutting measures.

■ **Debt funding**. While family, friends, and acquaintances are possible sources of loans, here is a look at the major business lenders:

   Banks. Though it's true that banks sometimes make short-term (up to one year) unsecured loans to small businesses, these loans almost always go to established businesses and are used most often to finance accounts receivable for 30 to 90 days. The majority of bank loans are secured by tangible assets used as collateral, and often require that the business owner personally guarantee the loan.

   Besides the cost of interest, bank loans often include an origination fee and require that certain balances be maintained at the bank. Most commercial bank loans are for working capital, equipment, and expansion. Use the "Capital Sources Contact Log" at the end of this section to organize your search for funding.

   The best time to approach a banker is when you don't need the money. Try to set up a line of credit when you're in great financial shape, then use it when cash needs arise. It's also a good idea to request loan packages from banks in your community. Just call them on the phone and ask for the package without saying anything about yourself or your business. Then look over their requirements. Make sure you're prepared before you actually start talking to anyone about your specific loan. The "Loan Package Checklist" at the end of this section provides an overview of the requirements for getting bank loans.

   SBA guaranteed loans. If you've tried to get bank loans and failed, the Small Business Administration may be able to help. It can guarantee loans for businesses that can't borrow through conventional channels and, on rare occasions, may even lend you the money themselves.

   Personal guarantees from the owner are required and the loans are almost always for machinery and real estate that can be used as collateral.

   The SBA requires a lot of paperwork to process its loan guarantees (see "Loan Package Checklist"), so be prepared to do some work. With a well-prepared business plan (see "Business Plan Guide" in the *Business Plan* section) you'll already have most of the information required to apply for an SBA loan.

   Other sources of debt funding. Savings & loan associations, commercial finance companies, leasing companies, life insurance companies and pension funds are also possible sources for business loans.

Existing businesses can sometimes get loans from suppliers, and at times even from customers. They can also use their accounts receivable as collateral for loans.

Another way for existing businesses to raise fast cash is through **factoring** their accounts receivable. Factors buy a company's current receivables at a discount, then have the payments sent to them instead of the company that issued the invoice. The discount may range from 7-15% or more depending on how creditworthy the companies owing the money are.

The Old Pro says: *"Raising money is a time consuming process.*

Don't wait until you are desperate for money before trying to raise it.

If the lender or equity investor senses you are in a pinch, they will either demand more in return for their investment or turn you down.

If you have a completed business plan, you should allow at least 3 months to raise equity and 2 months to get your first loan.

If you don't have a business plan, get one!"

■ **Equity funding.** Getting equity investors means giving up some of your ownership in the business. Passive investors (limited partners and some shareholders) contribute capital only, while active investors (partners, venture capitalists, and some shareholders) may participate in running the business as well.

Partners. When you take on partners, you not only get their investment, but also their skills and expertise, which can be a real plus. On the other hand, your partners will have a say in the business, so you'll be sharing control.

Venture capitalists. There are a number of venture capital firms who finance new businesses. In addition to money, venture capitalists can provide a wealth of business expertise. They expect start-up entrepreneurs to have prior managerial or entrepreneurial experience.

Venture capitalists are sometimes maligned because of their frequent insistence on receiving a controlling interest in any venture they fund. On the other hand, venture capitalists point out, "Any percent of something is better than 100% of nothing." Venture capitalists need big returns from their successful investments because many of their investments don't succeed.

Large venture capitalists probably won't be interested in any investment less than $1 million. They feel it's just as much trouble monitoring a $50,000 investment as it is one of $1 million or more. See the National Venture Capital Association in **Resources.**

Wealthy individuals. Also called "angels," private investors are one of the largest sources of capital for business investment. Each year they invest nearly twenty times the amount of money in businesses that venture capitalists do, frequently investing in start-ups, which often have difficulty raising capital. An investor may be someone you know, like your rich Aunt Tillie, or a total stranger looking for a good investment.

Investors have various investment strategies. Conservative investors are interested in a "sure thing" and they want a large share of the equity or ownership. Another type of investor is more interested in making substantial capital gains quickly. Some investors want to tell you how to run your business, while others are thrilled just to be a part of something new and exciting. Some have ceilings on how much they are willing to invest, while others won't invest below a certain amount. With the right preparation and a thorough search, you'll be able to find the investors best suited to your situation. See the Venture Capital Network, Inc. in **Resources.**

Small Business Investment Companies.
There are over 300 SBICs licensed by the SBA to fund small high risk businesses. They may purchase up to 50% of a company's stock and make below market rate loans with a minimum term of five years. In considering a business for investment purposes, the SBICs are looking for the following:

1. A product or service with a strong marketing niche

2. An experienced, well-rounded management team

3. Super high growth prospects (40% + a year).

See the National Association of Small Business Investment Companies in **Resources.**

Equity partners are other companies in the same or related market who are interested in your niche. Strategic alliances are formed so that the smaller partner gets the capital it needs, while the larger partner gets a share of a market or technology it wants.

Other sources of equity funding. Corporations have the option of selling stocks and other securities to the public. A public stock offering can be extremely expensive, but it can raise massive amounts of capital for an established business.

Where the Money Comes From

In 70% of new businesses, the amount of capital invested before the business makes its first sale is less than $50,000. Under $5000 is invested in about 18% of new businesses. The figures given below for 1988 (the most recent year for which figures are available) will give you a better idea of where investment capital comes from.

By far the largest source of outside investment capital is from private investors, who invested some $56 billion, much of it going to start-ups. By comparison, venture capitalists made investments totalling $3 billion, the vast majority of it in established businesses.

Leasing companies provided $94 billion of asset-based capital, factors contributed $46 billion, and the Small Business Administration made nearly $3 billion in loans. Existing businesses where the recipients of virtually all the capital from these three sources.

The average amount raised for each deal worked out to about $2 million for venture capital firms, $165,000 for SBA loans, and $65,000 for private investors. Use the "Start-Up Financing Planner" to keep track of how much money you've lined up for your new business.

Tips for Getting a Bank Loan

The difference between getting a loan and being turned down can often be attributed to one of the following factors:

■ **Planning ahead.** Know what you're going to need and start laying the ground work for it before you actually need the money.

■ **Cultivating a number of relationships.** Don't rely on just one banker. Meet a number of lenders and maintain an on-going relationship with them.

■ **Targeting the search.** Look for lenders who specialize in your field. Trade associations and others in your field are often aware of the most active lenders.

■ **Shopping for the loan.** Don't just look at the interest rate. Also compare the amounts of financing available and the terms of the loan.

■ **Asking for more than the immediate need.** Ask for 25% more than what you think you'll need. That way you'll have a "cushion" and won't have to go back and ask for more capital.

■ **Timing loans to favorable developments.** When things are looking up – increases in sales or profits, product introductions, winning major contracts — your business will look better to lenders.

- **Thinking of capital as a resource to have in inventory.** Put excess borrowed funds in certificates of deposit or money market accounts as a contingency fund. The difference between the cost of the borrowed money and the interest the money earns is the cost of having capital available.

- **Getting a time commitment.** Ask the loan officer what date a decision on your loan is expected. Then call back on that date. Don't let the approval process drag on; ask for definite time commitments.

- **Being persistent.** Even when money seems tight, some money is always available, so keep trying.

How to Raise Equity Funds

Everything that has been said previously about preparing for a loan is also true for raising money through investors. It takes a great deal of serious, time-consuming effort to raise equity funds. Your business plan is particularly critical to this effort. Here are the questions your plan should answer for investors:

- How much cash is needed?

- What the money will be used for?

- How much can I make and how much can I lose?

- How can I cash out my investment?

When searching for equity investment, it's helpful to review all your options with regard to potential investors. Here are the most common sources along with the typical range of investment for each:

- Family and friends ($5,000 to $25,000)

- Business associates ($10,000 to $50,000)

- Private investors ($50,000 to $1,000,000)

You can cultivate interest from family members, friends, and business associates by networking. Tell them your story and if they're not interested ask them to recommend someone who might be. Finding private investors can be a little different. You can run a newspaper classified ad under "Money Wanted," get personal referrals to local investors from friends, or make contact through a capital network (see the discussion of Wealthy Individuals above under Equity Funding).

In addition to these sources, there are two others, venture capitalists and corporate partners. But these types of investors are looking for high growth businesses in which to invest over $1,000,000.

Remember that the less developed your business is, the larger share of ownership investors are going to want for their money. You'll be in the best position to approach investors when you are seeking capital for expansion of an existing business. You have somewhat less strong a position when you approach investors with a working prototype or a just-opened store. Your least strong position in raising capital is when all you have is a fully developed idea (explained, of course, in a well-written business plan). With only a plan you may have to give up a large share of ownership in the business. Without a plan you will be wasting your time.

> *"An insufficiently capitalized organization will die— good and bad alike."*
>
> Peter J. Boni, President
> Summa Four

Tips for Using the Following Forms:

Note: You are encouraged to copy these forms for your own use. Keep the unmarked originals in a safe place and make copies of them to work from.

Start-Up Financing Planner – This form shows you how much capital you have available to start your business. Each time you find an additional source of funds add it in the appropriate place on the form. Your total start-up capital will be used in the "Cash Forecast." You'll need enough start-up financing so that when it's added to your first year's projected sales, your business will maintain a positive cash position. This information will also be used in your business plan.

Loan Package Checklist – Giving lenders what they're looking for is the best way to improve your chances of getting a business loan. This checklist makes this easy for you by listing everything that most lenders request and referring you to the appropriate sections in this manual containing more information about those particular subjects and/or forms or worksheets to make assembling the needed information easy. These references are shown in parentheses.

Virtually everything that a lender could ask for is included in this checklist. The first section lists the standard requirements for all applicants. Following that are the additional requirements for existing businesses. The next section contains a number of items that may or may not apply to your business. Then a section devoted to real estate and construction loans follows. The last section is a listing of forms required by the SBA in addition to the other items. The Small Business Administration form numbers are shown in brackets. Cross off any items that don't apply to your business.

START-UP FINANCING PLANNER

(BP)

Type of Financing	Source	Comments	Amount
Owner's Equity			$
Partner's Equity			
Bank Loans			
Finance Company Loans			
SBA Loan			
Loans from Individuals			
Venture Capital			
Individual Equity Investors			
Trade Credit			
Other Financing			
		TOTAL START-UP FINANCING	$

For All Businesses

- ❏ Credit Request, which is a letter stating how much you want to borrow, what you're going to do with the money, and how you intend to pay it back.
- ❏ Business Plan (see "Business Plan Guide" in *Business Plan*). A must for all new businesses, but may not be needed for established businesses.
- ❏ Federal Income Tax Returns covering the last three years for each proprietor, partner, or shareholder holding over 20% of the stock.
- ❏ Projected Income Statement for three years by month for the first year and quarterly for the second and third years (see "Projected Income Statement" in *Budgeting*).
- ❏ Projected Cash Flow for three years, by month for the first year and quarterly for the second and third years (see "Cash Forecast" in *Budgeting*).
- ❏ List of all fixed-term personal and business debt. Include the name and address of each creditor, original amount, original date, present balance, interest rate, maturity date, monthly payment, collateral security, and whether it is current or delinquent.
- ❏ Resume for each owner, partner, major shareholder, and top manager.
- ❏ Source of Equity, which is a statement from each proprietor, partner, or major shareholder indicating the source of his or her equity contribution to the business.

For Existing Businesses

- ❏ Income Statement for last three years and current interim dated within 90 days.
- ❏ Balance Sheet for last three years, and current interim dated within 90 days.
- ❏ Federal Income Tax Returns for the business for the past 3 years.
- ❏ Accounts Receivable Aging, within 90 days.
- ❏ Accounts Payable Aging, within 90 days.
- ❏ Business Credit References, three with names, addresses, and phone numbers.
- ❏ Copy of the Lease Agreement for your facilities.

For Real Estate and Construction Loans

- ❏ Purchase Agreement.
- ❏ Environmental Questionnaire and Disclosure Statement.
- ❏ Construction Contract.
- ❏ Bond furnished by contractor.
- ❏ Plans and Specifications.
- ❏ Contingency Fund.

If Applicable or Requested by Lender

- ❏ Estimated costs of construction, remodeling, and improvements.
- ❏ List of machinery, equipment, and inventories by major items or categories and their estimated costs.
- ❏ Buyout or Buy-Sell Agreement.
- ❏ Franchise Agreement.
- ❏ Sales or Distributorship Agreement.
- ❏ Articles of Incorporation.
- ❏ Corporate By-Laws.
- ❏ Resolution of Board of Directors on borrowing.
- ❏ Certificate of Corporation in Good Standing issued by state Secretary of State.
- ❏ Partnership Agreement.
- ❏ Personal Budget for professional loans (doctors, dentists, etc.).

Additional SBA Requirements

- ❏ Application for Business Loan [SBA-4].
- ❏ Personal History Statement [SBA-912].
- ❏ Personal Financial Statement [SBA-413].
- ❏ Request for Counseling [SBA-641].
- ❏ Compensation Agreement [SBA-159].
- ❏ Statement Required by Laws and Executive Orders [SBA-1261].
- ❏ Certification Pursuant to Immigration and Nationality Act [SBA-1261A].
- ❏ Certification Regarding Debarment [Temporary SBA-1624].
- ❏ Certificate as to Partners [SBA-160A] for partnerships only.
- ❏ Resolution of Board of Directors [SBA-160].

Other

Though not actually included as part of the loan package, many lenders also require the following:

- ❏ Life Insurance on principals for the amount of loan, with the bank as beneficiary.
- ❏ Hazard Insurance for collateral on the loan, with the bank as beneficiary.
- ❏ Guaranty. All principals may be required to personally guarantee the loan by pledging their personal property.

GOALS, MOTIVATION & TRAINING

Goal Setting:
The Systematic Way to Success

Success in business, or in anything else, is a matter of accomplishment – of getting things done. Your business success is measured by how well you do what you set out to do. Goal setting is a tool that helps you achieve success by helping you reach your objectives systematically.

A goal is different than a wish or a hope. Wishing and hoping are passive, dreamy states of mind without much power. A goal on the other hand is conscious and active. Goal setting produces positive results in a number of ways. First, having a goal focuses your attention, causing you to think about the goal more, and become more aware of opportunities related to it. Goals also provide a criterion for making important decisions and a reference point for planning.

Each goal is a clearly defined objective to be reached at some specific time in the future. When you accomplish the goal within the specified time frame, you are successful with regard to that goal.

Leading figures in business and sports repeatedly link their success to the goals they set for themselves. But just how important is goal setting on a practical level?

Some years ago a study was done at Yale University. Seniors were asked whether or not they had written goals. Only 3% of them did. Some years after graduation, these former classmates were interviewed again. Difficult as it may be to believe, among the findings were that the 3% who had written goals earned more than the other 97% of their classmates combined.

Success is achieving your goals.

Goal Setting in Business

What works for individuals works for businesses too. The specific business goals you set will depend on your business and your definition of success. Some of the more common types of business goals are increases in sales, profits, gross margins, and inventory turnover, to name a few.

It is difficult to overstate how critical the goal setting process is to business success. Setting and accomplishing goals keeps a business moving in the right direction. Without goals, there isn't an objective way to determine whether the business is successful or not; it is the achievement of goals that makes a business successful.

Business owners are often task oriented. They get caught up in the day-to-day activities of running a business instead of focusing on what they're trying to accomplish. A more achievement-oriented approach is to emphasize results instead of activities. This means viewing each activity in terms of how it affects the goals that have been set.

Many small business owners feel they don't have the time to set goals. That's another reason why so many small businesses fail. Successful business owners make the time to plan because they know how crucial it is to success.

Some business owners feel having their goals in their heads is sufficient, but unwritten goals are often vague and sometimes even contradictory. Writing out goals clarifies them and provides an objective way of tracking them against actual results.

Every business consists of a number of ongoing activities involving many tasks. The overall success of a business depends on how well each task is done. Setting a goal for each major area of your business helps ensure that the tasks necessary for your business to succeed are accomplished.

How to Set Goals

Setting goals is the surest way to get from where you are to where you want to be. But a goal is more than a desire, wish, or hope; to work most powerfully a goal must be:

- **Specific.** The more precisely you define your goals, the easier it is to achieve them. Saying you want your business to be successful isn't going to get you far. What exactly do you mean by successful? A certain level of sales? Profits? You might decide that business success means $250,000 in sales, or 20% net profits. Or it could mean that your business has to provide you with $50,000 a year income. You alone determine what success is for your business.

- **Measurable.** Goals expressed in numbers make it easy to measure your progress. Making your goals measurable also ensures that they are specific enough. Dollars are the numbers that most often measure business success. What exact amount of sales do you want? How much profit do you expect to make? What exact amount of personal

income do you want your business to provide for you? Is a business with sales of $5 million per year successful? It all depends on what its goal was. If, for instance, the goal was $4 million a year in sales, then it is successful because it exceeded the goal by 25%. But if the goal had been $10 million, the business would not be successful with regard to that goal since the actual results were only half of what had been set as a goal.

- **Set in a time frame.** Having definite dates for accomplishing goals provides a convenient context for judging success. Sporting events are generally played within some clearly defined time limit. At the end of the game, the successful team is determined by which one has the higher score. It's similar in business, at the end of a month, or a quarter, or a year, measure your actual results against the goals you had set to determine whether you've succeeded in accomplishing them. Even if you don't accomplish a particular goal within the time frame, use that experience to learn more about what it will take to succeed the next time.

- **Written.** Until goals are written down, they don't have any power. Once they're committed to paper, they become a reference point – something concrete that you can keep referring back to. The act of expressing your goals tangibly in writing gives them the power of your conviction. And because they're written out, they can be a constant reminder.

- **Planned out.** Develop a strategy for achieving your main objectives. Then put together an overall plan that includes the most essential steps for achieving the goal. Large or long-term goals should broken down into smaller short-term goals. Assign a time frame for each short-term goal. Identify resources that can help you achieve your goals. Anticipate possible obstacles and develop a plan for dealing with them.

- **Monitored.** Periodically review your results. When the results fall short of your goal, identify any problem areas and take corrective action. If your actions are working, keep on doing the same things. But if they aren't working, then try something else. Monitoring goals daily or weekly gives you more opportunity to gauge your progress. Frequent monitoring keeps you on track.

All your goals should be achievable, but they should make you stretch. As you accomplish more and more goals, you will experience success after success, and accomplishment will become a habit.

Long-Term Goals

Long-term goals are those things you want to accomplish three or more years into the future. They would include sales, profit, and competitive position goals. The goals set for the current year should be designed to facilitate the accomplishment of your long-term goals. Use the "Goal Setting Worksheet" at the end of this section to record your goals.

Use your long-term business goals as the foundation for your business planning. When setting these goals get your employees and associates involved in the process. They'll be more committed to achieving the goals if they've had a role in setting them.

Short-Term Goals

In order to accomplish your long-term goals, you have to break them down into short-term goals. A three-year goal would be broken down into three one-year goals. Then each of the yearly goals would be broken down into twelve monthly goals, which could be further subdivided into weekly goals, and finally into daily goals.

As each of the smaller sub-goals gets accomplished, you move closer to accomplishing your long-term goal. Use the "Planning Calendar," "Daily To Do List," and the "Project Schedule" to keep track of your goals.

Seeing the Big Picture

When choosing your long-term goals, it's a good idea to view the future of your business in terms of "the big picture." No business operates in isolation, each one is part of an industry, an economy, and a society. That's why business decisions have to take in much more than just what is happening at the present time.

"Seeing is believing" is a good motto for judging whether your efforts are achieving your goals. But before setting your goals, you should realize that the reverse is also true – when it comes to business, "believing is seeing."

How we see things – our perspective – is like a lens, through which we view the world. Our beliefs about something can determine to a great extent how we see it. This is important to know because how you view your business will affect your business goals; it will help determine which target market you go after, which products you develop, what equipment and facilities you acquire, what your financial requirements are, and how many employees you'll need.

> *No wind serves him who has no destined port.*
>
> Montaigne

Before setting long-term goals, ask yourself this question: "What business am I in?" This question is important because it will determine your expectations for your business. Is your definition of your business right for today's market? Tomorrow's market? Are there emerging customer needs that will require a new definition of your business in the next few years?

The railroad industry is one of the best examples of the importance of asking this question. At one time railroads were the dominant industry in the country, but they went into decline and virtual extinction because the railroad owners and managers saw themselves as being in the railroad business instead of the transportation business. Rather than broadening their services into trucking and aviation, they vainly fought against these transportation improvements, missing opportunity after opportunity. Because of their mindset, the railroad barons perceived these opportunities as threats.

Keep this in mind as you plan for the future. Don't expect circumstances to remain the same; expand your vision to include innovations and trends instead of resisting them. Make sure your beliefs are based on what's actually happening. If they are, the goals you set will be much more likely to be accomplished.

Base your beliefs on facts and you will be successful more often.

How to Stay Motivated

As a business owner, you are the chief factor in how successful your business becomes. It can grow as large and profitable as you're willing and able to make it. And at the same time, your business is primarily limited by you and your limitations. So it's important for you to continue learning and growing. The more you develop yourself, the more you can accomplish, and the more your business can grow.

School is never out for anyone serious about business. What you've learned so far has taken you to this point, and in order to go farther you have to learn more. There are two distinct areas of personal growth you need to develop as a business owner. The first is self-motivation.

Almost by definition a new business owner is a self-starter. Just about everyone is excited and highly motivated when they start their business, but as time goes by, enthusiasm can wane. Unexpected problems and difficulties can take a toll on your commitment to your business.

That's why it's so important to maintain a success-oriented attitude. Experts in every field of achievement agree that attitude plays a major role in success. This is especially true in business, where your enthusiasm about, and confidence in, your business are often your major assets when starting out.

To become successful, business owners need to find ways to keep the excitement and energy flowing into their businesses after the initial enthusiasm has worn off. Here are some ways to stay highly motivated:

- **Focus on positive outcomes.** Create clear mental pictures of how you want things to turn out, then work to turn those pictures into reality. Keep clearly focused on what you're trying to achieve, not on the obstacles you may encounter.

- **Think and speak positively.** According to trainer Brian Tracy, 85% of success is based on positive mental attitudes. How you think determines what you do, and what you say influences how you are perceived by others. What's even more important is what you say to yourself. It's been estimated that 70% of the things we say to ourselves about ourselves is negative. Make sure the things you say to yourself are positive.

- **Associate with positive people.** Your reference group has a lot to do with your degree of success, so make sure you're in the company of winners, not whiners. Make the acquaintance of highly motivated and successful people. If you use successful people as your reference group, you'll be associating yourself with success instead of mediocrity. People tend to mirror those around them, so make sure you surround yourself with the kind of people you admire and respect.

Skills Training

The second area of personal growth you'll have to develop as a business owner is skills training. Although most new business owners already have a number of talents and skills, it's the rare individual who is expert in every phase of starting and operating a business.

In addition to the specialized knowledge you already have regarding your product or service, there are a host of other areas where you'll also need knowledge. Business ownership requires a variety of skills that most of us have to learn on the job: planning, selling, negotiating, delegating, finances, etc.

Whenever you find yourself with a lack of necessary skills in any area, look for ways to improve those skills, such as community college classes, attending seminars, reading books, listening to audio tapes, and talking with other business owners.

While it's true you can learn from your own mistakes, the "College of Hard Knocks" exacts a very high tuition. By meeting regularly with other business owners, you can discuss your problems and get the benefit of their experience without having to make the same mistakes yourself.

By using **Building A Profitable Business** you've taken a significant step toward increasing your business knowledge and improving your chances of business success.

Employee Training and Development

Employees are any company's most valuable resource. In order to get the maximum value out of employees, wise business owners invest in employee training. Training benefits employers in a number of ways. Most significantly it can improve employee job performance, thereby increasing productivity.

For training to be effective, it has to be designed to achieve a specific objective. It can prepare employees for new jobs, or to use new equipment. Training is also helpful in preparing employees for

promotion and is an ideal way to reduce accidents and waste. Once you know what the goal is, then you can determine the subject matter to include in the training.

There are a number of ways to train employees and you'll need to choose the appropriate methods for your particular needs. While most skills training is held on-the-job, in some instances training may be given in a classroom setting. Off-premises seminars are often used for career development training for management employees. You also need to decide if any special equipment or materials, such as slide projectors, workbooks, or videotapes will be needed. How long the training sessions should last is another important consideration.

While training employees takes time and costs money, it can be the best investment you make. Employees are the assets of a business with the most potential for growth. Every dollar you spend for training and developing your employees can come back to you many times over in improved results – and increased profits.

The Old Pro says: *"An employee is the business asset with the greatest potential for growth."*

Tips for Using the Following Forms:

Note: You are encouraged to copy these forms for your own use. Keep the unmarked originals in a safe place and make copies of them to work from.

Goal Setting Worksheet – This worksheet provides a convenient place to commit your goals to writing. Follow the instructions at the top of each column when filling in your entries. It's best to have only a few major goals at one time to keep your energy focused. Pick the three goals most important to your business and concentrate on them.

Daily To Do List – Use this guide to keep you focused on the steps needed to achieve your goals on a day-to-day basis. The first two parts of the form are to list the tasks you want to accomplish that day. Be sure to include at least one task for each of the three goals you set in the "Goal Setting Worksheet." At the end of the day, carry over uncompleted tasks to the next day's list, along with any new tasks you've noted in the last section of the form.

GOAL SETTING WORKSHEET

GOAL	DESCRIPTION OF GOAL — Be specific. Business goals are generally expressed in dollars or some other measurable quantity.	COMPLETION DATE — Having a completion time gives you a way to measure your progress and it also creates a sense of urgency.	RESOURCES — List the things you already have that can help you achieve your goal. These could be money, people, tools, or information.	OBSTACLES — The better you understand the things standing in your way, the better you'll be able to turn these obstacles into stepping stones.	REASONS FOR GOAL — This is what you hope to gain as a result of achieving the goal. Knowing this adds the power of emotion to your efforts.	TASKS — Breaking a goal into a series of smaller tasks makes it easier to accomplish. Use the "Project Schedule" to keep track of the necessary tasks.
#1:						
#2:						
#3:						

GOALS, MOTIVATION & TRAINING — BUSINESS DEVELOPMENT

THINGS TO DO:

Action Items (List in order of importance)   **Notes**

❑ 1. _____   _____
❑ 2. _____   _____
❑ 3. _____   _____
❑ 4. _____   _____
❑ 5. _____   _____
❑ 6. _____   _____
❑ 7. _____   _____
❑ 8. _____   _____
❑ 9. _____   _____
❑ 10. _____   _____
❑ 11. _____   _____
❑ 12. _____   _____

PHONE CALLS TO MAKE:

Name   **Number**   **Notes**

❑ 1. _____   _____   _____
❑ 2. _____   _____   _____
❑ 3. _____   _____   _____
❑ 4. _____   _____   _____
❑ 5. _____   _____   _____
❑ 6. _____   _____   _____
❑ 7. _____   _____   _____
❑ 8. _____   _____   _____
❑ 9. _____   _____   _____
❑ 10. _____   _____   _____

ACTION ITEMS FOR TOMORROW'S TO DO LIST:

❑ _____
❑ _____
❑ _____
❑ _____
❑ _____

MARKETING

MARKETING PLAN

MARKET RESEARCH

SALES &
DISTRIBUTION

PROMOTION

PRODUCT
DEVELOPMENT

MARKETING PLAN

The Marketing Plan: Developing a Winning Game Plan

Sports are often used as a metaphor for business. And it's easy to see why; both fields are highly competitive, require preparation, and serve as a vehicle for personal achievement and public rewards.

In short, sports and business both produce winners and losers. Anyone seriously engaging in either one of these activities does so with the expectation of victory – of becoming a winner. People who don't care whether they win or lose generally won't last long in either of these competitive arenas because they won't do the things necessary for success.

The key element to winning in business is the same as in sports: preparation. Winning teams don't just start playing, they have a game plan before they step out onto the field; they know what they're going to do before the contest begins.  The same is true for successful business owners. They have a game plan too – a business plan. Both these plans lay out the necessary ingredients for achieving victory, they are recipes for success.

A marketing plan is an integral part of any business plan and a result of the market planning cycle. This cycle consists of setting objectives, developing a strategy, implementing tactics, evaluating the results, and then, on the basis of year-end results, setting new objectives for the coming year, thus beginning the cycle anew.

Winning plans aren't based on wishful thinking,

they're based on facts. Game films and statistics provide the basis for game plans in sports, while basic market research and previous results are used by businesses to formulate their plans.

Gathering the Facts

Researching your market needn't be elaborate to be helpful. It can be as simple as determining:

- **Your market segment.** Who are the customers you want to attract? What are their characteristics? What are their wants and needs? Where are they? Is this market increasing or decreasing? Unless you know these basics it'll be difficult to know how to attract customers, how to persuade them, and in some cases, even how to find them (see "Customer Profile Worksheet"). During your first year of business, you'll want to look frequently at how much you sold, who you sold it to, and when it sold.

- **Your competition.** Who are they? What are their strengths and weaknesses? How does their product, service, or store compare with yours? The more you know about your competition, the more opportunity you'll have to emphasize your strengths and capitalize on the weaknesses of your competition (see "Competitor Review Worksheet").

■ **The business environment.** What is the general outlook for your field? Are there regulatory, economic, cultural, or technological factors that could have a major impact on your business? Since no business exists in a vacuum, knowing the environment you're operating in allows you to make plans for seizing opportunities and avoiding potential problems (see "Industry Review Worksheet").

The information about these aspects of your market will help you use your resources to maximum advantage and guide you in formulating your objectives, strategy and tactics.

Objectives:
What You Want to Accomplish

Preparing for success in either sports or business begins with knowing what the objective, or definition of success, is. In sports it's fairly simple, the objective is to have more points on the scoreboard at the end of the game than your opponent.

In business it's a little more complicated. Even though you're not usually competing directly against just one opponent, there is still a way to determine your success. And this is whether your business has reached its objectives, the goals that you have previously set.

For established businesses, objectives may include increases in sales, profits, market share, etc. New businesses, which often can't expect immediate profits, may choose a certain sales volume as a goal to strive for. While a large company typically has its objectives set by its board of directors, in a small business it's up to the owner to choose which objectives are most important for their business.

Here are some examples of the kinds of objectives set by small business owners:

■ When Trina Ross-Bell started The Write Stuff, a Kansas City-based word processing service, her objective was to bill $50,000 worth of business the first year.

■ In Massachusetts, Todd Spinelli wanted to double the sales of his successful two-year-old sporting goods store, Clubhouse Connection.

■ Dr. Arnold Essery wanted to increase the number of patient visits to Brentwood Chiropractic by 50%.

Strategy:
Positioning for Success

Once you know what you want your business to accomplish, you're ready to plot your strategy – how you're going to achieve your objectives.

An important element of any strategy is positioning your product or service in the marketplace. By evaluating the strengths and weaknesses of your competition, as well as those of your own business, you can begin to see areas of opportunity that you can benefit from.

A clear objective is critical to the development of a sound plan.

Your business should be positioned to match its strengths against the weaknesses of its competitors. This means giving customers a reason for buying from you rather than your competition.

Todd Spinelli, for instance, opened a second store in a new mall as a strategy for meeting his objective of doubling sales. As the mall's first sporting goods store, it gave people in that area a good reason for shopping at the Clubhouse Connection – a convenient location.

While there are many different strategies available to small businesses, they are all variations of four basic options:

Business Strategies

WHO YOU SELL TO \ WHAT YOU SELL	Current Products	New Products
Current Markets	Market Penetration	Product Development
New Markets	Market Development	Diversification

Please note that "products" also refers to services and retail merchandise selection.

Market penetration involves selling your current product line to the same type of customer you've been selling to. In essence it means doing more of what you're already doing. It may involve running more advertising, cutting prices, increasing selling space, or adding more salespeople.

Market development entails finding new markets, locations, or territories for selling your current products. This could mean getting new types of customers to buy your product or service, or, for retailers, opening another store.

Product development means introducing new products to your current customers. Two ways to do this are by increasing the variety of current products (new models, features, colors, or styles) or by adding completely new lines.

Diversification involves selling different products to new markets. Generally this strategy isn't used by small businesses because it spreads their resources too thin. Because it's like starting a new business, it is risky. However, when a business has achieved all the market share it's likely to, diversification may be the only strategy available for continuing growth.

Which strategy you select will be based, at least in part, on the following considerations:

■ **Cost.** Is the strategy you have in mind affordable? No matter how good an idea looks on paper, it's not practical unless there is enough money to do it without jeopardizing the business.

■ **Probability of success.** How likely is it to work? New businesses need to focus their precious resources on a few things having a high likelihood of success.

■ **Response.** What kind of reaction do you expect from your competitors? Try to think out what kinds of counter-moves your competitors may make so you're not caught off-guard.

■ **Profit potential.** Where will you be able to get the most "bang for your buck?" The more money you get back from your marketing investment, the more you'll have available to spend to keep the ball rolling, to reinvest in the business, and to reward yourself and others for the time, money, and energy invested in the business.

Your business strategy will be influenced by the nature of your business and by your objectives. And the strategy you choose will also affect which tactics you choose to implement your strategy.

Tactics: How You Play the Game

Having a winning strategy won't lead to success unless it's put into action. Tactics are the day-to-day actions, the steps necessary to implement your strategy.

In a sense, tactics are like tools. Specific plays are the tools used in sports. Football, for instance, consists of a number of different running and passing plays. In business there's an even wider variety of tools, though they can be categorized as either:

■ **Product** - what you sell

■ **Price** - how much you sell it for

■ **Place** - where customers buy it

■ **Promotion** - how customers learn about it.

Taken together these marketing variables, sometimes called the four Ps, constitute the marketing mix. These elements are designed to work together to encourage demand for the product or service. For a strategy to be successful, it is necessary for the tactics to be consistent with one another and to complement each other. Then all the marketing efforts will support and reinforce each other, and work together to accomplish your objectives.

You'll find more detailed information in the following marketing sections that will allow you choose the best tactics for your situation. For now, so you can see how these elements work together, here is an overview:

Product. Obviously, the product or service you sell is an important part of your marketing plan. But the term "product" has far broader implications; it is the product and how the product satisfies customer needs and wants. Included in it are such things as the product's:

- features and how they benefit the customer; unique features and benefits are particularly powerful
- quality and whether that level of quality is in alignment with what the customer expects
- packaging and package design, which often give customers their first impression
- brand name and image, which helps create an identity in the customer's mind
- available services, enhancements, and upgrades, which add value to the original purchase
- guarantees and warranties, to reassure the customer by providing a way to remedy any problems
- product selection, having a sizable selection to choose from, gives customers a sense of getting a personalized product.

Your product, service, or store will be most successful when presented to potential customers the way they want, need, or expect it. The tactics you choose will depend on which of the above product elements are most important to your customers.

Price. Regardless of how much demand there is for a particular product or service, for it to become successful, it has to be affordable. While prices are influenced by the cost of materials, labor, and overhead (because recovery of these costs is necessary before a profit can be made) they also have to be set with regard to the prices of competitive offerings. If your price is higher than those of your competitors, you're going to have to provide additional value to the customer to justify the difference.

Other factors that go into "price" are:

- **list prices** are the prices that are recommended by the manufacturer
- **credit terms** are often made available to increase the number of sales
- **discounts** for the various resellers in the distribution channel
- **allowances**, which are reimbursements for freight and advertising.

Place (Distribution). The process of getting a product or service to the ultimate consumer is called distribution. Often there are a number of steps in the process, which together are called the channel of distribution. Related considerations involve storing and transporting the products. But the crucial factor is how the product or service gets into the hands of the customers.

For a retail store or a restaurant this would include the location, where accessibility, convenience, physical appearance, and the quality of its staff are of major importance. Each of these factors can be a tactic to support the business owner's strategy. For a service business, location could be just as important as for a retail business if customers come to the place of business.

A manufacturer, on the other hand, usually distributes through a sales force* or through "middlemen."

---

* Traditional marketing textbooks generally regard personal sales as a function of promotion because of its role in promotional strategy. In actual operation, though, the sales function is usually organizationally separate from other promotional activities. And because of its actual operational similarity to the other distribution channels, it is included here.

The choice of which distribution tactics to use depends a great deal on how your target market is accustomed to making similar purchases, what the prevailing distribution practices are in your field, and an analysis as to whether the benefits of adding additional channels of distribution out-weigh the costs and time involved.

> "The theory behind a marketing plan is that it gives management a map with clear directions to where it should be going."
>
> Joseph Mancuso, President
> The Center for Entrepreneurial Management

Promotion. Promotion is the communication between a business and those it seeks to influence, usually customers and prospective customers. Other audiences might include the general public, investors, government officials, employees, suppliers, and distributors.

The aim of promotion is to inform, persuade, and influence – most often to get the customer to buy the product or service being promoted. Promotion is considered by many business people to be the most important marketing variable, as well the most difficult to master.

There are four distinct activities included in promotion:

- **Advertising** consists of paid messages, such as newspaper and magazine advertisements, radio and television commercials, and direct mail.

- **Publicity** involves unpaid communications, such as feature stories and product an-nouncements which appear as news.

- **Sales promotion** consists of such things as samples, premiums, coupons, and contests.

- **Marketing communications**, which include the elements – logos, brochures, and catalogs – that go into building a company's identity.

Letting people know who you are, what you do, where you are, and why people should buy from you should be the aims of your promotional efforts.

Evaluation: Keeping Score

In sports, the team with the highest score at the end of the game wins. While the game doesn't end in business, you can select certain time periods, like fiscal years, to review the results of your efforts and determine if your strategy has been working. This is done by monitoring the results you've gotten and evaluating those results in terms of the objectives set out in your marketing plan. There are three main areas to review:

- **Objectives.** The first thing to look at is whether the objectives set in your marketing plan have been met. As the results come in, they should be monitored to ensure that they're on target with your objectives. While business objectives are generally planned for a year, more frequent monitoring is neces-sary in small businesses where survival of the business often depends on meeting the objectives. Monthly, or even more frequent, monitoring allows for adjustments to be made on an on-going basis. At the end of the fiscal year, the current year's results become the basis for setting the next year's objec-tives.

- **Strategy.** If your objectives were met or exceeded, it means that your strategy has succeeded, and you'll probably want to stick with it. If, on the other hand, your objectives aren't being met, that doesn't mean you should change your strategy. Since that strategy was based on your perceived "best shot" against your competitors, it's still probably the most likely way to meet your objectives. When the results don't match your expectations, it's best to look first at the tactics you're using to implement the strategy. It's only after you've tried a num-ber of tactics without success that you should consider changing your strategy.

- **Tactics.** Review the tactics to see if they are contributing to the forecasted results. Did your tactics achieve what you thought they would? Tactics that are not achieving expected results should be examined and, if necessary, replaced by other more promising tactics. Do more of what works and dis-continue any tactic that doesn't produce results. Patience is required because rarely do tactics pay off quickly and dramatically. Usually the tactics will reinforce each other over time, so that at some point a certain momentum becomes established. Until this happens, it's important to stick with what seems to be working reasonably well instead of switching tactics in an attempt to force dramatic results.

After you've been in business a while, your financial records will provide a clear indication of where you are and how your business has performed financially. By comparing the actual results with your objectives, you can pinpoint the problem areas in your marketing plan. Find the underlying causes for problems before trying to initiate solutions. Keep looking for the root causes, so that your marketing plan can address the areas that will have the most impact on your business.

Bankers can give you insight into how your financial performance looks to an "outsider," but you'll have to find other measures for your non-financial objectives. One way to gauge customer satisfaction, for instance, is to use simple customer survey cards, asking how they rate you on the objectives you're trying to achieve.

Just as a sports team needs a game plan to win, for your business to succeed, you're going to need a marketing plan – one that has clear objectives and a workable strategy supported by effective tactics. "Your Marketing Plan," at the end of this section, will help you to set your objectives and develop a strategy. The other marketing sections on *Product Development*, *Sales & Distribution*, and *Promotion* will help you select the tactics that best support your strategy for achieving your objectives.

The Marketing Planning Process in Action

Business	Objective	Main Strategy	Tactics	Evaluation
The Write Stuff	$50,000 in annual billings.	Increase amount of work from existing clients.	Acquire desktop publishing skills and equipment to increase types of services offered.	Compare monthly, quarterly, and year-end revenues to projections. Check what percentage is coming from the new services.
Clubhouse Connection	Double annual sales.	Open a 2nd store.	Hold a grand opening. Saturate surrounding areas with 15% off coupons. Run ads in local newspaper.	Keep track of what percentage of sales come from the coupons and ads. After giving new location six months to ramp up, check to see if the new store's sales are at or above the old locations.
Brentwood Chiropractic	Increase patient visits by 50%.	Acquire new patients.	Give free seminars on back care. Give discounts to patients who refer others. Send free exam coupons to surrounding area homes.	Keep track of what percentage of the free exam recipients have become patients. Prepare a weekly report showing number of new patients.

Tips for Using the Following Form:

Note: You are encouraged to copy this form for your own use. Keep this unmarked original in a safe place and make copies of it to work from.

Your Marketing Plan – Your marketing plan is a key component of the business plan necessary to make your business successful. It's composed of four major components: objectives, strategy, tactics, and evaluation. All of these elements are interconnected. Your objectives state what it is you want to accomplish, strategy tells how you intend to achieve your objectives, tactics are the steps for implementing the strategy, and evaluation is the way you tell if your plan is working.

1. Objectives. Your marketing plan describes your objectives, which may include sales and profit levels, growth rates, and market share. Objectives should be stated in clear, measurable terms, such as "$250,000 in sales," "20% growth per year," "$3 in traceable sales for each $1 spent on marketing", or "10% market share." Your own personal goals also play a large part in determining your objectives (e.g. do you want your business to provide a steady, comfortable source of income for many years, or do you want to grow it to a certain size and then sell it?). Describe your objectives in clear, measurable terms:

_____

_____

_____

_____

2. Strategy. How you're going to accomplish these objectives, your overall marketing strategy, is the next part of developing your marketing plan. Most new businesses concentrate on market penetration as their basic strategy. Another important element of your strategy involves how you're going to position your product or service in relation to the competition. Your "strategic advantage" (see "Product or Service Worksheet") is the source of your most effective promotional positioning. Briefly describe your strategy: _____

_____

_____

_____

3. Tactics. How you're going to implement your strategy is one of the most important parts of developing your marketing plan. Tactics are the stepping stones to the achievement of your objectives. As mentioned earlier, you'll find extensive discussion of the individual tactics in the sections on *Product Development*, *Sales & Distribution*, and *Promotion*. Worksheets and forms in these sections will help you choose the right tactics to achieve results you have set as objectives. Then use the "Marketing Calendar" to list the tactical marketing activities you plan to use. _____

_____

_____

_____

4. Evaluation. Once your objectives, strategy, and tactics are established, you'll need to monitor the results of your actions on a periodic basis, and compare them to your forecasts. Any failure to meet objectives should be examined carefully and corrective action taken. Describe how you'll monitor and evaluate the results of your marketing efforts: _____

_____

_____

_____

_____

MARKET RESEARCH

Look Before You Leap Into That New Business

Many failed businesses should never have been started in the first place, as their owners would have discovered with a little preliminary investigation. That's why market research is necessary even before a business opens its doors. Answering a few questions before launching a new business can save time, trouble, and money later.

Before starting a business, you should perform an informal feasibility study. If this study indicates the business isn't feasible, you've saved your time and money for a more promising enterprise. But if this study shows your business idea has good potential, you'll have the satisfaction and increased confidence from <u>knowing</u> you have a sound business idea. You'll also have gained an increased understanding of the business.

While the terms "market research" and "feasibility study" may sound complicated and technical, they merely involve getting the answers to a few simple questions, and then thinking about how the answers apply to your venture. When considering any new venture, use the checklists in the *Business Assessment* section to determine whether that particular business is right for you, and whether the business idea has any serious flaws. Once you've done this, you're ready to conduct some market research.

The Role of Market Research

Launching a new business, introducing a product or service, and buying advertising are all so expensive that misjudgments can mean disaster for a small business. Market research can avoid costly errors by telling you what people want to buy and how they want it presented to them.

Regardless of how great you think your product is, it's virtually impossible to sell any product or service that people don't want. On the other hand, it's very easy to sell people what they do want. That's the whole point of market research – to find out what people want so you can provide it for them. To be successful, a business has to know its market – who its customers and potential customers are and how they perceive its products and services.

Market research is the way to obtain, analyze, and interpret the information necessary for making marketing decisions. It provides the timely information you need to:

- reduce your risks
- identify and profit from new opportunities
- improve existing products
- plan and refine advertising campaigns
- spot problems and potential problems
- evaluate alternative distribution channels

Fortunately market research doesn't have to be expensive. Although large corporations often spend millions of dollars for market research, a small business owner can accomplish much for very little money. Initially you need to determine such things as whether there is a market for your product or service, how that market can be reached, who your competitors are, and the current condition of your industry or field and its future outlook.

Key Market Research Questions

In order to make a sound decision about starting any business, you need the answers to the five key questions below. At the end of each question you'll find references to which worksheets to use for developing the answers. As you answer each of the questions and enter your responses in the appropriate places on the forms, you'll also be gathering information that can be used to create your business plan (see "Business Plan Guide" in *Business Plan*). If you can't answer these questions, you don't have enough information to start your business:

1. **Who will buy your products and/or services?** Customers are the most important element of any business. Successful marketing depends on reaching customers most efficiently. This is done best by targeting your market carefully. Target marketing means using your marketing resources more like a rifle than a shotgun – going after only those customers most likely to want your product or service. The more certain you are about who your potential customers are, the more likely your efforts are to be successful. When entrepreneurs say that "everyone" is a potential customer for their product, it usually means they haven't really targeted their market; this can lead to wasting huge amounts of money on inappropriate and ineffective marketing. The more you know about who you're trying to reach, the more efficiently you'll be able to market to them. In addition to knowing who your customers are, you'll need to know how many of them there are, where they are, and what their wants and needs are. The "Customer Profile Worksheet" found at the end of this section will help you to develop a complete customer profile for your business.

2. **What benefits will customers receive from your product or service?** Customers purchase products and services for the benefits they expect to receive from them. The most important benefits are the ones customers consider to be most important, not the ones you think they should care about. Many business owners make the mistake of emphasizing what they consider to be the main benefits their product or service has to offer, instead of discovering what their customers are actually looking for. For your product or service to be successful, you'll have to answer the question customers will be asking themselves: "What's in it for me?" Make sure your answer is from the customers' perspective and takes into account their wants and needs. The "Product or Service Worksheet" (see *Product Development*) gives you a place to describe the benefits your customers will receive when they purchase your product or service.

3. **How will customers obtain your product or service?** Distribution, or getting the product into the hands of customers is vital to the success of any business. Having a great product or service isn't enough; what counts is how well you are able to get what you're selling into the hands of your customers. You need to learn where your customers expect to find products like yours, and then find a way to make sure your products are there. Retail, mail order, and most service businesses sell directly to customers, while manufacturers generally have at least one intermediary, or middleman, between themselves and their customers. The "Sales & Distribution Planning Guide" (see *Sales & Distribution*) provides a handy way of compiling the information you need to help in developing your distribution channel.

> *"The secret of business is to know something that nobody else knows."*
>
> Aristotle Onassis

4. Who are your major competitors? Find out as much as you can about your competitors. The more you know about them, the better you'll be able to compete with them. You need to know who they are, where they are, and why customers buy from them. By studying your competition, you can discover information useful to your own business. Identify direct competitors, by product line and/or location, and also investigate indirect and marginal competitors. Even though other businesses may not offer the same product or service as you, if their product or service is related to yours, they may still be competing for the same dollars you are. Collect samples of competitors' advertising, brochures, and other written materials. Then analyze them to learn their prices, terms, and selling points. You can also learn a lot from observing your competitors' operations and by talking to their present or former customers and employees. If you can't find any competitors, it may not mean you've hit upon an overlooked "gold-mine." It could simply mean there isn't a demand for what you're offering. Use the "Competitor Review Worksheet" found at the end of this section to compile information about your major competitors.

5. What is the current status of your industry or field? One of the best ways of finding out what kind of financial results you can expect from your business is to find out how similar businesses are doing. Most businesses are part of an industry for which average sales and profit figures may be available. Getting this information early will help you determine if your business idea has a good chance of providing the kind of return you expect from it. Trade associations often provide industry ratios. Other sources of industry specific information include Accounting Corporation of America, Dun & Bradstreet, National Cash Register Co., Bank of America, and the Federal Trade Commission (see the **Resources** section). It is often possible to determine the future outlook for an industry by doing a little library research. A business librarian can direct you to many valuable sources of information. Use the "Industry Review Worksheet" at the end of this section to guide the investigation of your industry or field.

Basic Market Research Techniques

In some ways, small businesses have a distinct advantage over large ones, in part because small business owners are usually much closer to their customers than executives in large companies. Because of this they can learn much more quickly about what their customers want, and can react more rapidly to any changes in their customers' buying habits and preferences. New businesses can use the first two research techniques below, while established businesses can and should use all of them:

■ **Consult secondary sources of information.** There is an enormous amount of information on specific types of business and market trends already available in books, magazines, newspapers, directories, and published surveys. The business department of your local library is a good place to start. Colleges, trade associations, and government agencies are also fruitful sources of information.

■ **Interview customers and suppliers.** If you haven't started your business yet, try to talk with potential competitors, their customers, and suppliers. If you're already in business, you can use normal contacts with customers and suppliers to sound them out to get their perspectives. Ask questions; people generally like giving their opinion. You can learn a lot by asking customers in your target market about their wants, needs, likes, and dislikes. Suppliers often have keen insight into what's happening in their field. They may also be able to give you some idea how your business compares with those of your competitors.

- **Review internal records and files.** After you've been in business a while, your sales records can tell you who your best customers are, what your best selling products are, what the market area for your business is, and much more. You can also get valuable information from credit records, receipts, complaints, and just about any other paperwork your business generates.

- **Interview employees.** Employees deal with customers on a day-to-day basis, so they could be an important source of customer information. They hear customer complaints about your product or service, and they know what customers are asking for. Because of their daily contact with customers, employees can probably provide a fairly accurate customer profile too.

Advanced Market Research Techniques

To obtain all the information you need, more sophisticated techniques of market research may be required. These include direct mail questionnaires, telephone surveys, focus groups, and test marketing. To ensure the most reliable results, these kinds of research should be designed by a professional market researcher, who can also conduct the study. To save money, you may want to gather the information yourself or have your employees gather it. Regardless of who compiles the data, have the market researcher interpret the results. You may be able to obtain low-budget research by contacting the marketing department of a local college or university. Often professors and graduate students are willing to do some moonlighting.

One word of caution about market research is in order. Be on guard against "paralysis by analysis." As valuable as market research is, it isn't a substitute for good business judgment. Many important business situations require that decisions be made without all the facts being known. Remember that the role of market research is to guide your decisions, not make them for you.

Telephone surveys are an excellent way to help find out how customers perceive your business.

Tips for Using the Following Forms:

Note: You are encouraged to copy these forms for your own use. Keep the unmarked originals in a safe place and make copies of them to work from.

Customer Profile Worksheet – Use this worksheet to describe your customers as accurately as you can. Identifying your best prospects will enable your marketing efforts to achieve better results and can save you lots of money too. Answer these questions to get a clear idea of who your target customers or clients are. This will help enormously by providing you with valuable insights on how and where to advertise for maximum results. And it will help you determine the proper look and tone of everything you do. This information will also be included in your business plan.

Competitor Review Worksheet – Put your main competitors' names in the spaces along the top of the form. Then enter the rest of the information in spaces provided. Some of the information, such as their addresses, prices, product lines, and reputation, will be relatively easy to discover, but other information will require some digging. Talk with competitors about each other, and talk with customers of each of the competitors. When you've got a good profile of each of your major competitors, you'll be in a good position to fill in the important information in the last two spaces at the bottom of the form. Based on each competitor's strengths and weaknesses, how will you position your business to compete with them? And how you expect they'll react will also be included in your business plan.

Industry Review Worksheet – To get a comprehensive view of your industry, use the sources mentioned in question 5 earlier in this section to answer the questions on this form. These answers will let you know whether the business you're contemplating has the potential to provide you with return you expect. The information from this form will also be included in your business plan.

CUSTOMER PROFILE WORKSHEET

Describe your ideal customer or client (after answering the questions below): _____

_____

_____

_____

1. Are they men, women, or both? _____

2. What is their age group? _____

3. What is their approximate average income? _____

4. What is their employment type (blue-collar, white-collar, managerial, professional, homemaker, etc.)? _____

_____

5. What is their lifestyle (personality, self-image, etc.)? _____

_____

6. Where are they located (local, statewide, national, international)? _____

7. How many of them are there? _____

8. How many do you expect to get as customers? _____

9. What percentage of the market do you expect to get? _____

10. What's the growth trend of your target market? _____

_____

11. How much will they pay for your product or service? _____

12. What are their buying habits? _____

_____

13. What are their attitudes toward what you're offering? _____

_____

14. What magazines do they read? _____

_____

15. What organizations do they belong to? _____

_____

16. What conventions or events do they attend? _____

_____

17. Is there a directory that lists them? _____

18. Are there mailing lists of them available? _____

_____

19. What's the best way to reach them? _____

_____

COMPETITOR REVIEW WORKSHEET

	Competitor #1	Competitor #2	Competitor #3	Competitor #4
Location				
Prices				
Product Lines				
Target Markets				
Positioning				
Unique Selling Points				
Your Strategic Difference				
Their Major Strengths				
Their Major Weakness				
Promotional Activities				
Reputation				
Market Share				
Financial Condition				
How You Will Compete				
Expected Responses				

Industry Trends

1. What are the annual sales, in dollars, of your industry or field? _____

2. How large will it be in five years? _____

3. Is this industry growing, stable, or declining? _____

4. Is your industry dominated by a few large companies or many small ones? _____
_____

5. What effect are regulatory or legal issues likely to have on this industry? _____
_____
_____

6. What important economic events could affect this industry? _____
_____
_____

7. What effect are cultural trends (life styles, demographics) likely to have on this industry? _____
_____
_____

8. What technological changes could affect your business or this industry? _____
_____
_____

9. Are other products or services like yours already offered in this industry? _____
_____

10. How does your business fit into the industry? _____
_____

Industry Financial Performance

11. What are the average sales and profits for your type of business? _____
_____

12. What is the gross margin (sales minus cost of items sold) as a percentage of sales? _____

13. What are the average expenses as a percentage of sales? _____

14. What is the average net profit (sales minus all expenses) as a percentage of sales? _____
_____

15. What is the normal markup (dollar markup divided by cost of merchandise) as a percentage? (if applicable)? _____

16. What is the annual inventory turnover rate (total sales divided by average inventory value)? (if applicable)? _____
_____

SALES & DISTRIBUTION

The Heart of Business

It's been said that nothing happens in business until somebody sells something. The significance of this is that for a business to be successful, it has to get its products or services into the hands of its customers. A business can have the best products or the finest services, but unless they find their way to customers in sufficient quantities, the business won't have a chance of succeeding.

That's why the process of getting your product or service to the ultimate consumer plays such a crucial role in your marketing mix. Sales and distribution is the "place" in the four Ps mentioned in the *Marketing Plan* section, it's where the customer buys the product or service, and includes all the steps involved in getting the product from where it originates to where it finally becomes available for purchase by the customer.

Personal Selling

Every business owner is a salesperson whether they realize it or not. In order to create a successful business, it's necessary for a business owner to know how to sell – not only their product or service, but themselves and their business as well. You may have to sell your business idea to a banker to get a loan, or to a prospective employee.

Though few would deny the importance of sales ability to business success, many small business owners find personal selling either distasteful or downright frightening. It doesn't have to be either if you understand the important role that sales plays in any business, and learn the selling skills necessary to be a good salesperson.

Just remember this: to be a successful business owner you're going to be a salesperson whether you want to be or not. What you have to decide is whether you're going to be a good salesperson or a mediocre one.

The Sales Process

Regardless of your type of business, it is important for you and any sales employees you hire to understand the selling process. This process consists of a series of steps, each one of which is the foundation for the following step. When each is done correctly and in the proper order, the result is another sale for your business. The following overview will introduce you to the basic selling process, which you can adapt for your business:

1. **Preparation.** Make sure you have as complete a knowledge of your product or service as possible. Think of yourself as a problem solver or consultant to your customers, and prepare to be an expert for them. At the minimum you should be aware of all the features, benefits, and prices of your product or service. No less important is to have the most thorough knowledge of your customers you can. It's also necessary to know ahead of time what your company sales policies and procedures are, and how to correctly fill out order forms or use the cash register. Every one of your employees should also be familiar with, and comfortable about, these mechanics too.

2. **Prospecting.** Today's competitive business environment ensures that tomorrow's successful business owners aren't waiting around for the phone to ring, or for the customers to come to them – they're taking the initiative and going out looking for sales. To get your business started off right and to keep it healthy, continually search for new business leads. Use the "Prospect Profile" found in this section to keep track of your hottest prospects. After you've been in business a while, you'll find that your best prospects are the ones most similar to your customers. Remember that business growth depends on continually adding new customers. So keep prospecting.

3. **Initial contact.** It's important to get off on the right foot. Start with a smile (even if the conversation is taking place over the telephone) and a cheerful greeting. Make the prospect feel important by being attentive and courteous. Listen carefully to everything the prospect says to determine if you should try to make a presentation. What you're trying to discover is whether the prospect is qualified, whether they are actually ready and able to buy. You'll learn this by asking questions. You'll learn a lot more with your ears open than you will with your mouth open, so probe to find out as much as you can about what the prospect wants. Once you have determined that the prospect is qualified and the time is right, you can begin your presentation.

4. **Presentation.** If you've done a good job of asking questions, you'll be prepared to tailor your presentation to your prospect's particular needs. In other words, first find out what the prospect wants and then present your product or service in those terms. Begin with a statement or question that will grab the prospect's attention, based on what they've told you so far. Concentrate on the benefits the prospect will receive from your product or service – always focus on what's in it for them from their point of view. Get the prospect involved as much as possible, don't

> *"Nothing happens until someone sells something."*
>
> Red Motley, Publisher
> Parade Magazine

just rattle off a canned sales pitch. Instead, adapt your presentation to the prospect's needs. Be creative, use showmanship – showing is a lot more persuasive than telling.

5. **Handling objections.** Welcome objections as a natural part of the sales process. Each objection you overcome means that you're one step closer to the sale. While it isn't a good idea to argue with customers, there are effective ways to handle objections. Start out by agreeing with the prospect as much as possible: "Yes, I can see why you'd think that, but...." Or you can ask them: "Why is it that you feel that way?" When price becomes an objection, and it often does, turn the discussion to value and point out why your product or service is a better value and will save them money in the long run; perhaps it will last longer, be more effective, need fewer repairs, etc. A good way of turning objections into sales is by asking something like this: "If the product did have the features you're asking for, would you buy it today?" If the answer is "no," then probe to find out why. Often the first several objections are merely "good reasons" given because they sound good. But they mask the "real reasons" which aren't immediately stated because they could make the prospect lose face: perhaps they don't have the buying authority, or maybe they just signed a contract that wasn't nearly as favorable as your deal, etc.

6. **Closing.** While many business people are uncomfortable asking a prospect for the order, it's the fastest and surest way to make the sale; and not asking for the order is the biggest reason for losing sales. Because timing is important, and building up to the close can create a high level of anxiety in both the prospect and the salesperson, don't wait until the end of your presentation to

"pop the question." Several times during your presentation, try to gauge the prospect's interest with a series of trial closes. When you perceive some interest on the prospect's part, ask, "When do you need delivery by?" or "Which color do you like better, the tan or the gray?" If you use these trial closes too early, or too often, they could sound manipulative. While offering choices is one of the best ways to close a sale, limit the choices and options so the prospect doesn't get confused. If a prospect is hesitating, creating a sense of urgency may help: "If you order today, I can give you a 10% discount." Even though closing puts you at risk of being rejected, always ask for the order. You're wasting your time and your prospect's time if you don't. Since most salespeople don't ask for the order, you'll have a competitive advantage if you do.

7. **Add-ons**. Right after making a purchase, a customer is most receptive to making additional purchases. So once the customer has made a purchase, suggest something to go along with it, ordinarily something that complements it well. For instance a toy store owner could suggest batteries for the toy, or even better, rechargeable batteries and a recharger. Someone who sells equipment could suggest an extended service contract. The more a customer buys from you, the more they are committed to you as a vendor.

8. **Follow-up**. Make your customers feel as though they made the right decision in buying from you. Thank them for their order. Later, check to make sure the delivery was made on schedule. Sales follow-up builds goodwill and repeat business. Don't limit your thinking to making that particular sale, think instead about creating a customer who will make numerous purchases from you over time. Satisfied customers are usually your best bet for new business. It takes a lot less effort to get a reorder than it does to get an order from someone who has never dealt with you before.

Selling takes perseverance. The average sale occurs on the seventh call.

Sales Tips

Many business owners find selling difficult and even uncomfortable. While this feeling is understandable, it's neither necessary nor useful and will disappear with experience. You may find it helpful to read books and listen to audiotapes on selling. Attending sales seminars is another good way to brush up on your selling skills.

Whenever you're in a sales situation don't worry about whether you're going to make the sale or not. Instead of focusing inward on your own thoughts and feelings, focus outward on the prospect. Subtly adapt your posture and breathing to that of the prospect, without obviously imitating each of their movements. This "mirroring" and "pacing" will help create rapport because the prospect will begin to feel more relaxed around you and more receptive to what you have to say.

One thing you should always keep in mind is that you're not going to make every sale. Typically, you'll hear "no" a lot more often than "yes." Don't take it personally, "no" isn't a personal rejection. It's merely a "no," which could mean "not at this time," or something similar. So you've got to keep going without being discouraged. Try to think of each turndown as a neutral outcome that you can learn from, and use each selling situation to learn how to be more effective.

Top salespeople have found, that on the average, their sales are made on or after the seventh sales call. Persevering that long is what separates them from average salespeople, who generally give up after two or three tries. Stick with the process outlined above, believe in yourself and your product or service, and keep at it. Pretty soon you'll be hearing "yes" a lot more often.

Sales Environments

Depending on the type of business, selling can take many forms:

Retail Sales. Because of the large number of stores, shops, and restaurants, people are probably more familiar with retail sales than any other kind. What makes retail sales different from other types of selling is that the customers come to your place of business instead of you going into theirs. Here are some things to remember about retail sales:

■ Customers expect assistance from sales clerks. Don't make them wait while you or your employees re-stock, tidy up merchandise, or engage in personal conversations.

■ Sales clerks are responsible for making customers feel welcome and comfortable. Remember that all customers want to be waited on promptly and to be treated with respect.

■ A frequent customer will become a loyal customer when you remember their name and use it while serving them.

■ Sales clerks need to know the store's policies and procedures concerning credit, discounts, layaways, returns, deliveries, and upcoming sales. One of the biggest complaints customers have about retail sales is that sales clerks are often uninformed about these things.

■ How customers are treated on the telephone is as important as how they're treated in person. When a customer calls for any reason, use that occasion to make them feel good about dealing with your business by handling their call courteously and efficiently. If a caller is dissatisfied with the service they receive over the telephone, it's unlikely they'll want to shop in person.

■ In the event of a dispute or misunderstanding, resolve it in the customer's favor. Customers may not always be right, but if you treat them as though they were, you'll gain a loyal customer base.

Outside Sales. Whenever you go to your customer's location to deliver your product or service, you're acting as an outside salesperson. This is true whether your customer is a consumer or another business. The overview of the sales process outlined above will acquaint you with how the sales process works, but there are a number of other things you should know:

■ Before meeting with any prospect, rehearse your presentation. In your mind picture the prospect saying "yes."

■ When you enter a prospect's home or office, remember that you're a guest and act accordingly.

■ It's better to call ahead for an appointment than to drop in unannounced.

■ People expect sales representatives to be presentable and professional. The best way to dress is similarly to, but a little better than the people you're calling on. If you're not dressed as well as the prospects, you'll look unsuccessful to them, but if you're overdressed, you may appear intimidating or phony.

■ Don't smoke or chew gum even if it's offered to you by the prospect.

■ Look for something personal in the prospect's immediate environment, such as a trophy or photograph, to comment on as an "ice breaker."

■ Once you've established rapport, get right to your presentation. Don't tell jokes or "shoot the breeze." Nobody wants their time wasted.

■ Stay focused on how your product or service can be of benefit to the prospect. Don't get sidetracked.

■ If the prospect is being constantly interrupted, say something like, "I can see how busy you are today, when would be a better time to talk?" Don't make your presentation until you have the prospect's full attention.

■ Make notes on what the prospect says, so you'll have more information to work with the next time you visit.

■ If you've told the prospect you'd take only ten minutes of their time, when that time has elapsed, mention it and prepare to leave. Allow the prospect to ask you to stay.

■ Never seem desperate for a sale. Think about the sales process as a long term relationship. Be better prepared the next time around.

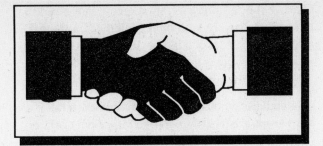

Professional Sales. In keeping with their status, professionals generally take a low-keyed approach to personal selling. Unlike the business person who engages in outside sales, lawyers, accountants, consultants, and other white collar professions find ways of building a client base without making sales calls. Some of the considerations that go into selling professional services are:

■ Clients expect professionals to be professional. Everything about your business should reinforce your professional identity.

■ When discussing business with a client, use ordinary language instead of jargon.

■ Respect your client's time by being on time and prepared for meetings and appointments.

■ The way most professionals get clients is by referral, or "word of mouth." So the more satisfied your clients are with your service, the more associates they'll refer to you.

■ Another important source of referrals is networking, which entails getting out of your office and meeting people at business and social events (networking is fully discussed later in this section).

■ A good way to become known locally, or even nationally is to establish yourself as an expert in your field. Write books, articles, or columns to reinforce your status as an authority. Make yourself available for interviews with the media.

■ Further enhance your identity as an authority by giving seminars or making speaking engagements.

■ Put out a newsletter that is of interest to your clients and prospects.

■ Offer free initial consultations to attract new clients.

Wholesale Sales. A form of business-to-business sales, wholesaling is much different than retail sales. Retailers typically sell only a few items at time to individual customers, while wholesalers sell large quantities to commercial accounts. Here are some of the keys for selling successfully at wholesale:

■ Establish a schedule for calling on customers and prospects so you don't go too long between visits. Doing so helps ensure your customers don't run out of stock, and it keeps you visible to your prospects.

■ As soon as up-to-date price lists are available, distribute them to customers and prospects. Out of date price lists can cause confusion and problems.

■ Respond quickly to requests for literature and samples. Follow up with a phone call to make sure the requested items were received.

■ Become a valued source of information by passing along industry news to your customers. But don't spread rumors or gossip. If your customers are given inside information about your other clients, they'll wonder what you say to others about them.

■ Don't "bad mouth" your competitors. Keep focused on how your business provides the most value to its customers.

■ Take personal responsibility for checking to make sure factory-shipped orders go out on schedule.

Telephone Sales. Any type of business can use the telephone to generate sales. Some businesses can also benefit from outbound telemarketing departments whose only job is to call customers and prospects soliciting business. Other businesses, particularly in the service field, find the telephone useful for cold calling to set up sales appointments. All types of business, from retailers to manufacturers, have found that inbound toll free (800) numbers can generate increased orders. Here are few tips about how to use the telephone as a sales tool in your business:

■ Courtesy is the main thing to remember about telephone sales. Treat callers with the same respect you would if you were face to face with them.

Any type of business can use the telephone to generate sales.

- Have incoming calls answered by people instead of machines whenever possible. While voice mail and other telephone answering mechanisms are convenient, many people don't like them.

- Have enough phone lines so that customers don't get busy signals when they call.

- Use scripts for outbound sales calls. Have scripted answers for the most common questions. But don't make the responses sound "canned."

- Don't call a prospect with the same offer until at least three months have passed since the previous call.

- Make sure your order form is easy enough to fill out that the telephone salesperson can use it while talking with the customer.

Distribution Channels

Getting products and services from producers to customers requires channels of distribution. Each channel is an organized network established for expediting the flow of product from the source to the ultimate consumer. Some distribution channels are simple and straightforward, going directly from the producing or providing company to the customer. Other channels have two or three layers between the producing company and the buyer.

Consultants, accountants, and other professionals provide their services directly to their clients. Similarly, most personal service businesses

barber shops, laundries, shoe repair shops and the like, deal directly with their customers, although they may be part of a larger distribution system if they sell products to their customers in addition to providing their primary service.

Retailers, wholesalers, and manufacturers, however, are usually part of a larger network, or chain of distribution. The main links in this chain of distribution are:

- **Retailers.** Stores, except for those that make everything they sell, are part of a channel of distribution; as are manufacturers, except for those that sell directly to their customers. The role of retailers is to purchase and stock goods for resale to consumers who come to them to make the purchase. Retailers may purchase their merchandise from manufacturers, wholesalers, or agents. Discounts and markups vary depending on the particular type of retail establishment, but generally retailers expect discounts of around 40-50% off list price.

The main consideration in retail sales is the store location, where accessibility and convenience are the keys to success. Other factors include the store's physical appearance, and the quality of its salespeople. Each of these factors can be a device, or tactic, to support a retail marketing strategy. Retail is the most popular form of distribution for most products, so manufacturers are usually desirous of gaining widespread retail distribution for their products. The resulting competition for shelf space has led those who want to sell through retail to find non-traditional outlets for their products. Some businesses are now seeking additional retail distribution through stores that normally don't stock their kind of product, but whose customers are nevertheless prospects for it. Selling home repair books through hardware stores is one example. This trend can also open up opportunities for retailers to add new profit centers to their business. Everyone realizes that a shoe store sells shoes, but it can also sell hosiery, shoe laces, and shoe polish. Other retail strategies for businesses that manufacture products include selling only through a few exclusive shops, through mass market retailers like K Mart, or through deep-discount warehouse-type outlets like the Price Club.

A product won't be successful until you have found a way to get it into the customer's hands.

■ **Wholesalers/ Distributors.** Depending on the industry, the "middlemen" who purchase and stock goods for resale to retailers or commercial accounts are called either wholesalers or distributors. They are extremely important in many fields because many manufacturers don't want to go through the trouble and expense of selling directly to individual stores. In some fields, selling through wholesalers is a necessity, but even where it isn't required, it can be a good way increase distribution. While the wholesaler's discount varies from industry to industry, 10 to 15% is a rough average. Wholesalers typically operate within a given geographical territory. Exclusive distributors are the only wholesaler in a specific territory to sell a particular manufacturer's line. Since they most often stock the products of several manufacturers, wholesalers usually sell in large quantities. In some industries wholesalers and distributors function merely as order takers who don't aggressively promote the products they carry, seeking only to satisfy existing demand, while in other industries distributors actively solicit new business by making sales calls.

■ **Agents/Brokers.** Many fields also have agents or brokers, who also sell to retailers and commercial accounts, but who don't usually purchase and stock the goods themselves. Agents are sometimes called manufacturers' reps. They can be an excellent channel for a company who either doesn't have its own sales force, or whose sales force is too small to reach all the available customers, either because of high demand or because the customers are geographically remote. Agents and brokers also represent several manufacturers, and they tend to be pursue sales aggressively. Typically, they expect a 10 to 15% commission on their sales. More information on this topic can be found below under the heading, "Independent Sales Agents."

■ **Sales Force.** Sales forces are generally used by businesses that sell to other businesses or professionals, but some businesses that sell directly to retailers or the public also employ them. Company salespeople are paid by salary, commission, or some combination of the two. Sales commissions depend both on the amount of salary a salesperson receives and the type of product or service being sold. Since salespeople represent only the company that employs them, they can concentrate exclusively on selling their employer's products. Unlike most other channels of distribution, employing salespeople can add substantially to a company's overhead.

No matter how good your product is, or how much of a demand your advertising creates, unless your product is widely available, it won't find its way into your customers' hands. The choice of which distribution methods you use depends a great deal on how your target market is accustomed to making similar purchases, the prevailing distribution practices in your field, and an analysis as to whether the benefits of adding additional channels of distribution outweigh the costs and time involved.

If your business is manufacturing or wholesaling, use the "Sales & Distribution Planning Guide" at the end of this section to determine the distribution channels you'll want to put into place for your business, and the "Sales Planning Worksheet" to plan your sales force if you intend to use one.

Manufacturer's reps can be your no-overhead sales force.

Independent Sales Agents

If you have difficulty selling, or have a product with national sales potential and don't want to miss sales opportunities, you may want to consider independent sales agents, or manufacturer's reps, as an alternative to hiring a sales force. Independent sales agents represent several clients on a commission basis. They call on clients in specific geographical territories and they generally insist on exclusive rights to sell in that territory. This can lead to conflicts if you're trying to put together a nationwide chain of reps, who may already have overlapping territories.

The commission manufacturer's reps charge varies, but is roughly in the 15-20% range. In a few cases, manufacturer's reps expect commissions on all sales made in their territories even if they didn't directly generate the sales. This isn't a condition you shouldn't agree to unless you don't intend to have any other source of sales. Before signing any contracts, make sure the rate and payment schedule for commissions, and how they are earned is clearly spelled out.

You can find out more about independent sales agents by consulting the directory put out annually by the Manufacturer's Agents National Association (MANA), which is listed in the **Resources** section. It contains a great deal of valuable information about dealing with manufacturer's reps as well as listings of the leading rep firms around the country. Your library may have a copy.

Networking

Every business owner can benefit from networking because everything that happens in business happens through people. Networking is the process of connecting people with each other to make things happen. It's a valuable tool to connect you with other people who can help your business succeed. It's also a great way to meet others with whom you share common interests and to make new friends.

Networking involves making contact with other people, usually to give and get referrals. Anytime you need something from someone in business – some information, an appointment, etc. – a referral makes it a lot easier to get because people are more comfortable dealing with a person referred by someone they already know. Though every type of business can benefit from networking, it is particularly effective for consultants, professionals, and services, all of which may get the bulk of their new clients through referrals.

Another benefit of networking is that interacting with others on a regular basis, particularly other business owners, gives you exposure to knowledge and experience you don't personally possess. You don't have to know everything yourself, or make every mistake yourself, because you can use networking to profit from the knowledge and experience of others. This is a valuable shortcut that high achievers have always used to help take some of the bumps out of the road to business success.

But there's a lot more to networking than just getting things for yourself. Networking is a two-way street where you give help as well as receive it. And it has its own set of rules:

■ **Be willing to help others and be open to letting them help you.** Don't just network for what you can get. Instead, help other people get what they want. Sometimes you'll give someone a name and a phone number, other times you'll make the call for them, and at other times, you'll just give them the name and let them look it up. Don't try to do everything for them, let them experience the challenge and satisfaction of making efforts in their own behalf. Also allow others to experience the satisfaction of helping you.

■ **Be clear about what you're looking for and stick to the point.** Don't use each conversation to drone on endlessly about yourself and your business. Instead ask the people you meet about themselves, their businesses, and their needs. When giving information, don't overload people – just give them enough information to be useful. When they give you leads, don't keep pumping them for more. Follow up on what they've already given you before asking for more.

■ **Listen carefully to everything you are told and are asked.** Make a sincere effort to listen from the other person's point of view. Ask a lot of questions about what they want and try to remain free of assumptions.

Use the "Effective Networking Checklist" at the end of this section to guide your networking efforts.

Where to Network

You already belong to several informal networks: friends, business associates, your church, social clubs, and various organizations, like the PTA. With the recent growth of groups devoted exclusively to networking, more opportunities for networking exist than ever before.

These groups can be identified by certain words in their titles, such as "contacts," "leads," "connections," and "referrals," as well as "networking." Look for announcements in your newspaper's business section for the location and meeting times for the groups near you.

If your community doesn't have formal networking groups, you might consider starting one. You can also join Toastmasters (a nationwide group dedicated to public speaking) and your local Chamber of Commerce. It's also a good idea to join the local chapter of the trade or professional association related to your business.

Notes:

Tips for Using the Following Forms:

Note: You are encouraged to copy these forms for your own use. Keep the unmarked originals in a safe place and make copies of them to work from.

Sales & Distribution Planning Guide – Manufacturing and wholesaling businesses should use this guide to help them plan the distribution channels they'll want to establish for their products. Retailers need only answer the questions in part A, Personal Sales. Pay special attention to the items marked with an asterisk, they are meant to be included in your business plan.

Sales Planning Worksheet – This form is designed for any business using an outside sales force. Answer all these questions before any salespeople are hired; and even if you're going to be the only salesperson, answer the first eleven questions to help plan your sales strategy.

Prospect Profile – Any business using outside sales needs to compile prospect data. This form should be good for most prospecting purposes, though you may want to adapt it for your own special needs. Harvey Mackay, the popular business author, uses a profile consisting of 66 questions. You probably won't need that much information, but you do need enough to get the order. The more you know about the prospect, the better chance you have of making the sale.

Effective Networking Checklist – Networking is an important activity for any business owner. It gives you a chance to let others know about your business. Successful business people are often great networkers. To hasten the success of your business, use this checklist to guide your networking efforts. Place a checkmark in each box you can answer "yes" to. The more checkmarks you have, the better you are at networking. The questions you don't check indicate the things you have to do to become a better networker.

SALES & DISTRIBUTION PLANNING GUIDE

A. Personal Sales

*1. Which kinds of sales effort do you intend to use?

❏ In-store ❏ Outside sales ❏ Telemarketing ❏ Other

*2. What kinds of salespeople do you intend to use?

❏ Yourself ❏ Inside salespeople ❏ Outside sales force ❏ Manufacturer's reps

*3. How many salespeople will you need? _____

B. Retail Distribution.

*1. Type of stores (if applicable): _____

*2. How many of them are there? _____

*3. How many of them do you expect to get as customers? _____

4. Where are they located? _____

5. What discounts do they expect? _____

6. Who does the buying (owner or buyer)? _____

7. What are their trade customs (payment terms, etc.)? _____

8. What trade publications do they read? _____

9. What trade groups do they belong to? _____

10. What trade shows do they attend? _____

11. Is there a directory that lists them? _____

12. Are there mailing lists of them available? _____

*13. How do you intend to reach them? _____

C. Wholesale Distribution.

*1. Type of distributors (if applicable): _____

*2. How many of them are there? _____

*3. How many of them do you expect to get as customers? _____

4. Where are they located? _____

5. What discounts do they expect? _____

6. What are their trade customs (payment terms, etc.)? _____

7. What trade publications do they read? _____

8. What organizations do they belong to? _____

9. What trade shows do they attend? _____

10. Is there a directory that lists them? _____

11. Are there mailing lists of them available? _____

*12. How do you intend to reach them? _____

Items with * are for inclusion in your business plan

SALES PLANNING WORKSHEET

1. Who are the decision makers within the companies you've targeted as potential customers? _____
   _____

2. How will you decide which prospects to contact first? _____
   _____

3. How many sales calls per day will each salesperson make? _____
   _____

4. How many sales calls will it take to get a presentation or demonstration? _____
   _____

5. How long will it take to get each presentation? _____
   _____

6. How many presentations will it take to get one sale? _____
   _____

7. How long will it take to get each sale? _____
   _____

8. What will be the dollar value of the initial order? _____
   _____

9. Will you be able to get repeat orders? _____
   _____

10. What will be the dollar value of each repeat order? _____
    _____

11. What volume of sales will each salesperson produce annually? _____
    _____

12. What is the commission structure for your salespeople? _____
    _____
    _____

13. Will the commission increase or decrease once the quota is met? _____
    _____

14. When are the commissions payable? _____
    _____

PROSPECT PROFILE

Company: _____ **Date:** _____

Contact: _____ **Title:** _____ **Phone:** _____

Address: _____ **City:** _____ **State:** _____ **ZIP:** _____

Type of Business: _____

Decision maker(s): _____

Influencer(s): _____

What are this company's main goals and objectives?: _____

_____

What is their current situation?: _____

_____

What problems or needs do they have?: _____

_____

What questions can I ask to clarify this company's needs?: _____

_____

What are their decision making criteria?: _____

_____

Which benefits are most important to this company?: _____

_____

What objections does this prospect have?: _____

_____

What are the answers to these objections?: _____

_____

What is my specific goal in calling on this account?: _____

_____

How will I accomplish this goal?: _____

_____

Contact date: _____ Results: _____

_____

Contact date: _____ Results: _____

_____

Contact date: _____ Results: _____

_____

Contact date: _____ Results: _____

_____

Basic networking:

❏ Do you attend at least one meeting a week where you can make contacts?

❏ Do you go out of your way to introduce yourself to other people, tell them what you do, and ask them what they do?

❏ Do you give them your business card?

❏ Do you ask for theirs?

❏ After you've talked with someone, do you jot down key information about them on the back of their business cards so you don't forget it?

❏ Do you ask for specific referrals?

❏ Do you write them down?

❏ Do you follow up on them?

❏ Do you write a "thank you" note to the person who gave you the referrals and let them know how you used their leads?

❏ When giving referrals, do you limit them to three, so the person you're giving them to won't be overwhelmed (and to ensure they are serious)?

❏ Do you avoid sending too many referrals to the same resources?

Advanced Networking:

❏ Do you go to conferences and trade shows in your field?

❏ Do you write articles for trade journals or other publications in your field?

❏ Do you send people you meet copies of articles they would be interested in receiving?

❏ Do you send people copies of articles about your business?

❏ Do you call people and ask them for advice on your current projects?

❏ Do you ask people to recommend others who might be able to help you?

❏ Do you invite the people you've met to parties or special events?

❏ Are you listed in all relevant directories for your field?

❏ Are you listed with your alumni association?

❏ Are you listed in local business publications?

Networking Opportunities (List places where you can network):

_____   _____

_____   _____

_____   _____

_____   _____

_____   _____

PROMOTION

Promoting Your Business

Every successful business uses some sort of promotion to influence certain audiences by informing or persuading them. Promotional activities are usually directed at customers and prospects, but other audiences may include the general public, investors, government officials, employees, suppliers, and distributors. Persuading customers to buy the product or service being promoted is the most frequent use of promotion.

Promotional activities are tactics that support your marketing strategy. They are the vehicles for getting your message out to those you want to purchase your product or service. Promotion is an umbrella term that covers a wide range of activities. It is considered by many business people to be the most important aspect of marketing, as well as the most difficult to master. Promotion includes:

■ **Advertising.** Unless people know about your business and your products or services, they're not likely to become customers. Advertising is a way to let prospects know who you are, what your product or service is, and how they can purchase what you have for sale. It consists of paid messages in media such as newspapers and magazines and on radio and television to attract customers. Which media you advertise in depends on the audience you're trying to reach and how effectively a particular medium can present your product or service.

■ **Sales promotion.** Sales promotion is a kind of advertising that doesn't involve paid display ads or broadcast time. Samples,

premiums, trade shows, reduced price coupons, contests, introductory offers, and imprinted calendars are all effective sales promotion tactics. Which ones you choose depends on the nature of your business and what you're trying to achieve.

■ **Publicity.** Publicity consists of unpaid communications, such as feature stories and product announcements appearing as news in either print or broadcast media. Announcing new products, having a grand opening, offering seminars, or providing helpful hints are just a few of the tactics you can use to get free publicity for your business. Hooking up some aspect of your business into a current event is another good tactic. Publicity stunts, such as having people dress in costumes or wearing masks, are time-honored ways of getting publicity. Many businesses can benefit quickly and dramatically from publicity, particularly if the business has a newsworthy or attention-getting aspect.

■ **Marketing communications.** In this usage, marketing communications refers to the various elements – logos, brochures, and catalogs – that go into building a company's identity, as well as other communications, such as invoices and company stationery. In addition to building an identity, marketing communications materials can also be used to sell: the backs of business cards can be used as mini-billboards, new offers can be sent out with invoices and statements, etc.

Advertising

Advertising consists of paid sales presentations and informational messages intended to communicate with large numbers of people at the same time. Common types of advertising include newspaper and magazine ads, radio and television commercials, direct mail, billboards, and the like. The purpose of advertising is to inform customers about a company's products or services, persuade them to buy, and, in the case of well-known businesses, to remind customers of their company name and products.

Many business owners don't understand advertising or why they might need to advertise. Every business needs to attract customers, and because advertising can reach large numbers of people, it may be an effective way to build your business. But there's nothing magic about it. You can't just buy some ads and expect business to boom. It doesn't work as simply as that.

Often small business advertising is wasted on a shotgun approach that doesn't focus on the company's best prospects: those who are ready, willing, and able to purchase the product or service. In an attempt to reach "everybody," these advertisers either miss their true target market or spend far more than necessary to reach it.

Advertising is most effective when done in support of an overall marketing strategy. Your marketing strategy should be based on who your best prospects are and what's important to them. Because you can't be all things to all people, position your product or service to appeal directly to your target market and concentrate your advertising budget on trying to attract them.

You'll find more information on creating a marketing strategy for your business in the *Marketing Plan* section. Use the "Customer Profile Worksheet" in the *Market Research* section to help target your market.

Developing An Advertisement

Before spending any money on advertising, the first thing to do is to clearly determine what you want the ad to accomplish. Each ad you do should have the goal of achieving one of the following results:

- **Generate immediate orders.** Wally Javitz used direct mail advertising to get immediate orders for his book on off-shore corporations.

- **Promote special events such as sales, business openings, new products.** When Todd Spinelli open his second Clubhouse Connection sporting goods store, he advertised the grand opening in local newspapers.

- **Generate inquiries for follow-up.** Doug Alejandro, owner of Bottom Line Consulting, offers free reports for business owners on such things as "The Seven Biggest Causes of Business Failure" and "How to Raise Capital for Your Business" in a local business newspaper. He then follows up on the enquiries, seeking an appointment to assess their needs, with the intent of signing them on as clients of his firm.

- **Build recognition of your business and create a favorable image.** Many large companies, including ITT, TRW, Greyhound, Beatrice, and Chevron, have run advertising designed to gain public awareness. Instead of trying to sell products, these ads were intended to create a favorable image for each of these companies in the minds of their audience.

As a new business, your advertising should be designed to accomplish one of the first three goals on this list. It's a rare start-up that can afford to put money into "image" advertising like the major consumer product companies. Instead, use the look and tone of your regular advertising and other marketing communication materials to create and reinforce your business identity, and put your advertising dollars to work getting people to buy your products or services.

Generally, the most effective ads focus on the customer's needs or wants, and describe the product or service in terms of the benefits it provides for the customer. The ad needs to tell the customers how they will be better off from having purchased the product or service. Emphasizing a key benefit, such as saving the customer time, and building the ad around that is one of the best tactics to use.

Other tactics include comparisons with competitive products, two-for-one offers, special one-day discounts, and offers of free information. These tactics all involve the content of the ad, but there are other kinds of advertising tactics as well: the tone of the ad (humorous, friendly, informative, etc.), the ad's design, the timing of the ad, and the offer itself.

Which tactics you use in your advertising will help determine the media you select and the exact message you communicate. One of the best ways to get familiar with the tactics in your field is to take a careful look at how your competitors are advertising. What tactics are they using? Can any of them apply to your business? Collect your competitors' advertising materials and use them to stimulate your thinking.

The most important things to take into consideration in any ad are the audience and the offer. Who is the ad trying to reach? If the ad isn't presented to the right audience and addressed to them in their own language, then it isn't going to get noticed. And if the offer isn't something that interests them and gets them excited, then they're not going to pay attention to it even if they do notice it.

> **Your ads should have one specific goal, either to:**
> - generate immediate orders,
> - generate inquiries about your product or service, or
> - promote a special event, a sale or a new product.

Creating effective advertising is an art that requires special writing and artistic skills. Advertising messages consist of copy (words) and graphics (pictures). Some ads, particularly smaller ones, are made up entirely of copy, but even when an ad has graphics, the copy is still what does the bulk of the selling.

So unless you're an expert copywriter, don't write your own advertising copy, and don't design your ad unless you have a graphic design background. If your ad is weak in either copy or design, you'll most likely be wasting your money running it. See the "Advertising Design Checklist" at the end of this section to get an idea of what it takes to create an effective ad.

Where To Get Advertising Help

Large companies often pay huge amounts to ad agencies for creating their advertising, but most small businesses don't have this luxury. Fortunately there are more reasonably priced alternatives for small, and even new, businesses. You could try some of the smaller ad agencies, whose fees aren't as high as those of large agencies. But even if their fees are too high, you could hire freelance copywriters and designers, who will work on an hourly or project basis. To find advertising agencies and freelancers, ask business associates for referrals. If you happen to see an ad you like, call the advertiser and ask who did it for them. Business owners living near colleges, may be able to find a talented marketing or advertising student who can do good work inexpensively.

Before hiring someone to create your advertising, ask to see samples of their work. You should be comfortable with what you see. If you don't like the work or don't understand it, then move on to someone else. Be skeptical of anyone who tries to explain why their ads are good. Ads are supposed to do their own talking, if they don't, they're not good ads. Ask about results. An ad that increases sales 20% is worth more than one that wins a shelf full of awards, without improving sales.

When interviewing agencies or free-lancers, make sure they understand both your product and your market. Unless they do, you could end up with a costly disaster instead of a winning ad. It's best to work with someone who has small business experience and who understands the importance of staying within budgets.

If you intend to run newspaper or yellow pages ads, you can usually have them done free by the publication's staff as part of the cost of the ad. Though the ad will probably be done by someone who has already created a number of other ads, the person isn't likely to be proficient at copywriting, nor are they likely to know much about your product or market.

The point isn't to get the lowest priced ad you can, but rather to get the best ad you can afford. A truly effective ad will pay for itself many times over, while a poor ad will cost you money to prepare, to run, and to replace.

Deciding Where to Advertise

Where you choose to advertise will depend on the audience you're trying to reach, the geographical range of your business, where your product or service can be most effectively presented, and your budget. For a few businesses, a simple Yellow Pages ad will reel in customers. Most businesses, however, need to put considerably more thought into how and where they advertise. Here is a discussion of what you need to know in order to make a good decision:

■ **How well the medium reaches your target audience,** or how many qualified prospects see your ad, how many times they are exposed to it, and how long that exposure lasts. This is the main consideration for choosing an advertising medium. Getting your message in front of those who are interested in what you have to sell is the key to advertising success. If you've profiled your customer accurately, you know who you're trying to reach. It doesn't matter how many readers a publication has, or how large the audience is for a radio or television show, the real question is how many of them fit your customer profile. Another factor that comes into play is the geographical region you're trying to reach. If all your business comes from a highly localized area, advertising far and wide will be a waste of money. On the other hand, if you have a product with national distribution and

you're only advertising in local media, you could be ignoring the major part of your market. Place your advertising in the media that do the best job of reaching your target audience.

■ **How effectively the medium communicates your main selling points.** The second consideration is whether your product or service can be effectively presented in that particular medium. Your ad has to be able to tell your product's story in the length of time the customer is exposed to it. Exposure time refers to how long the message lasts (a radio commercial has a short exposure time, while a newspaper ad can be read as long as the reader desires), and life span refers to how long people can be expected to keep the medium around for reference (newspapers have a short life span, magazines have a long life span). Products and services whose sale requires lengthy explanations or demonstrations cannot use a medium that doesn't allow for this, though it may be possible to use that medium to get inquiries. Following up the inquiries with a brochure or a sales call to give the required explanation or demonstration is called a "two-step" sale. Make sure any medium you choose allows you to give the customer all the information they need to make a buying decision or to request additional information.

■ **How much that particular medium costs,** usually measured in terms of cost per thousand prospects reached, or CPM. Advertising is expensive, so it is important to have a way of comparing the prices of various media. This is done by dividing the cost of the ad by the number of people reached expressed in thousands. If an ad in one medium with a circulation of 100,000 costs $200, and a similar ad in another medium with a circulation of 500,000 costs $500, you can use the CPM to judge which is the better buy. The first ad has a CPM of $2 ($200 ÷ 100), while the second ad has a CPM of $1 ($500 ÷ 500), making the second ad a better buy. But how many people will see an ad is only part of the story. What is more critical is how many of the people seeing the ad match your customer profile. How many qualified prospects it reaches, not how many people in general see it, will determine the response your ad gets. Intelligent media buying decisions can't be based on price alone. A better measure is the cost of reaching qualified prospects. That's why the best advertising medium isn't necessarily the least expensive one, but the most effective one.

When you're considering advertising in a certain publication, call or write their advertising department and request a rate card and a readership survey. Most often these will be sent to you as part of a media kit. The rate card contains information on ad costs and production specifications. The readership survey indicates how well that publication's readers match your customer profile. A good survey will tell you the readers' average age, sex, income level, and other demographic information. If there is a good match with your customer profile, and the rates are reasonable, then this could be an excellent place to advertise. Radio and television stations may also provide information of this sort, but it usually isn't as comprehensive.

"Many a small thing has been made large by the right kind of advertising."

Mark Twain

Media Comparison

To give you a better idea of how the various media stack up against each other, here is an overview which includes the advantages and disadvantages of each:

Newspapers (Daily and Weekly) – Newspapers reach large numbers of people and can be targeted geographically. Their short lead times mean that ads can be placed quickly. Because you can run different ads in the newspaper at different times, they provide flexibility. Larger newspapers offer zoned advertising, where you can reach just the part of the community where the bulk of your customers live. The prestige of the newspaper can add credence to your ad. At the same time, newspaper ads have a short life span, their production quality is poor, and many people scan newspapers quickly. Newspaper advertising can also be relatively expensive. Generally newspaper ads work best for retailers whose market lies within the circulation area. You can find directories that list daily and weekly newspapers at your local library.

Magazines (Local and National) – Magazine ads can be targeted to specific geographic and demographic markets. The quality of reproduction is high and the ad has a relatively long life. The credibility and prestige of the magazine can benefit your ad. Some magazines provide extra services such as reader response cards to make lead generation easier. On the other hand, ads are often costly to prepare and run, and they must be placed well in advance of the issue's appearance, so there's very little flexibility. As an advertiser, you'll have very little control over where your ad appears in the magazine. Magazine ads are best suited for mail order businesses, national services, and brand name merchandise. Some products and services, most notably books and big-ticket items, don't generally sell well through magazine ads.

Trade Journals – Trade journals are the most highly targeted publications because they're dedicated to a single topic. Like other magazines, they have relatively long lead times and very good reproduction quality, but may be costly. Steady advertisers in trade journal publications may find it easier to get preferred placement than is the case in general interest magazines. Trade journals are used primarily in business-to-business marketing for products and services directly related to subject matter of the publication. They often provide a number of other services such as product announcements, reader response cards, and mailing list rental.

Yellow Pages – Customers with a need or desire to buy most often turn to the yellow pages, so most businesses will want to advertise or list themselves in the local directory. Directories provide an opportunity to describe all your products, services, hours of operation, location and phone number in one easily accessible place. They also allow you to advertise head-to-head with even your largest competitors, and to target customers by advertising under appropriate headings. Ads can only be changed once per year and reach customers only within the directory area, but are relatively inexpensive so you can easily advertise in more than one at a time. Because the directory is annual, be sure you do not miss the deadline.

Direct Mail – The most personalized of all media, direct mail advertising provides a great deal of flexibility in reaching targeted market segments. It also offers great flexibility for what can be said and shown. And there isn't any clutter from competing ads. Direct mail allows the presentation of complete information in a way not possible in other media. Yet some people view direct mail as "junk mail" and throw it away without reading it. Direct mail is best suited for mail order and catalog businesses, but also works well for some services and retailers. The success of any mailing is tied primarily to the quality of the mailing list. The per person cost of direct mail can vary greatly depending on the quality and complexity of the mailing piece.

Radio – Radio reaches large audiences and lends itself to demographic and geographic segmentation. It also provides audio capability, adding another dimension. Radio commercials are relatively inexpensive, have short lead times, and can reach audiences in their cars. On the other hand, the message is temporary due to its short exposure time. And the market is fragmented because of the large number of radio stations. Radio works best for businesses whose customers fit a station's demographics, but there isn't as much demographic information available on radio as there is on other media.

Television – Television is best used for mass coverage to large audiences. TV commercials have high impact because of their video and audio capabilities, and their short lead times mean that response will follow quickly. Flexibility is high with regard to large scale geographical targeting because every major geographic region has its own TV stations. There is prestige attached to quality television advertising. The other side of the coin, however, is that television ads are very expensive and require

---

Advertising In a Nutshell

To get the best results from your advertising:

- **set an objective for your advertising** – be sure about want you want to accomplish

- **target your market with precision** – know exactly who you're advertising to

- **develop an advertising plan** – choose the media that reaches your target market most efficiently

- **offer your prospects something they want** – make the offer easy to understand and emphasize the benefits they will receive by acting immediately

- **tell your story in the prospects' language** – make sure the ad reads like a conversation to a friend, using words the readers will be comfortable with

- **make it easy for them to respond** – tell them what action to take and include coupons, an 800 number, and business reply envelopes

- **follow through** – ship promptly and stand behind what you sell

- **track your results** – be sure to find out what's working so you can do more of it.

---

costly professionals to produce. The ad's message is extremely temporary because of its short exposure time. And targeting specific demographic markets can be difficult. Television is best suited for products and services with wide appeal to the mass market.

Outdoor and Transit – Billboards and transit ads are relatively inexpensive and people view them repeatedly. At the same time, both are limited to simple messages. And people only see the ad for a very short period of time while driving or commuting. Billboards are best used for attractions and entertainments located near the billboard, while transit ads work best for businesses along the route.

Other – Flyers, handbills, and posters can be effective for most types of business. They're inexpensive and can be distributed in selected areas. While they are sometimes seen as "tacky" and ignored, adding a coupon can help to increase their perceived value. Other low cost media include coupon books and cooperative mailings, with several businesses sharing the costs. These "guerrilla" methods are well suited for introducing a new business or service or for advertising a special sale. For more ideas see the discussion on Sales Promotion immediately following this introduction to advertising.

For easy comparison, you'll find the major advertising media and the characteristics of each on the accompanying "Advertising Media Comparison Guide."

Other Advertising Considerations

This discussion of advertising is intended to acquaint you with the major considerations you need understand to make good advertising decisions. Here are a few more:

Advertising Plan. After you've found what you think are the best media for advertising your product or service, use the "Advertising Placement Planner" at the end of this section to plan your program systematically. It gives you a convenient way to list your options and to compare their costs. Each column indicates a critical item that needs to be addressed. Filling in each item will assure that you have all the

information you need to make a sound advertising decision. Having a plan can help you prevent costly mistakes arising from poor decisions caused by lack of complete information.

Testing. Advertising experts say that testing is indispensable for creating a successful advertising program. Testing can measure the effectiveness of different elements in an advertising campaign. Test different ads against each other in the same medium, test different media against each other using the same ad, test mailing lists against each other using the same mailing piece, and test different mailing pieces by dividing a mailing list and sending one mailing piece to part of the list and a different mailing piece to another part of the list. To make identifying the source of an order easier, include a key code in all ads, preferably on a coupon, and on all mailing labels. A key code is simply a few letters or numbers that tell you the origin of the order. Putting a department number in your return address is a common way to key a promotion piece (e.g. Dept. SI902). When people come in, or call in, ask where they heard about your product or service. The more you can to determine where your sales dollars are coming from, the better able you'll be to plan your advertising. When you know which parts of your advertising plan are working well, keep repeating them as long as they continue to be successful.

Measuring Results. Many advertisers judge the effectiveness of an ad by its response rate, or the number of people who respond to the ad as a percentage of the total audience exposed to the ad. For example, if a business gets 500 responses from 40,000 mailing pieces their response rate would be 1.25%. A more meaningful way to judge results is by comparing the amount of money returned by the ad to the amount of money spent on it. If one ad draws $17.85 in sales for each $1 spent while another ad brings in $2.23 for each $1, the first ad is clearly more effective than the second.

If you intend to be heavily involved in the advertising of your product or service, read some of the books on marketing and advertising mentioned in the **Resources** section at the back of this binder.

ADVERTISING MEDIA COMPARISON GUIDE

Characteristic	Daily Newspapers	Weekly Newspapers	Local Magazines	National Magazines	Yellow Pages
Market Area	City-wide or metro area coverage. May be divided into zoned editions.	Localized community coverage.	Metropolitan area or regional coverage. May have zoned editions.	National coverage. Regional editions are often available.	City-wide or metro area coverage. Individual directories for each community.
Audience	General.	General.	General. Often better educated and more affluent than the average consumer.	Generally highly targeted to specific interest groups.	General.
Best Suited For	Retailers who serve a relatively wide market area that matches the circulation area of the newspaper.	Retailers serving a local market.	Restaurants, entertainment businesses, specialty retailers, and mail order businesses.	Brand name items. National services. Mail order businesses.	Services, retailers of speciality or brand name items.
Advantages	Large numbers of people can be reached with short lead times. Easy to change ads.	Targets specific locations. Short lead times. Easy to change ads.	Loyal special interest audience. Relatively long life. Reproduction quality high.	Targeted to highly loyal special interest and demographic markets. Long ad life. Excellent reproduction quality.	Long ad life. Used often by consumers.
Disadvantages	Audience not targeted. Short life span for ad. Relatively expensive. Poor reproduction quality.	Audience limited. Readers may not pay much attention to it. Short life span for ad. Poor reproduction quality.	Audience limited. Little control over ad placement. May be costly to prepare and run.	Long lead times. Little or no control of ad placement. Can be costly to prepare. Relatively expensive to run.	Only those with immediate need use it. Doesn't work well with some types of business.
Approximate Cost	Type: Metropolitan Daily Rate base: 1,380,000 Size: 4" x 5" (1/12 page) Color: black/white Run: 3 days @ $1425. Cost: $4275. CPM: $1.03*	Type: City Weekly Rate base: 200,000 Size: 6.5" x 5" (1/8 page) Color: black/white Run: 3 days @ $500. Cost: $1500. CPM: $2.50*	Type: Local Lifestyle Rate base: 175,000 Size: 4.5" x 2.5" (1/6 page) Color: black/white Run: 3 months @ $800. Cost: $2400. CPM: $4.57*	Type: National General Interest Rate base: 1,800,000 Size: 2.5" x 4.5" (1/6 page) Color: black/white Run: 3 months @ $8,760. Cost: $26,280. CPM: $4.87	Type: Metropolitan Area Rate base: 1,000,000 Size: 3.5" x 2.5" (1/8 page) Color: black/white (yellow) Run: 12 months @ $232. Cost: $2784. CPM: $2.78*
Comments	Production costs included in price.	Production costs included if no art work is required.	Does not include the cost of designing and producing the ad.	Does not include the cost of designing and producing the ad.	Production costs included in price.

* CPM is the cost of getting your message in front of one thousand members of a medium's audience. It should be used in conjunction with likely response rates when selecting advertising media.

ADVERTISING MEDIA COMPARISON GUIDE

Characteristic	Direct Mail	Radio	Television	Outdoor	Transit
Market Area	Coverage may be as wide or as narrow as the advertiser chooses, even down to a single zip code.	Market area defined by the station's location and strength of signal.	Broadcast market area defined by the station's location and strength of signal. Cable requires special hook-up.	Coverage may be as wide as an entire metro area or as narrow as a single neighborhood.	May cover an entire metro area or a few transit routes.
Audience	May be targeted to any audience for which a mailing list exists.	Specific audiences may be targeted on the basis of the station's programming format.	Time of day and program determines viewer profile. Tend to be younger than average.	General, but specifically drivers.	General, particularly workers and pedestrians.
Best Suited For	Mail order and catalog businesses. Also services and retailers, particularly new businesses.	Businesses with easily identifiable demographics (age, sex, lifestyle, etc.).	Products and services with wide appeal. Also good for businesses whose owners have dynamic personalities.	Attractions, amusements, and entertainments. Tourist related businesses. Brand names.	Businesses located along the transit route.
Advantages	Personalized approach to large numbers of qualified prospects. Allows complete presentation. No competing ads.	Large audience reach with demographic and geographic selection. Relatively inexpensive. Reaches people in cars.	Mass coverage to large audiences. Combination of audio and visual elements creates dramatic impact.	Frequent exposure.	Repeated lengthy exposures.
Disadvantages	Negative image: "junk mail." Often ignored by recipients.	Temporary message because of short exposure time. Fragmented market because of large number of stations.	Expensive to buy and requires costly professionals to produce.	Limited to very simple messages. Short exposure time because people are driving by.	Audience limited to passengers who ride that route.
Approximate Cost	Type: "Standard" Mail Package Quantity mailed: 100,000 Size: 8.5" x 11" letter & brochure Color: full color Frequency: 1 mailing Cost: $60,000. CPM: $600*	Type: Metropolitan Area Rate base: 130,000 Time: 60 seconds Frequency: 1 spot for 5 days Morning drivetime cost: $3750. Late night cost: $50. CPM: $5.77*	Type: Network Affiliate Rate base: 194,000 Time: 30 seconds Frequency: 1 spot for 5 days Primetime cost: $ 40,000. Off hours cost: $250. CPM: $41.24*	Type: Metropolitan Area Rate base: varies Size: 14' x 48' Color: full color Frequency: 4 months @ $3800. Cost: $15,200. CPM: $63.33*	Type: Metropolitan Area Rate base: 240,000 Size: 12'x25' Color: full color Frequency: 1 month, 24 posters Cost: $14,760 CPM: $61.50*
Comments	Letter, brochure, order form, envelope, return envelope, labels, mailing, postage, art and copywriting all included.	Production costs included in price. "Celebrity" DJ voices available at additional charge.	Does not include the cost of producing the commercial.	Production costs included in price.	Production costs included in price.

* CPM is the cost of getting your message in front of one thousand members of a medium's audience. It should be used in conjunction with likely response rates when selecting advertising media.

Sales Promotion

Though often necessary, traditional advertising is not only expensive, it's also impersonal. Sales promotion, on the other hand, can be relatively inexpensive and provide a more personal way of relating to customers. People like to receive things for free, so sales promotion often involves giving away samples or free gifts. Here are examples of some typical sales promotion activities:

- **Samples**. There's no better way to let customers know how good your product or service is than by letting them sample it. Stores that sell cookies, candy, or ice cream know the power of samples. When major companies introduce a new soap, shampoo, or detergent, large numbers of selected households get a free sample. Some businesses mail out samples, some have them hand delivered, and others require that the customer come into the place of business to receive the sample. Even attorneys are offering free introductory consultations.

- **Reduced price coupons**. If you can't provide samples of your product or service, you can still offer it at a reduced rate to attract customers. Coupons are becoming increasingly popular because they appeal to a customer's desire to get a good deal. Reduced price coupons are an especially good way to introduce prospects to your product or service. Once they try it and like it, they'll be more likely to purchase it at the full price. Coupons can be part of your regular ads, mailed out to prospects, or be included in coupon books or cooperative mailings.

- **Premiums**. The good thing about premiums is that if they are well chosen, the customer will keep them a long time. And each time they look at the premium, they'll be reminded of you. That's why it's a good idea to have premiums personalized with your business name and address or phone number. The best premiums are ones the customer will want to keep or use. Imprinted pens, calendars, and note pads are commonly used as premiums. Paperweights, letter openers, and key chains can also be good choices. The more related a premium is

to your business, the better reminder it will be to the receiver. One floppy disk manufacturer gives away chocolate computer disks. Some firms give away private label wines and other exotic fare, but for most small businesses it's probably best to stick with less expensive items. One of the most popular premiums at a nurses convention a few years ago was a little furry ball about the size of a marble with eyes, a nurse's cap, and feet. Peeling away a strip on the bottom of the feet exposed an adhesive that allowed the little "nurse" to be affixed to practically any surface. Even though this item was inexpensive the nurses loved it.

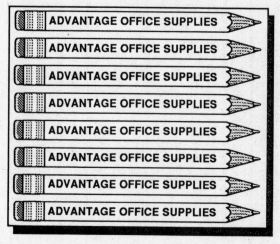

- **Contests**. People like the idea of winning something and for this reason are attracted to contests. Large companies conduct million dollar sweepstakes to gather prospect names, but you don't need to offer a huge prize to attract attention. You can offer modest cash prizes, merchandise, or gift certificates instead. The more related the contest is to your business, the better its goodwill value. Contests that judge customers' use of your product are ideal: a model building contest in a hobby shop, a cooking or baking contest at a kitchenware store, or a home-made clothing contest in a fabric shop. Not all contests require skill. Some businesses have monthly business card drawings, others have contests where customers try to guess how many coins, marbles, or jelly beans are in a container. One retail store has monthly drawings of copies of its cash register receipts – the more purchases customers make, the more chance they have to win. Stay alert for contest ideas that you can adapt to your business.

■ **Trade shows.** Every major industry has trade shows, often organized by the industry trade associations. Exhibitors rent booths to display and demonstrate their products and services to the association's members. These shows are an excellent opportunity to meet buyers face to face and get your promotional materials into their hands. They also provide a good opportunity to learn more about the buyers, suppliers, competitors, and opinion makers in your field. Buyers go from booth to booth examining products and talking to the exhibitors, often placing orders at the show. Reporters also attend looking for interesting stories about new products. There are also shows aimed at consumers and end users. Trade shows are a great way to introduce a product, but they require a great deal of preparation, and can be quite costly.

Which sales promotion activities you choose will depend on your type of business and what you're trying to achieve. With a little imagination you should be able to come up with a number of promotional activities that will work well for your business.

Notes:

Publicity

Your business can benefit from the fact that half of all the stories in the daily media are the result of a publicist's efforts. Even if you can't afford a public relations agency, by following the guidelines below, you'll be well on your way to launching a successful publicity campaign for your business.

Drawing favorable attention to your business and its products or services is a necessary ingredient of business success. Large, well-funded companies can spend a fortune in advertising to let everyone know about them. Most small businesses, however, can't afford to follow suit. Fortunately though, even without a massive promotion budget, a small business can still get publicity in local and national print and broadcast media. In many instances publicity is much more effective than advertising for making customers aware of a new business or product. And it certainly is less expensive.

Having your business written up favorably in a local newspaper or magazine can be a real boon to your business. When this happens, either request reprints or cut out the article and reproduce it. You can use the copies of the article to send along when you're trying to get more publicity. Copies of articles about your business can also be sent out to prospects and/or customers, and hung in attractive frames at your place of business for added credibility.

Being on radio and television can also get you exposed to large numbers of people, and it can also be a lot of fun. So don't be intimidated by the thought of going out over the airwaves. It's a lot easier than you think. And you can make it even easier by knowing exactly what you want to get across to the audience.

As with any promotional activity, the goal of your publicity program should be to generate a positive response from your customers and prospects. In many ways it's easier to do this with publicity than with advertising since stories about a business are believable because they're perceived as news, while advertising is regarded with skepticism.

The secret to creating successful publicity is having a newsworthy angle. Regardless of which media you've targeted, you're going to have to answer the same question: What about your business is interesting enough to be considered newsworthy? Only if your story is of interest, benefit, or entertainment value to their readers, viewers, or listeners will the media give you coverage. This means that your news release should read more like news than advertising. Blatantly self-serving news releases are virtually certain to be tossed out. But enough of what doesn't work, let's look at what does work.

Getting Publicity

Since a properly produced news release is the backbone of any publicity campaign, follow the instructions given below and be sure to look at the sample news release as you read to make sure you understand what all the elements look like in actual use.

While sending out news releases is the most obvious part of getting mentioned in the media, creating real news about your product or service is actually the first step. The next step is identifying and contacting the appropriate media to receive your news release. To get the best results, send your news releases only to those media whose audiences are very likely to be interested in what you have to say.

Follow-up often gets overlooked, but it is crucial to any publicity campaign. Make follow-up phone calls to the media contacts to make sure they received your release, but don't try to pressure them into running it. If they don't run it, don't call and complain.

If you're certain your releases would be of interest to a certain medium's audience, keep sending them new releases and following-up. The more releases you send, the more likely one of them will eventually be run. Don't get discouraged, just keep trying. If your releases are newsworthy, with enough patience and persistence, you'll get them placed.

Use the "Publicity Planning Guide" at the end of this section to plan your publicity campaign. Then use the "Publicity Contact Log," also found at the end of this section, to maintain a record of the news releases you send out and keep track of the responses you get. Any medium that produces high levels of response to your news releases, is probably an excellent candidate for inclusion in your advertising plan.

The News Release

The basic tool for generating publicity is the news release. With it you can get free publicity from newspapers, magazines, radio, and television. Most of the news in newspapers and magazines comes from news releases sent out by companies, government agencies, associations, and various individuals and groups.

Since a properly prepared news release is the backbone of any publicity campaign, follow the instructions given below to ensure that you create a good one. While some room for creativity exists, there is a common, easy-to-follow format for successful news releases (see the accompanying "News Release Sample"). It has several key elements: the originator (you), the release date, the contact, a headline, and the double-spaced copy itself.

If you send out the news release on your company stationery, that will take care of the originator. All you have to do is type NEWS or NEWS RELEASE in capital letters at the top of the letterhead. Having special news release stationery may have more visual impact, but it isn't necessary.

The release date is the date you want the story released. In many cases, it can say FOR IMMEDIATE RELEASE. This is probably best, unless there is some overriding reason why the story can't be released before a certain date. Also necessary is the name of a person to contact for further information. Along with the name, include the telephone number and area code where that person can be reached. In cases where the material is extremely time-sensitive, you may want to include an evening phone number as well as the daytime number.

The headline should appear in capital letters, six spaces below the contact line. It should be as clever and catchy as possible so it captures the attention and arouses the interest of the editor or producer. Newspaper headlines can be used as models of how to write news release headlines. Try for a headline that compels the reader to read the entire release.

Tips for More Effective News Releases:

■ Unless the story is extremely important to the recipient, keep the release to one page.

■ Use a colorful or graphically interesting envelope to catch the editor's attention.

■ Reproduce by high quality photocopying, instant printing, or laser printing. Don't use dot matrix printers, mimeograph, or carbons.

■ If you've already talked to the editor or reporter, it's OK to include a handwritten note.

■ Photographs sent to newspapers should be either 5" x 7" or 8" x 10" black and white glossies.

■ If you send photographs, tape the captions to the back of the photo so that the caption is readable while looking at the front of the photograph.

Eight spaces below the headline, you should begin the body of the release. It should be double-spaced and written like a newspaper article, with the most important information in the first paragraph, the supporting information next, and the least important information last. A news release can be any length, but a one-page release is probably best. If you do use more than one page, place the word "MORE" at the bottom center of the first page.

You can use news releases to announce the start of your company, new products and services, speaking engagements, and appearances on radio or television shows, or any other event connected with your company that has potential news value.

Whom you address your news releases to is extremely important. Newspapers and magazines have specialized editors, while each radio and television talk show has a specific producer. Your best chance for getting the publicity you desire is by directing your release to the appropriate editor or producer.

Because your release may be reprinted verbatim in some newspapers or organizational newsletters, spend ample time to compose clever, readable releases. In some cases, your release may even be used as the basis for a feature story.

It's a good idea for your news releases to end with a "For more information" paragraph. Use this to give your company's name, address, and phone number and to offer a free brochure or some other kind of promotional material. Doing this encourages people to contact your business, giving you new prospects and an opportunity to gauge the relative impact of that particular coverage.

If you are particularly interested in developing a high media profile, you may also want to add a line at the bottom of your release saying "Media interviews welcome." Professionals and others in personal service businesses can benefit most by being recognized as experts in their field by the media.

Be sure to key each news release so that you'll be able to know where your inquiries are coming from. A simple keying system involves placing a department code somewhere in your address on the release, for example: "580 Main Street, Dept. OT." This code could be for a release sent to *The Oakland Tribune*. You could use numbers as codes instead of letters, or a combination of both.

After you've prepared your news release, use the "News Release Checklist" at the end of this section to ensure that you've included all the necessary elements.

M MERIDIAN Learning Systems

4980 Appian Way, Suite 200
El Sobrante, California 94803
(510) 223-6800 Fax (510) 223-7014

NEWS

FOR IMMEDIATE RELEASE   Contact: Kathy Stevens
                                            (510) 223-6800

NEW BOOKLET CAN HELP EMPLOYERS CUT HEALTH CARE COSTS

Employers are finding the key to containing health care costs is their own employees. The choices employees make can cost a company money or save that company money.

The new 1988 larger type edition of the HEALTH CARE COMSUMER'S GUIDE: Your Guide to the Wise Use of Health Care Services has just been published by Meridian Learning Systems of San Francisco. It was created to inform and motivate employees to shop for health care services the way they would for any major purchase. This colorfully illustrated, easy-to-understand, 16-page booklet emphasizes educating employees to become skilled consumers as the key to cost containment.

Descriptive pictures and easy-to-read text show the employee how to get the most out of the health care system, proper use of the emergency room, the importance of second opinions, how to keep hospital costs down, how to save money on prescriptions, what tests can spot health problems before they become serious, and tips on prevention.

The HEALTH CARE CONSUMER'S GUIDE is specifically designed and priced to be distributed as take-home employee handouts to be shared with dependents. They are also ideal for retirees. For a free sample copy, write to Meridian Learning Systems, Dept. 204, 4980 Appian Way, Suite 200, El Sobrante, CA 94107 or call (510) 223-6800.

                              ###

Sample News Release

Dealing with Editors and Producers

Getting good media coverage requires contacting the proper people with something of value to them. Editors and producers are looking for something new, something different, or some quirky angle that will give your story appeal to their audiences.

The more personal involvement you have with any media contact, the more likely it is that your release will generate publicity. The tips given below can be adapted to any decision maker at any type of media company (newspaper, magazine, radio or television). The two main things to remember about contacting an editor or producer personally are:

1) **Be prepared.** Have your story down pat. Figure out everything in advance and then practice a few times before actually calling, and

2) **Think of the call you're about to make as an audition.** How you come across on the phone can determine whether or not you get the airtime or print coverage.

Editor/Producer Checklist

Use this checklist before making contact with editors or producers.

❏ Make a written outline of your proposed stories, being sure to include all the news hooks and angles you can think of.

❏ Study your outline carefully until you're completely comfortable with the information on it.

❏ List all the media sources you think might give your business coverage.

❏ Call each one and ask to speak with the features editor (print media) or the producer (broadcast media).

❏ Introduce yourself, mention your story idea, and give them "news hooks."

❏ Ask if you can send them publicity materials (news releases, copies of articles already written about your business, etc.).

❏ Ask about their lead times and deadlines.

❏ Follow up the phone conversation with a "thank you" letter.

Here are some tips that can help you keep on the good side of media people:

❏ Make sure your release is sent to the proper editor or producer.

❏ Try to see your story from the viewpoint of the media contact.

❏ Always be polite and friendly. Never be hostile.

❏ Be completely accurate. Have your facts at hand, ready to answer questions.

❏ Watch what you say. Nothing is really "off-the-record."

❏ Prepare for difficult questions. Don't get caught off guard.

❏ Be persistent. Keep sending news releases and following up.

Marketing Communications

Marketing communications are the communications a business has with its prospects and customers other than advertising and publicity. Besides the obvious message, every communication from a business conveys a more subtle, but no less important message about the business itself. The look and tone of these communications create a certain identity in the customer's mind.

The Importance of Business Identity

One of the most valuable assets a business can have is its identity. That's why large corporations spend so much money enhancing and promoting their identities. A corporation's identity influences the way customers, suppliers, investors, and employees think and feel about the corporation.

For a new or small business, the importance of identity is enormous. Usually the business owner doesn't have a proven business "track record." So it's vital for them to be able to communicate their business expertise and professionalism to others. The professionalism of your business communications can help you do that.

In order to be effective, however, an identity has to be true to the facts and believable. A business that wants to be seen as reliable, has to actually be reliable in its dealings with customers. No matter how relentlessly a business promotes itself as an excellent company, unless it performs in an excellent manner, its efforts to create that identity won't have the desired effect. After all, how a business actually performs has more impact on people than what it says about itself.

It's important for you to know how prospects and customers perceive your business because their perceptions will be more influential in determining your business identity than all your efforts. Whether your customers have a positive view of your business or a negative one, they'll tell their friends and associates about it. "Word of mouth" is one of the most potent marketing forces a business can have in its favor. What people say about your business can literally make or break it.

That's why it's so important for your business performance to be consistent with your business identity (see comments on positioning in *Advertising*).

Many people confuse identity with image, but there is a big difference. A business identity actually reflects what a business is or is striving to be, while an image is generally perceived as a false front meant to deceive. Use the "Basic Marketing Communications Checklist" at the end of this section to help ensure that your communications materials support the identity you've chosen for your business.

> *"A good image has to be earned by performance."*
>
> Robert Townsend, former CEO
> Avis

The Elements of Your Business Identity

The tangible elements that go into communicating your identity are your business name, your logo, and your printed materials, or collateral. Here are the chief things to remember about each:

■ **Business Name.** Your name can say a lot about your business. Words like "Economy" or "Speedy" in your business name give a specific impression. In general, your business name should say something about what you do without being too limiting. "Accurate Word Processing," "Mobile Photography," and "Taxsavers Bookkeeping Service" all convey something positive while letting others know what the business does. Avoid names like "A&B Enterprises" because they don't provide any meaning and they sound amateurish. Though it isn't usually a good idea to name your business after yourself, e.g. "The John Anderson Co.," certain professions that want to create a more dignified identity are common exceptions to this rule. Certified public accountants, consultants and ad agencies, for instance, often use their principals' last names as a firm name, e.g. Price Waterhouse, McKinsey & Co., Chiat/Day, etc.

■ **Logo.** A logo is a distinctive graphic element, either a symbol or arrangement of letters, that represents a particular business. It can provide instant recognition: What fast-food restaurant do you think of when you see golden arches? A well-designed logo also imparts an air of professionalism to all the printed materials of a new business. Through its design and color, a logo can also give a sense of continuity to all of a business's printed materials, signage, and advertising. Take a look around and notice the hundreds of logos you're exposed to every day. Use them for inspiration but don't copy them because they're probably protected by trade-mark laws. If you can afford it, hire a graphic designer to develop a logo consistent with your business identity. If you can't, you may be able to find an art student to design your logo economically.

■ **Printed Materials.** One of the first impressions people will have of your business will probably come from some piece of your printed communications. When a prospect receives one of your brochures, or a letter from you, or even your business card, they form an impression of your entire business. It's up to you to make sure the impression prospects have of your business is the impression you want them to have. Unless you have a considerable amount of graphic design skill, it's a good idea to have a graphic artist design your printed materials. The clearer you are about the identity you want your business to project, the better chance the graphic artist can come up with something that conveys exactly that identity. When interviewing graphic artists, be sure to review their portfolios to make sure you like their style.

At the minimum, most businesses need the following items:

Business cards. Your business cards set the tone for how your business is perceived. Regardless of the identity you want to convey, it's important to make sure that your card reflects an appropriate level of professionalism as well. In addition to your business name and address, make sure your name and business telephone number are on the card.

Choose your stationery to convey the identity you want customers to have of your business.

Letterhead and matching envelopes. As with your business cards, people are going to make judgements about your business based on the identity your stationery projects. You can help ensure that they perceive the identity you're trying to project by having a uniform appearance throughout your printed materials. A good way to do this is have your stationery and business cards designed as a "package." Always include your business address and telephone number, and your fax number if you have one, on letterheads to give people every opportunity to get in touch with you. When you send a letter out on your stationery make sure it's neatly typed.

Brochures. The purpose of your brochure is to explain your product or service. It can serve a multitude of functions. You can mail them to prospects (so design them to fit into a standard #10 envelope), you can hand them out when making sales calls, or you can keep them on display at your place of business in a "take one" rack. The most important thing about your brochure is that it be entirely clear as to what you are offering, what benefits customers will get, and what makes your business better than the competition. It should be designed to make your product or service understood even if the reader just scans it; most people won't read it word for word. Use large readable type, key word headings, illustrations or photographs where appropriate, and lots of white space (don't try to cram in a lot of type). Hiring a good copywriter to write your brochure copy is a must unless you are a persuasive writer. Remember that the brochure is intended for your customers and should be written from their perspective rather than yours.

Every element of your marketing materials should support the identity you're trying to promote. The texture and color of the papers, the colors of ink, the style of the type, and all the elements that go into the stationery should work together to enhance that identity. It doesn't have to be extremely costly to get stationery that fits your needs, but it will require some thought about what you want it to achieve in terms of creating the right identity for your business.

These days businesses generate lots of paperwork, so you may need more printed materials than just business stationery. Some examples are proposals, estimates, invoices, and the like. Though these items need not be of equal quality to your stationery, it is necessary to make sure they don't contradict your business identity, and that they support it as much as possible.

Now that we're in the electronic age, more and more businesses are using audiovisual materials to communicate. Many companies are marketing their products or services with video tapes and audio cassettes. Though these kinds of communications are costly to produce and require the help of professionals, you should be aware of their potential as promotional tools.

Notes:

Tips for Using the Following Forms:

Note: You are encouraged to copy these forms for your own use. Keep the unmarked originals in a safe place and make copies of them to work from.

Advertising Design Checklist – Each time you prepare a print ad for your business or review one that someone else has prepared, run down the checklist to make sure that the ad is ready to go. By doing this you'll be able to ensure nothing important has been left out of your ad. With the success of your business often riding on the results of your advertising, it's wise to use this checklist routinely, the way a pilot uses a take-off checklist. If you don't, your ad's chances for success will be reduced.

Advertising Placement Planner – Place the names of likely advertising media in the first column. Call each of these potential advertising vehicles and ask for a "media kit" and rate card. When you receive the media kits, double check that the demographics match your target audience. Using the information in the media kits and on the rate cards, fill out the rest of the form. The circulation or audience size will be found in the materials you've received. Place it in column 2. Then choose the size or duration of your ad and enter it in column 3. Add the space or time costs (how much it costs to run the ad) to the prep costs (how much it costs to prepare the ad) and place the sum in column 6. To calculate the CPM divide the Total Cost by the Circulation and multiply by 1000. Write the deadline, the date you must have your ad submitted by, in the next to last column. Then use the last column to enter the run dates, or any comments.

Publicity Planning Guide – The media have an insatiable appetite for news and information to keep their audiences informed and entertained, which gives you an excellent opportunity to get good publicity for your business – provided you make it easy for the media. Use this planning guide to help get your business mentioned in newspapers and magazines, and on radio and television. By answering each of the questions, you'll be developing the necessary elements of your publicity campaign.

News Release Checklist – After you've created a news release along the guidelines suggested in the text, use this checklist to make sure you've covered all the essential points. Put a check mark in the box in front of each question you can answer with a "yes." The more check marks you have, the more chance your news release has of getting the kind of coverage you desire. The questions not checked will show you where you can improve your news releases.

Publicity Contact Log – Fill in the name of the publication (magazine or newspaper) or station (radio or television) you want to contact in the first column. Next write in their phone number, and in the third column, the name of the person (editor or producer) you want to contact. Jot down the key words of your story idea in the fourth column so you'll remember what story you're approaching them about. Put the date of your first phone call in the next column, and the results of your call in the column following that. When you follow up with this contact, put the date in the next to last column and the results in the last one.

Basic Marketing Communications Checklist – In marketing communications as in any competitive endeavor, the basics are crucial. Before investing money promoting your business or having materials printed, make sure your most basic marketing tools reflect the business identity you've chosen. The clearer your business identity, the easier you can communicate it to your customers and prospects. Use this checklist to make sure your basic marketing communications are ready to do their job. Put a check mark in front of each question you can answer with a "yes." Any questions left without a check mark indicate areas that need to be examined more closely and corrected if necessary. Once you've created pieces that you are satisfied with, show the designs to friends or business associates, they can often see things you've overlooked.

Promotion Planner – This form provides a convenient way to list your promotional activities in one place. It will help you in coordinating these activities by showing you when the activity is scheduled and how much it costs. When all the costs are added up, it will also give you a figure for promotional expenses to be added to your "Projected Expense Budget & Capital Expenditures." First enter the advertising costs from "Advertising Placement Planner," then for each promotional activity you intend to engage in, enter the cost and date planned. Use the blank lines to add items not included on the form. Information from this form will be included in your business plan.

ADVERTISING DESIGN CHECKLIST

Planning – Know your objective and your audience
- ❏ Do you know what the purpose of your ad is?
  - ❏ Immediate orders ❏ Inquiries
  - ❏ Promote a special event
- ❏ Do you have a clear profile of your intended customer?
- ❏ Is this ad going in a publication specifically targeted to your customer profile?

Headline – Grab their attention
- ❏ Is the headline in a large easy-to-read typeface?
- ❏ Does your headline attract attention at a glance?
- ❏ Does it use short, powerful words (e.g. Easy, Free, Money, Proven)?
- ❏ Does it promise or suggest a benefit (e.g. Earn, Learn, Profit, Save)?
- ❏ Does it have action words in it (e.g. Be, Do, Have)?

Sub-head – Arouse their interest
- ❏ Is the sub-head type size in between the size of the headline and body copy?
- ❏ Do the sub-heads support the headline and lead into the body copy?
- ❏ Do the sub-heads give the major points of your message?

Body copy – The details of your offer
- ❏ Is the body copy written as though it were intended for just one person?
- ❏ Does it use short, common words and short sentences?
- ❏ Does the copy use "you" and "your" instead of "we" and "our"?
- ❏ Is your offer clearly stated?
- ❏ Are your claims believable ("long lasting") and documented ("tests show a 43% longer life") rather than exaggerated ("the world's finest")?
- ❏ Does the copy emphasize benefits instead of features ("easy to carry" vs. "weighs 6 lbs.")?
- ❏ Does the copy offer guaranteed satisfaction?
- ❏ Did you include a special offer to stimulate response ("introductory offer - save 20%")?
- ❏ Does the copy ask the reader to take action ("write," "call," "order now," "attend," "join")?

Graphic – Worth a thousand words, easily
- ❏ Is the graphic of high professional quality?
- ❏ Is it directly related to the headline and body copy?
- ❏ Is it a single large photograph rather than several smaller ones?
- ❏ Does the graphic show either the product or service in use, or a benefit of the product?
- ❏ If needed, does the graphic have a caption?

Guarantee – To reassure your audience
- ❏ Do you offer a money back guarantee?
- ❏ Does your guarantee have a special border around it to make it easy to see?
- ❏ Is your guarantee 100%, with no strings attached?

Response Device – Making it easy to say "Yes"
- ❏ Do you have an order coupon in your ad?
- ❏ Is it in the bottom right hand corner to make it easy to cut out?
- ❏ Does it have a dashed line around it to set it off from the rest of the ad?
- ❏ Is there enough room on it for all the necessary information?
- ❏ Do you provide a toll free telephone number for orders?
- ❏ Do you accept credit cards?

Signature – Letting them know who you are
- ❏ Is your company name at the bottom of the ad?
- ❏ Did you include your street address to enhance credibility?

Response-boosting extras – For even better results
- ❏ Does your ad use testimonials from satisfied customers or authorities in your field?
- ❏ Does your ad use at least one color in addition to black?

ADVERTISING PLACEMENT PLANNER

Magazines	Circulation	Size/Description	Space Cost	Prep Cost	Total Cost	CPM	Deadline	Run Dates / Comments

Newspapers	Circulation	Size/Description	Space Cost	Prep Cost	Total Cost	CPM	Deadline	Run Dates / Comments

Direct Mail	List Size	Type of Mailer	Mailing Cost	Prep Cost	Total Cost	CPM	Deadline	Run Dates / Comments

Yellow Pages	Circulation	Size/Description	Space Cost	Prep Cost	Total Cost	CPM	Deadline	Run Dates / Comments

Radio	Audience Size	Ad Length	Time Cost	Prep Cost	Total Cost	CPM	Deadline	Run Dates / Comments

Television	Audience Size	Ad Length	Time Cost	Prep Cost	Total Cost	CPM	Deadline	Run Dates / Comments

Billboard	Circulation	Size/Description	Space Cost	Prep Cost	Total Cost	CPM	Deadline	Run Dates / Comments

Other	Circulation	Size/Description	Space Cost	Prep Cost	Total Cost	CPM	Deadline	Run Dates / Comments

General Publicity Considerations:

Who will be responsible for getting publicity? _____

Have you selected the publications and broadcast media that you want to get coverage from? List them here: _____

_____

_____

Finding Newsworthy Angles for Feature Stories:

What are the things that people most want to know about a business like yours? (Usually this will be tied to the benefits of your product or service.) _____

_____

_____

What "news hooks" can you develop around the things that people want to know about your business? (Don't make media people try to figure out why they should be interested in what you're doing, give it to them on a silver platter.) _____

_____

_____

What current news stories or events can you tie your business into? (Accountants and financial planners find the tax season a favorable time for getting publicity, for example.) _____

_____

_____

Have you requested editorial calendars from the publications most likely to report on your business? (Knowing months in advance about feature stories and special issues can give you an edge in getting coverage.) List the publications: _____

_____

_____

Are there any celebrities or locally or nationally prominent people connected in any way with your business (as co-owners, investors, or customers) who might agree to be interviewed for a story about your company? To be most effective, celebrities should be well liked in addition to being well known. List them: _____

_____

Have you let editors and reporters in your field know that you are available as an authoritative "source" for stories related to your area of expertise? (Write your areas of expertise on your business cards and send them to local reporters and editors along with a note advising them of your availability as a source. Then follow up with a telephone call.) List reporters and editors who might use you as a source: _____

_____

What other aspects of your company could be considered newsworthy? Here are some ideas to help you get started thinking about getting news coverage for your business. Check the ones that may apply to your business:

❏ New business start-up

❏ New product introduction

❏ New facilities or location

❏ New employees

❏ Anniversary (e.g. in business for 5 years)

❏ Successes, such as big deals, large contracts, etc.

❏ Responses to new legislation (postal rate hike, etc.)

❏ Any seminars you may have conducted

❏ Any speeches you may have given

❏ Helpful hints (how to save on taxes, etc.)

❏ Expert opinion (on topical issues)

❏ Stands on current local issues

❏ Employee promotions

What story ideas do you have that would warrant publicity? (Now that you've done all the above, you should have some story ideas. What are they? Write some things down to get you started – you can always change them later after you've refined your focus.) List your story ideas here: _____

_____

_____

_____

What events can your business sponsor? (Little League teams, races, book signings, readings, lectures, theme parties, contests, awards, balloon rides, etc.) List them: _____

_____

_____

Checklist for Attracting Media Attention:

❏ Have people dress in costumes symbolizing something connected with your business.

❏ Use a hot air balloon to symbolize launching a new business or product.

❏ Do something jointly with a politician or celebrity.

❏ Create and present an award or a booby prize for something related to your field.

❏ Have a political leader issue a proclamation.

❏ Conduct a survey and publish the results.

❏ Give away something for free.

❏ Have a contest.

❏ Have an opening of something: an event, a season, a location, etc."

❏ Have a large celebration to mark some important achievement.

❏ Host a Chamber of Commerce "mixer."

❏ Attach your business to a cause. (e.g. literacy, the environment, etc.)

NEWS RELEASE CHECKLIST

Format Guidelines:

❑ Is it on one side of a standard 8-1/2" x 11" sheet (your letterhead for instance)?

❑ Are there ample margins (3/4" to 1") around the body of the release?

❑ Does it say "NEWS" or "NEWS FROM" near the top of the page?

❑ Is the release dated with the date you're sending it out?

❑ Does it say, "FOR IMMEDIATE RELEASE" or contain a specific release date?

❑ Does it include a contact name and phone number?

❑ Is your headline typed in all capital letters?

❑ Is body of the release typed normally (not capitalized)?

❑ Is body of the release double spaced?

❑ Does the last paragraph include where to write, or who to call, for more information so readers can follow-up?

❑ Does the release end with one of the three ways ("-30-", "end", or "###") publicists use to indicate the end of the release?

❑ In the rare instance a release has more than one page, does the first page end with the word "more"?

Writing Guidelines:

❑ Does the headline summarize the most important point of the story?

❑ Is the headline catchy?

❑ Does the lead sentence grab attention?

❑ Does the lead paragraph summarize most of the who, what, where, why, and when of your story?

❑ Does the second paragraph complete whatever information wasn't given in the first one?

❑ Does the release tell why this story is important to the contact's audience?

❑ Does the release state a benefit?

❑ Does the release provide evidence or examples?

❑ Does the release avoid stating opinions, except as a direct quotation?

❑ Are all quotes attributed?

❑ Is the release written in journalistic style, with the most important information at the beginning and the least important at the end?

❑ Are the words short and easy to understand?

❑ Is the release free of jargon and technical words (unless intended for a trade or technical journal)?

❑ Is the release easy to read and can it be understood quickly?

❑ Are the sentences short (about two lines long)?

❑ Are the paragraphs short (three or four lines long)?

Suggestions for Improving Your News Releases:

❑ Can you connect your story with a current event?

❑ Can you give your story a local or national angle?

❑ Do you include enough evidence to support your lead?

❑ Do you ask the reader to take some kind of action?

❑ Is the release clear on the first reading?

PUBLICITY CONTACT LOG

Publication / Station	Phone #	Contact Name	Story Idea	Date	Initial Contact Results	Date	Follow Up Results

Business Name:

❑ Does your business name let prospects know what your business does?

❑ Does it imply a benefit (economical, dependable, quality)?

❑ Does it avoid words that have negative or offensive connotations?

Logo:

❑ Is your logo different enough not to be confused with those of other firms?

❑ Does it project the identity you want for your company?

❑ Does it look professionally designed?

Business Cards:

❑ Do your business cards look professional?

❑ Do they match your business stationery?

❑ Do they include your name, your business name, and business address?

❑ Do they include your business telephone number, fax number, and other appropriate ways of contacting you (home phone, modem, etc.)?

❑ Do your business cards carry advertisements for your business, such as a motto or slogan on the front of them?

❑ Have you used the back of your business card as a mini-advertisement to promote your products or services, or to provide a map to your location?

Business Stationery:

❑ Are your letterheads and envelopes printed on good quality paper?

❑ Are they professional looking?

❑ Is the type face easily readable?

❑ Is your phone number clearly visible on your letterhead?

❑ Does the size and printing on your envelopes comply with postal regulations? (Your local post office can provide you with pamphlets explaining the most recent regulations.)

Brochures:

A brochure can tell the story of your business, explain your products or services, or provide background information on key personnel. To avoid confusing your customers, it's best not to cram too much information into a brochure, so you may need a separate brochure for the different messages you want to communicate.

❑ Will your brochure fit into a #10 standard business envelope?

❑ Does it look like it came from an established, quality-conscious business?

❑ Have you used heavy, good quality paper stock?

❑ Will a person, who is just glancing at it, be able to understand the main points even if they spend less than a minute looking at it?

❑ Is the type large enough to be read easily (no smaller than 10-point)?

❑ Is the copy written from the audience's point of view and in their words?

❑ Is your business address and phone number clearly displayed on it?

PROMOTION PLANNER

BP

Promotional Activity	Cost	Date Planned	Notes/Comments
Advertising (from "Advertising Plan")			
■			
■			
■			
■			
■			
■			
Sales Promotion			
■ Samples			
■ Samples			
■ Coupons			
■ Coupons			
■ Introductory offer			
■ Contests			
■ Premiums			
■ Premiums			
■			
■			
■			
Publicity			
■ Grand opening			
■ New product or service announcement			
■ Seminars or talks			
■ Helpful hints column			
■			
■			
■			
■			
Marketing Communications			
■ Business name and logo			
■ Stationery			
■ Business cards			
■ Brochure			
■ Other printed materials			
■			
■			
■			
■			
Total Cost	$		

PRODUCT DEVELOPMENT

Your "Product"

Whether you operate a retail establishment, provide a service, or manufacture something, your business provides a "product." That product may be a tangible product like a pair of earrings or a computer system, or it may be an intangible service like tax preparation or hair cutting. It might also be a retail store with its merchandise and decor, or a restaurant with its menu selections and ambiance.

The way your product is perceived by customers is how it's going to be compared with your competition. The critical factor for any product, service, or store is how well it satisfies its customers' wants and needs. The main components of any business "product" and how they affect the customer are:

- **Features and Benefits.** Features and benefits are the key factors in differentiating your product from your competitors'. Being the first to offer a desired feature or benefit can give a business a tremendous advantage. The Polaroid camera's ability to produce pictures on the spot made photography easy and fun for people who didn't have photographic skill. Offering instant tax refunds is a tactic one tax preparation organization has introduced to gain competitive advantage by giving customers an immediate and obvious benefit for doing business with them.

- **Quality.** The most important quality consideration is whether the customer's perception of the quality offered matches their expectations. Chrysler, after years of decline, used the increased quality of its products as a tactic to pull itself back from the brink of financial ruin. Chrysler gave the car-buying public the quality it demanded and had previously been getting from imported cars.

- **Packaging.** The perceptions customers have of a product are strongly influenced by its packaging. Cake mixes show a beautiful cake on their packages because people actually want a cake when they buy a mix. The package reminds them of their desire and offers itself as the fulfillment of that desire. In a retail store the layout and decorations set the tone for how it is viewed by customers. They don't expect fancy fixtures in discount stores or crowded displays, packed to overflowing with merchandise, in upscale stores.

- **Product (Brand) Name.** Brand names help create an image in the customer's mind. A name like Hefty for trash bags implies that these bags are durable even without saying it. Ivory soap is associated with purity because of years of advertising focusing on that feature. The Smile Clinic portrays itself as a friendly, maybe even fun, place to have your teeth cleaned and checked instead of the potentially painful dental office many people have come to fear.

- **Services or Enhancements.** A good way to differentiate a product from competing ones is to add value to the original purchase by including something extra that the customer wants. Many computer software companies provide newsletters and low-cost product upgrades to their customers. Some provide toll-free "help" lines for customers to receive technical assistance. Sharita Mosely offers office lunch delivery from her Veggie Heaven vegetarian restaurant. Her business district customers appreciate the convenience of being able to eat a healthy lunch at their desks and of being able to have a nearby source of nutritious food for business meetings and office parties.

■ **Guarantees and Warranties.** Since customers like to be reassured, many products, mufflers for instance, come with a lifetime guarantee. Money back guarantees help take the risk out of purchases. Some retail chains "guarantee" the lowest prices by offering a refund of the difference plus ten percent to any customer finding lower prices elsewhere.

■ **Product Selection.** When making a purchase, customers want to choose from an adequate selection. It gives customers a sense of the product being personalized for them. A shampoo manufacturer, for instance, may offer variations of their product for "dry," "oily," and "normal" hair. Because selection is so important, many stores today specialize in just one product: microwave ovens, fans, lamps, barstools, etc. George Olsen chose this tactic when he opened Recliner World, offering the widest available assortment of recliners in his area. For some businesses, selection means depth, or variations of a single product; and for others, like discount stores, selection means breadth, or a wide assortment of different types of products to choose from.

Each element of your "product" is a potential tactic that you may be able to use to gain competitive advantage. Any of the above elements you can offer that your competition doesn't can be an especially effective way to attract customers. But remember that your product, service, or store will be most successful when presented to customers the way they want, need, or expect it. So focus on which of the above product elements are most important to your customers to determine the tactics you use. Think about your business right now and identify for yourself just what "product" you're selling to the public. Use the "Product or Service Worksheet" at the end of this section to organize your thoughts.

The Old Pro says: *"Ideas are a dime a dozen. People who turn them into products and services are priceless."*

"How Should I Set My Prices?"

Questions about pricing are among the most commonly asked by new business owners. And understandably so, because pricing is one of the most important issues facing any business. Even when there is a high demand for a particular product or service, it still has to be reasonably priced to become truly successful.

Selecting the right price depends on a number of variables, the first of which is the cost of materials, labor, and overhead, since the recovery of these costs is necessary before a profit can be made. But the price of a product must not only provide a profit, it also has to be reasonably consistent with what competitors are charging. If your price is higher than your competitors', what do you offer that the competitors don't? In order to get a higher price than the competition, you're going to have add something of value that the customer wants. But avoid the trap of trying to justify a higher price by adding costly enhancements that customers don't really want.

Price is one of the main tactics to consider when creating a plan to implement your marketing strategy. How products and services are priced has a great impact on how well they sell. Not that the lowest price is always the best one – sometimes a product or service actually sells better at a higher price. There are other aspects that influence the price charged to the customer. Some of them may apply to your business:

■ **List prices** are the "suggested" prices to the ultimate consumer. One common tactic is to introduce a product at a low list price to create demand, and once the product is accepted in the marketplace, the price is raised. Another tactic used in some fields is to artificially inflate the list price to allow for much lower "sale" prices, which are actually closer to the intended selling price. Depending upon the type of business and its location, pricing may be subject to some legal restraints.

- **Credit terms** make what you're offering easy to buy. Once only relatively expensive items were offered on credit terms. Today, the convenience of ready credit is a tactic used to promote many products. In addition to the widespread use of major credit cards, many department stores offer their own credit cards. Magazine subscriptions are being offered for "just three easy payments." Many service businesses charge a portion of their price upon getting the job, another portion at some agreed upon interval, and then the balance upon completion of the job.

- **Discounts** are required for each step in the distribution channel. These discounts off the list price compensate the "middlemen" for their part in getting the product to the consumer. In book publishing, for instance, a distributor may get a 15% discount for selling to retailers, who get at least a 40% discount for selling to the public. This leaves 45%, at most, for the publisher to cover all the costs of production, marketing, overhead, and profit. In spite of this, many publishers offer even greater discounts to encourage distributors and retailers to handle their books.

- **Allowances** are reimbursements for freight and advertising given to resellers as inducements. A common tactic used by some companies is to pay some portion of the advertising costs of the retailers who advertise their products. Other businesses absorb the cost of shipping, particularly for large volume orders.

The Old Pro says:

"To get higher prices, do something different; something that no one else is doing."

The "Right" Price for Your Product or Service

Finding the "right price" for your product or service is the result of several considerations:

- **Your target audience.** How much do they now pay for similar offerings? What can they afford to pay? Most products or services are price-sensitive and have a price limit, above which they just won't sell. What is it in your business?

- **Your market position.** How do customers perceive what you're offering? Is it seen as high quality with excellent value? Or is it seen as too inexpensive to be of much value. People are willing to pay more for better quality.

- **Your competition.** How much are your competitors charging? Your price will probably have to fall within the range between what your lowest and highest competitors are charging.

- **How much your costs are.** Your price has to reflect not only what it costs you to produce the product or service, but there should also be enough included in it to cover overhead, sales and marketing expenses, and profit. Hidden costs mean less profit.

- **Your sales projections.** When you set a sales goal it is based upon selling a certain amount of product at a certain price. The higher your price is, the fewer units you have to sell in order to reach your goal. And the lower your price is, the more units you'll have to sell to reach your sales projections.

- **Your expected profits.** Some businesses that emphasize low prices, such as supermarkets, generally have relatively low per item profits, so they need relatively high sales volume to cover overhead and make a reasonable profit.

- **Other considerations.** Discounts, allowances, and the added cost of credit, have to be regarded as costs of doing business and must be accounted for in your pricing decisions.

While pricing is often more of an art than a science, there are proven ways to help you determine how much you should charge. Remember that the formulas given later in this section are merely guidelines. A product or service is only worth what it can be sold for. So regardless of the price a formula suggests, you still have to determine whether your target audience is able and willing to pay that much for it. If the market won't pay the price you ask, there are four things you can do about it:

- **Raise the value.** Your best option is to differentiate your product or service so much from those of the competition in your customers' minds that they'll pay your price. Adding value to a product or service helps to avoid price competition. One way to add value is to add features or benefits, but it isn't necessary to change the product to add value. As mentioned earlier, you can also add value through quality, service, performance, delivery time, terms, additional services, discounts, and packaging.

- **Lower the price.** Reducing the price is another option. While reducing the price and accepting a lower margin may be feasible, generally a small business shouldn't compete on price. Since larger businesses often have the advantage of purchasing in large enough quantities to obtain the maximum discounts, they can afford to sell at lower prices without affecting their margin. Usually when a small business lowers its price, the difference comes right out of the margin, and therefore the profit.

- **Cut costs.** One way to reduce the price without lowering margins is by cutting the costs involved in producing it. This can be done by either altering the product or changing the way it is produced. If you can reduce costs enough to allow you to lower the price significantly, it probably indicates the product or service was overpriced because of inefficiencies resulting from poor planning.

- **Exit the market.** Large companies can discontinue a product or service that won't sell at a reasonable price, but for a one-

product or one-service business, discontinuance means the end of the business. Instead of folding, explore ways to raise the perceived value of the product or service in the customers' eyes.

Setting an Hourly Rate for a Service Business

In trying to price your time, the first place to look is at your competition: those who are performing the same or similar service in your area. Find out what they're charging, what they're offering, and what qualifications and experience they have. This will give you a good idea of where you fit in.

If there is a lot of demand for your particular skills, and not many others are offering the same service, or if you do your work uncommonly well, then you should be able to command an hourly rate near the high end of the competitive range. But if there isn't great demand for your skills, or you're just starting out, then you will probably have to settle for less than premium rates. The value that you personally bring to a situation, is what makes your service worth more, as the following anecdote illustrates:

Some time ago Jerry, a retired boilermaker, was called out of retirement by his former employer to repair the boiler which he had kept going for many, many years. After the latest shut-down, numerous "experts" had been called in to repair it, but without success. With nowhere else to turn, the plant owner thought of Jerry, who said he'd be delighted to help. With the owner looking on, Jerry crawled through the maze of pipes surrounding the boiler until he found the one he was looking for and gave it three whacks with his hammer. Immediately the boiler came sputtering to life, much to the pleasure of the plant owner, who then told Jerry to send him a bill for his trouble. Hastily Jerry scratched out a bill for $1000 for "repairing boiler" on a piece of scrap paper. Mr. Krug, the plant owner was flabbergasted. "Jerry," he said, "This won't do. You'll have to submit an itemized invoice so it's clear just what you did to earn so much money." At which Jerry scribbled out the following invoice: "For banging on the boiler pipe, $25. For knowing where to bang and how hard, $975. Total, $1000."

Unlike employees paid by the hour, self-employed people who charge an hourly fee for their services don't receive payment for all the time that they work. A self-employed person may put in forty or fifty "working hours" a week, but can only charge for the "billable hours" spent working directly on clients' projects.

If you have a definite idea of how much you want to make in a year (see "What's In It For You" in *Business Assessment*), an estimate of what your expenses are going to be (see "Projected Expense Budget & Capital Expenditures" in *Budgeting*), and how many billable hours you want to work in a year, you can determine what hourly rate you'll need to charge to attain that income. This hourly rate can then be compared to the rates charged by others in your field who have approximately the same skill levels as you.

The following formula will help determine the hourly rate:

(Total Income + total expenses) ÷ Billable hours = hourly rate needed to earn desired annual income

Let's use an example to see how this formula actually works: A.J. Whitcombe is starting a personal computer consulting company in Illinois. She has decided that she'd like to earn the equivalent of a $30,000 a year salary. She figures she'll spend 30 hours per week working for her clients and work 50 weeks per year, for a total of 1500 billable hours (the rest of the time, she'll be marketing her services and doing paperwork).

A.J. also expects to have about $4000 in expenses during the first year and she decides to add 10%, or $3000, as a contingency against unexpected changes in her market or her business (always a good idea for new businesses). After adding both the known expenses

and contingency to the $30,000 she wants to earn, she comes up with $37,000, which she divides by the 1500 billable hours to get $24.66 per hour. Since this figure falls below the low end of the $25 to $75 range of hourly rates for similar consultants in her city, she decides to set her hourly rate at $30.

Her reasoning is that since she's just starting the business, she wants to "test the waters." Her experience is limited to the three years she was in charge of the PCs at the legal office where she worked, and to one operating system and only a few of the more popular application programs. As she gains experience, A.J. expects to raise her hourly fees to reflect her increased ability and competitive position.

One thing that A.J. didn't take into consideration was taxes. She was looking for a salary equivalent to match what she made previously as an employee. Someone who wants to earn $30,000 a year after taxes, would add 50% of their desired income, or $15,000 in this case, to (3) in the mini-worksheet below. Federal and state income taxes will come to approximately 35% and another 15% has to be added for self-employment tax. Remember that these are approximations and your particular tax situation could be different.

Here's a worksheet for you to use that's good for any service business that charges by the hour for its services and operates as a proprietorship:

Pricing Mini-Worksheet #1 – For Service Businesses

(1) Your desired annual net income
(from "What's In It For You") : $ _____

(2) Total annual expenses
(from "Expense Budget") :   + $ _____

(3) Taxes (see explanation above) :   + $ _____

(4) Add (1), (2) and (3) to get
total amount needed :   = $ _____

(5) Number of billable hours
you'll work in one year :   + $ _____

(6) Divide (4) by (5) to get hourly rate
needed to earn your desired income: = $ _____

How does this hourly rate compare with that of others in your community doing the same kind of work? Remember that in addition to satisfying your requirements, this rate also has to compare favorably with that of your competitors. Now that you have this preliminary hourly rate, it's time to ask yourself whether you want to add 10% for contingencies, as A.J. did?

Pricing Guidelines for Products

For pricing tangible products, here is one method that manufacturers have been using for some time:

Annual cost of materials & labor to make products
+ estimated other annual operating expenses
+ desired annual profit
= Required Revenue

Required Revenue
÷ number of units sold in one year
= Wholesale Price per Unit

Wholesale Price per Unit x 2
= Retail Price.

For example, Rob Archer, a retired firefighter, has created an emergency preparedness kit for homes and offices. To purchase the materials and assemble them costs $8.35 per unit. He can produce and sell 5000 units in one year, so 5000 x $8.35 = $41,750 is his product cost. To this he adds his estimated overhead costs for one year of $5500 to give a total cost of $47,250. Since he wants to make $20,000 in profit for the year, he adds this to the total cost to get $67,250. When he divides this figure by the number of units produced in a year ($67,250 ÷ 5000), he gets a wholesale unit cost

of $13.45. To determine the retail price he simply multiplies the wholesale unit cost by 2 to get $26.90.

In this example the retail, or selling, price seems reasonable. But there will be other times when the selling price derived from this method will be too high. When that happens, the first thing to look at is your cost of labor and materials. Is there a way to reduce them? If not, look to see if there is any way you can reduce your overhead. Once you've cut these costs as much as you can, you may want to see if you're willing to accept a lower profit. Of course, if you can position your product so that it has a higher value in the customers' eyes, then it might sell at the higher price.

Just as in the previous example, taxes can be computed in the following manner: estimate 35% for combined federal and state income taxes, and another 15% for self-employment tax.

You can use the following worksheet to calculate the pricing for any product:

Pricing Mini-Worksheet #2 – For Product Sellers

(1) Cost of materials and labor per unit (from "Product Cost Worksheet"): $ _____

(2) Number of units you'll sell in one year: X $ _____

(3) Multiply (1) times (2) to get total product cost: = $ _____

(4) Estimated annual overhead costs (from "Expense Budget"): + $ _____

(5) How much do you want to take out of the business (from "What's In It For You"): + $ _____

(6) Taxes (see explanation above): + $ _____

(7) Add (3), (4), (5), and (6) to get total amount needed: = $ _____

(8) Divide (7) by (2) to get the wholesale price per unit: ÷ $ _____

(9) Double (8) to get the retail price: = $ _____

How does this price stack up against the competition? If it's lower, is this part of your marketing strategy? If it's higher, do you have enough of a strategic advantage to position your product so that it's worth the difference to customers?

Here is a formula that's handy even if you're not sure of your overhead and desired profit figures. All you do is take your product cost for materials and labor (which you can compute by multiplying the number of units you intend to make and sell by the unit cost from the "Product Cost Worksheet" found at the end of this section) and subtract it from your total projected sales (which you derive by multiplying the number of units you intend to make and sell by your proposed wholesale price).

Now that you see how it works, let's try it with your product:

Pricing Mini-Worksheet #3 – Wholesale Products

(1) Your proposed wholesale
price per unit: $ _____

(2) Number of units you can
make and sell in one year: X $ _____

(3) Multiply (1) times (2) to
get total sales: = $ _____

(4) Total product costs
for materials and labor: - $ _____

(5) Subtract (4) from (3) to get
the amount left to cover
overhead, profit, and taxes: = $ _____

Proposed wholesale price
x number of units to sell
= Expected Revenue

Expected Revenue
- product cost for materials and labor
= Amount Remaining to Cover Overhead and Profit.

Mary Bemis makes gift baskets in northern California. She's put together a special basket called "Wine Country Memories" which costs $18.77 each for purchasing and assembling the components. She can make 500 of them and sell them for $29.95, for a total of $14,975. Since each one costs her $18.77, her total product cost is $9,385. After subtracting the $9,385 from the $14,975, there is $5,590 to cover overhead and profit. She has to decide if this kind of return is worth it to her. If not, she can look for ways to lower her costs, try to find a way to raise the selling price of the basket, or attempt to sell more baskets.

Will the amount in (5) cover all your operating expenses and taxes as well as providing enough money to support you in the manner you desire? If so, and the price is reasonable in terms of your competition, then this may indeed be a good price for your product. But, once you have gone through the worksheets above, you will want to test other prices in the range of the ones indicated above to determine the best selling price for your product. (Price testing is discussed in detail later in this section.)

Retail Pricing

For retailers and other businesses that resell someone else's products, the central pricing concept is markup, or the difference between what an item costs and what it sells for at retail. Retailers generally apply predetermined markups to their cost of merchandise. The markups used vary according to the type of retail establishment, and can often be obtained from that field's trade association.

To illustrate how markup works, let's look at an example. At Caren's Cotton Casuals, Caren Savage wanted to set a retail price for a dress that cost her $20, using her usual markup percentage of 100%. Here's how she did it:

Retail price =
Cost of merchandise +
(Markup percentage x Cost of merchandise)

Retail price = $20 + (100% x $20)
Retail price = $20 + (1.00* x $20)
Retail price = $20 + ($20)
Retail price = $40

Retailers usually know their cost of merchandise and standard markup percentage, and can use these figures to find their dollar markup. Using the same numbers as the example above, let's see how this works:

Dollar markup =
Markup percentage x Cost of merchandise

Dollar markup = 100% x $20
Dollar markup = 1.00* x $20
Dollar markup = $20

In some cases, retailers will know their cost of merchandise and how much money they want to make on certain items, and want to know what

markup percentage these figures represent. Again using the same figures as above, here's how to compute the markup percentage:

Markup percentage =
Dollar markup ÷ Cost of merchandise

Markup percentage = $20 ÷ $20
Markup percentage = 1.00*
Markup percentage = 100%

In this example, the markup percentage means that the retailer's markup is 100% of the cost of merchandise, which includes the invoice price of the goods plus any transportation charges, but minus any discounts given by the supplier.

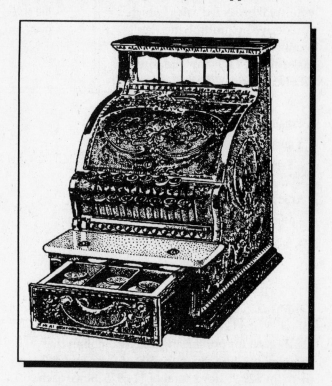

A rule of thumb used by many different kinds of retailers is to set the retail price of an item by doubling its cost. This automatic doubling is called "keystoning." Though convenient, it may be too low if the store has particularly high overhead, or too high if the item is particularly competitive. A better policy is to price high enough to cover expenses and profits, and low enough to build up

---

* Convert percentages to decimals by dividing by 100

* Convert decimals to percentages by multiplying by 100

sales volume. A thorough knowledge of your customers will tell you whether in general your prices need to be in the high (above prevailing prices for your market), medium (equal to prevailing prices for your market), or low (below prevailing prices for your market) ranges.

It may be that a "blanket" markup isn't feasible for your type of merchandise, particularly if many items are selling elsewhere for less. In this case, establish individual markups based on competitiveness of each line. It is often better to "mark down" slow moving items to encourage their sale. While the margins will be lower, at least the merchandise will be converted into cash. Another aspect of pricing that retailers need to consider is "shrinkage," the losses from theft, damage, and spoilage. Unless a certain percentage is added to the markup to cover shrinkage, these losses will come directly out of profits. Experience will dictate what your actual losses are, but until you have at least one year's operating history, you can probably be guided by the averages supplied by your field's trade association.

In this test, the middle price brought in $552 more total sales than either of the other prices; yet the highest test price brought in more than $450 in additional profits, even though it had the least total sales. Wally therefore chose $49.95 as the selling price to use for marketing his book nationally. These differences are clearly shown on the accompanying chart:

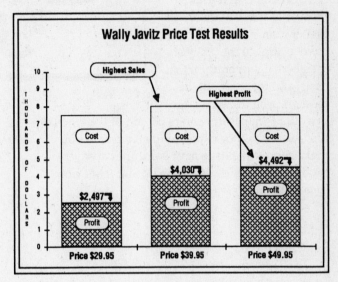

Price Testing

The best selling price is the one that brings in the most profit. To make an informed choice between potential prices, do price tests. Wally Javitz, of New Jersey, did three test mailings for his book on how professionals can reduce their taxes by setting up off-shore corporations. His total cost for each book was $20 and the only thing that varied between these mailings was the price of the book. The following table shows the results of Wally's price testing:

Discount Retailers

In some fields pricing is done much differently than in the formulas given earlier. Mail-order catalog houses and warehouse-type chain stores, for instance, need more of a discount than the 50% shown in the previous examples. Traditionally for an item that costs $10 at retail, the retailer gets a 50% discount, and pays a wholesale price of $5. This retailer then marks up the $5 wholesale price to arrive at the retail selling price of $10.

With a reseller who operates with larger markups, the figures are different. Let's say your retail price is the same $10, but the reseller wants a 75% discount. Then your share is no longer

Wally Javitz Price Test Results

Units Sold	Test Price	Total Sales	Unit Costs	Total Costs	Profit
251	$29.95	$7,517.45	$20.00	$5,020.00	$2,497.45
202	$39.95	$8,069.90	$20.00	$4,040.00	$4,029.90
150	$49.95	$7492.50	$20.00	$3,000.00	$4,492.50

50%, but 25%, or $2.50. The reseller can then mark up the price three times to $7.50 and still be able to under-sell the suggested retail price of $10 by 25%, giving the discounter an advantage over the competition.

Pricing right is the first step to nailing down a profit.

If you find that it's not profitable to sell at discounts higher than 50%, then you'll have to stick to the types of retailers who operate on that basis, and forget about the resellers who insist on larger discounts. Make sure you're certain of the kinds of discounts you'll be expected to give before you make commitments to have someone carry your products, or you could end up losing money on each sale.

Break-Even Analysis

Using a break-even analysis is another good way to get additional information for determining your price. It lets you see how many units you have to sell at what price in order to have your sales cover your expenses. This "break-even" point is important because it is the point at which your sales equal your costs, and any sales after this point contribute to profit. Up until the break-even point, all sales go toward recovering the costs of producing and selling the product and running the business. The two kinds of costs being recovered at break-even are:

Fixed costs are usually incurred prior to any sales being made and continue on regardless of any major fluctuations in sales volume. Fixed costs typically include salaries, rent, utilities, insurance, and the other operating costs. Generally, the higher the fixed costs, the higher the risk of loss, or "downside."

Variable costs, on the other hand, are directly related to sales or production volume. The greater the level of production, the higher these variable costs are; conversely, the lower the production volume, the lower the variable expenses. Variable costs typically include the cost of materials and labor going into making the product.

Another important aspect of break-even is that it is an estimate of average costs and sales over a certain time period. It assumes that neither costs nor the selling price will change dramatically. Any significant changes in these factors can have a pronounced effect on the break-even point.

It's important to remember that the sales volume at break-even isn't a forecast of sales that can actually be achieved, but rather it is the level of sales necessary to recover costs. While forecasting sales accurately can be very difficult, it's considerably easier to judge whether sales will exceed break-even. A break-even analysis can be a quick indicator of whether the required sales volume is attainable.

A break-even analysis is more than an academic exercise. Not only can you use it as a planning tool, but lenders and investors will want to know the break-even point of any venture before they become involved. To figure your break-even point, use the "Break-Even Worksheet" at the end of this section.

Here's an example that shows how break-even analysis works. Kelly Nguyen's Kosmic Ear Kreations makes designer earrings. Her annual overhead (fixed expense) is $21,000, while the cost of producing and selling each pair of earrings is $2. She receives $5 for each pair of earrings she sells to retailers, giving her a gross margin of $3 ($5-2) per pair.

Kelly's break-even analysis looks like this:

■ With fixed costs of $21,000 divided by the $3 gross margin per pair, we see she has to sell 7,000 pairs to cover overhead

■ When she adds her $14,000 cost for those 7,000 pairs she gets $35,000 as her total costs ($21,000 + $14,000)

■ Since each pair sells for $5, she receives $35,000 in revenues (7000 x $5)

■ Subtracting the $35,000 total costs from the $35,000 in revenues leaves $0 profit, because 7,000 pairs is her break-even point, and every pair she sells after that contributes to profit, which is illustrated in the accompanying chart:

Pricing Tips

Here are some basic pricing considerations you should be aware of:

■ When you use retailers to sell your product, while at the same time selling the product yourself, be sure to sell at the suggested retail price. Don't sell to the public at wholesale prices and under-cut your retail buyers. When they find out about it, not only will your reputation suffer, but they'll stop doing business with you.

■ Use the "Pricing Plan Worksheet" at the end of this section to establish and justify pricing policies for your business. Develop new policies for pricing questions that keep arising. Have specific prices and policies for each channel of distribution. That way you'll be able to respond quickly when asked for prices by a particular type of reseller. You may want to print up price lists for different types of resellers.

■ The main thing to remember about pricing is that it's what the customer is willing to pay that will determine the success or failure of a product or service. If you keep raising the suggested retail price to make up for giving higher discounts, you could lose business as your prices increase beyond the perceived value of your product. So always know how big a factor price is to your target audience and keep it in mind before making pricing decisions.

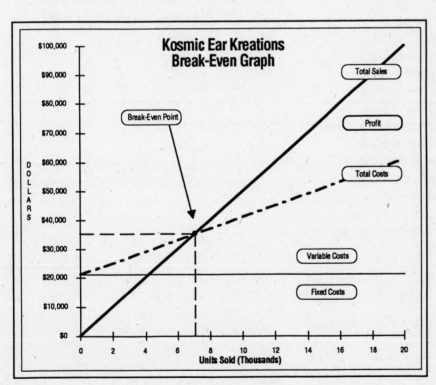

Kosmic Ear Kreations Break-Even Graph

Tips for Using the Following Forms:

Note: You are encouraged to copy these forms for your own use. Keep the unmarked originals in a safe place and make copies of them to work from.

Product or Service Worksheet – One of the most important things you can do in a new business is to describe your product or service clearly and concisely so that it is recognized and accepted by those who want or need it. Another benefit of having a clear, concise statement of your product or service is that it helps you position it in the marketplace, allowing you to differentiate it from what your competitors are offering. This statement will also provide the essential details for you to build your advertising and marketing materials around. Just provide the information each question requests. Where to use this information in the "Business Plan Guide" is indicated by a key (either * or +) before each question.

Product Cost Worksheet – Use one of these forms to determine the unit cost of each product you manufacture. This form is designed to allow you to account for all the variables that go into the production of any item. First under Part #1, write in the name of the first component. Use the Description column to describe the items listed on its left, then enter the unit cost where shown. To determine the total cost, multiply the unit cost by the quantity entered in the upper portion of the form. The total unit cost information will go into the Pricing subsection of the Marketing Plan in the "Business Plan Guide."

Pricing Plan Worksheet – Use the Pricing Mini-Worksheets found in the text above to develop your prices. Enter them on this form and answer the accompanying questions in Part A. The information you enter on this form will be included in your business plan (under Pricing Policies in the Marketing Plan section of the "Business Plan Guide"). Then based on your type of business, complete the questions under either Part B, C, or D.

Break-Even Worksheet – This easy to use worksheet will help you determine the sales volume necessary for you to cover your fixed and variable expenses. Just fill in your information in the blanks provided and follow the instructions on the form.

A. Product Concept (for all types of business)

*1. Describe your primary product or service in 45 to 50 words: _____

_____

_____

_____

_____

+ 1a. Now describe it again in only 12 to 20 words, keeping only the key points, the essence, of what you're

offering so you can quickly communicate it to others: _____

_____

_____

*2. What benefits does your product, service, or store offer customers or clients?: _____

_____

_____

_____

*3. What is special or unique about what you're offering that will give you a strategic advantage over your

competitors?: _____

_____

_____

_____

*4. List the other products and services you plan on selling initially: _____

_____

_____

_____

*5. What additional products, services, or locations can you introduce in the future?: _____

_____

_____

_____

Continued on next page

B. Product Specifics: Service Businesses

*1. Will you be providing a specific service to a wide range of clients, or a broad range of services to a specific group of clients?: _____

_____

*2. What means (educational materials, seminars, free consultations) will you use to add value to your services?: ___

_____

_____

_____

C. Product Specifics: Retailers

*1. Will you focus on providing a deep selection of a single product category, or a wide assortment of related goods?:

_____

_____

*2. What services (delivery, alterations, repair, etc.) can you provide for your customers?: _____

_____

_____

D. Product Specifics: Product-Based Businesses

*1. What stage is your product currently in?:

❏ Existing   ❏ Ready to manufacture   ❏ Prototype   ❏ Model / Drawing   ❏ Idea

*2. What's your product's status with regard to patent or trademark protection?:

❏ Protectable   ❏ Protection applied for   ❏ Protection granted   ❏ Not Protectable

*3. Will you produce a single version of one product, several models of a single product, or a wide range of different products?: _____

_____

_____

* To be included in the Product or Service subsection of the Marketing Plan in the "Business Plan Guide"

+ To be included in the Company subsection of the "Business Plan Guide"

PRODUCT COST WORKSHEET

BP

Product:		Quantity:		Date:	
Item	**Description**		**Unit Cost**	**Cost**	
Part #1:			$	$	
Materials					
Set-up charge					
Tool cost					
Freight in					
Labor					
Part #2:					
Materials					
Set-up charge					
Tool cost					
Freight in					
Labor					
Part #3:					
Materials					
Set-up charge					
Tool cost					
Freight in					
Labor					
Part #4:					
Materials					
Set-up charge					
Tool cost					
Freight in					
Labor					
Part #5:					
Materials					
Set-up charge					
Tool cost					
Freight in					
Labor					
Product Packaging					
Set-up charges					
Tooling costs					
Freight in					
Labor					
Assembly Labor					
Finishing Labor					
Royalty					
Overhead					
Other					
Other					
TOTALS			$	$	

A. For Retailers

1. What percentage will you mark up merchandise by? _____
   _____

2. What range does this put you in compared to your competitors (high, medium, low)? _____
   _____

3. How do you justify this price range? _____
   _____

B. For Service Businesses

1. What price or hourly rate have you established for your service? _____
   _____

2. What range does this put you in compared to your competitors (high, medium, low)? _____
   _____

3. How do you justify this price range? _____
   _____

C. For Product Based Businesses

1. What wholesale price have you established for your product? _____
   _____

2. How do you justify this price? _____
   _____

3. What retail price have you established for your product? _____
   _____

4. How do you justify this price? _____
   _____

5. What range does this put you in compared to your competitors (high, medium, low)? _____
   _____

6. How do you justify this price range? _____
   _____

In order to determine your Break-Even Sales Volume you need to know:

1. Price - What you intend to charge for your product
   or service (from Pricing Mini-Worksheets). $ _____

2. Variable Cost per Unit - The cost per unit of producing
   your product or service (from "Product
   Cost Worksheet") plus shipping and
   handling. $ _____

3. Total Fixed Cost - The total costs of operating your
   business; includes all the expenses listed
   on the "Projected Expense Budget". $ _____

By subtracting the Variable Costs per Unit from your Price you can determine
your Gross Margin per Unit:

Price   -   Variable Cost per Unit   =   Gross Margin per Unit

_____   -   _____   =   _____

Dividing your Total Fixed Costs by your gross Margin per Unit gives you
your Break-Even Sales Volume:

Total Fixed Costs   ÷   Gross Margin per Unit   =   Break-Even Sales Volume

_____   ÷   _____   =   _____

The Break-Even Sales Volume is the number of units you need to sell to generate enough
revenue to cover all of your fixed and variable expenses without generating any profit or loss.

All sales made above the Break-Even Sales Volume contribute to Net Profit.

OPERATIONS

CUSTOMER SERVICE

PURCHASING

INVENTORY

PROCEDURES

EQUIPMENT

CUSTOMER SERVICE

Focus on the Customer

If aspiring business owners were asked what one ingredient is necessary for starting a business, some would say money, others a good idea or product, some would say motivation and hard work, and others would say customers. What would your answer be?

When successful business owners were asked this same question, most of them choose customers as the most necessary ingredient for starting a business. Successful business owners realize that without customers, no amount of money or hard work can make a business successful.

Having an excellent product or service isn't even enough to guarantee business success. Customer service, or the way that a product or service is delivered and how the business interacts with its customers is a more crucial factor. Business owners who aren't aware of this make the mistake of focusing almost exclusively on the product or service they provide rather than the customers who do the buying. This can be a costly mistake.

The idea that the purpose of a business is to get and keep customers is a very profitable point of view because it focuses attention where it belongs: on the customer, who is the source of the money the business needs to operate. When you look at your business and how it operates, try to see it as customer would. Do you like what you see from that viewpoint?

For your business to grow to its full potential, it must satisfy your customers. Providing excellent customer service is the way to keep your customers satisfied and coming back to do more business with you. You can use the "Customer Service Planning Guide" and the "'Customer-Friendliness' Checklist" at the end of this section to plan or evaluate your customer service.

What is Customer Service?

Every contact with customers is an opportunity to render excellent customer service. This is important to remember for owners of one-person businesses, who often have so much else to do that they may sometimes be tempted to treat a customer as an interruption or an inconvenience. Here are some common customer-contact situations along with suggestions on handling them effectively:

■ **Telephone inquiries.** Always answer your business phone in a business-like manner, such as "O'Brien Technologies. How may I help you?" or "Hello, Davis, Wilkes & Company. Al Wilkes speaking." If you're working at home, be sure to instruct your children not to answer your business phone. In many cases, the initial telephone contact will be the first impression a potential customer will have of your business, so make it positive. Smiling while answering the phone makes you sound friendlier. Treat callers with respect; make them feel important; listen to them without interrupting. Ask questions to be sure you understand the caller completely. Have enough incoming phone lines so that customers don't get busy signals or put on hold when they call.

■ **Requests for printed materials, samples, estimates, etc.** Treat each request for printed materials, samples, and estimates as an opportunity to make a new customer. Find out exactly what the caller wants and send it to them as quickly as possible. A national study found that often information wasn't sent out until two to six weeks after the request. By then, your prospect has probably already forgotten about you and about making the request. You can make your business stand out by sending out literature and samples the same day they're requested. Provide estimates as soon as possible and then follow up each estimate with a phone call to determine if the prospect has any further questions and whether they are ready to order.

> *"Make the other person like himself a little bit more, and I promise you that he will like you very much indeed."*
>
> Lord Chesterfield

■ **Problems and complaints.** Whenever customers call with problems or complaints, don't transfer them to someone else to get rid of them. Instead, try to determine the exact nature of the problem. If the caller is irate, don't get defensive or get into an argument. Apologize for their inconvenience (even if you're certain they're mistaken) and get all the facts. Once you're sure what the problem is, ask the customer what they would like done about it. Take responsibility for correcting the problem. Offer suggestions for proposed solutions. Don't place blame on others, stay focused on finding a solution. A customer whose problem is successfully resolved tends to become an even more loyal customer and spreads good word of mouth advertising about your business.

■ **Service.** If you sell it, service it – or at the very least be able to direct the customer to authorized repair facilities. Never say, "We only sell 'em, we don't fix 'em."

How Customer Service Helps Your Business

One of the biggest misunderstandings business owners have about customer service is that it's too expensive. Customer service is actually an investment that more than pays for itself. Many businesses have found that every dollar spent improving service results in several dollars of additional revenue.

Business success depends on satisfied customers, who express their support of a business by spending their money there and recommending the business to others. Dissatisfied customers withdraw their support of the business by finding somewhere else to spend their money and they often tell ten to twenty other people about their dissatisfaction. Once lost, a customer is usually lost forever. And since it costs about eight times as much to make a sale to a new customer as it does to sell to an existing customer, losing customers can have a severe economic impact on a business.

Customer service can literally make or break a company. By providing superior customer service, customers will want to keep doing business with you. And they'll be more likely to recommend others to you as well. Here are some of the areas where your business can practice good customer service:

■ **Delivery.** Prompt, accurate delivery is essential for creating and keeping satisfied customers. Everyone who takes orders should know the importance of taking down customer information accurately to ensure correct handling of the order. Process orders immediately, the same day if possible, or at least according to some timely schedule. Don't let them sit around collecting dust and customer resentment. Ask customers if they need the shipment by a certain date. Make provisions to handle rush orders. Be prepared to ship by alternative methods to meet a deadline. Do a good job of packaging everything you send out to avoid having it damaged in transit. Use shipping services, like UPS and Federal Express, that allow you to trace shipments.

■ **Ease of ordering.** The easier you make it for people to order your product or service, the more orders you'll get. Your order form should be so simple and straightforward that it would be easy enough for a child to fill out. Use a toll-free telephone number to make it convenient for your customers to phone their orders in. That way you'll get orders a week or two earlier than by mail. Accept credit cards because people like to use them, and spend more when using them. Consider using a fax machine to speed up communications with your customers, perhaps even taking orders over it.

■ **Helpful, friendly service.** When customers call or visit your business, how they're treated is a big part of the impression they have of your company. It could very well determine whether or not they ever do business with you again. Answer inquiries the same day you receive them. Resolve complaints immediately, giving the customer the benefit of the doubt. If you can't ship an order immediately, acknowledge the order as soon as possible and let the customer know when to expect shipment. Answer the phone as soon as it rings. Use an answering machine or answering service when no one is available to answer calls. After you receive messages, return the calls right away.

■ **Confidence.** Keep your promises and follow through on your commitments. Honor your guarantees. If someone requests a refund, send it out immediately. Know your products or services thoroughly. It's also important to be able to track an order through your system to find out its status. If a customer asks you a question about a product or the status of an order that you can't answer immediately, get right back to them. Shipping delays due to lack of inventory should be kept to a minimum. Stay abreast of inventory levels so that customers can get what they order when they want it.

Customer service is one area where small businesses can shine.

Your Winning Edge

Customer service is one of the areas where a small business can effectively compete against larger companies. Smaller businesses tend to be in closer contact with their customers and have the ability to respond more quickly to questions and complaints. This gives them the opportunity to get to know and serve their customers better.

People almost expect poor service from larger companies, which they often perceive as bureaucracies providing poor, impersonal service. But they expect good service from small businesses because of their smaller size and more personal nature. Given these perceptions, providing poor customer service is much more damaging to a small business than to a big business.

Talking with customers is one of the best ways to build relationships that result in a loyal customer base. Use every interaction as an opportunity to get to know your customers and to ask them about their likes and dislikes. Making the commitment to provide extraordinary customer service an integral part of the way you do business will give your business the winning edge.

Tips on Using the Following Forms:

Note: You are encouraged to copy these forms for your own use. Keep the unmarked originals in a safe place and make copies of them to work from.

Customer Service Planning Guide – Even if your business is a start-up, you'll benefit from reviewing this questionnaire. It will help you become aware of the customer service guidelines to keep in mind when planning your operations. The questions in this action guide are designed to get you thinking about how you can make your business more customer-oriented.

"Customer - Friendliness" Checklist – New businesses should use this checklist to plan their operation to be as "customer-friendly" as it can be. Existing businesses will find it a useful way to review their current operations. Not all the questions apply to every business, so just cross off the ones that don't apply to your business.

Even though customers are the most important component of any business, many businesses, large and small, have forgotten this. Every business needs to have satisfied customers. After you've been in business a while, one of the best ways to assure this is to keep track of problems and customer complaints. Then review them to determine the ones that show up again and again. Ask yourself:

What are the most common problems customers have with us? _____

_____

_____

_____

_____

What can we do to prevent or minimize these problems? _____

_____

_____

Have you done everything you can do to assure your customers of the best possible service? The following questions will help show you the current level of your customer service. Every "no" responses indicates where you can improve service:

Yes No

❏ ❏ Is it easy for customers to do business with you? How can you make it easier? _____

_____

❏ ❏ Do you put customers through a series of procedures to receive service? How can you cut the "red tape?" ___

_____

❏ ❏ Do your policies benefit the customer? What policies can you develop that will be of real benefit to your customers? _____

_____

❏ ❏ Do you and/or your employees try to solve problems immediately instead of referring the customer somewhere else? How can you work with customers to solve their problems? _____

_____

❏ ❏ Does your product or service give the performance and results promised by your advertising and promotion? How can you improve the product or service so that it does what you claim for it? _____

_____

❏ ❏ Do you make it as easy as possible for customers to place orders? How can you make it easier for customers to order? _____

_____

❏ ❏ Do your credit and return policies show customers that you value their business? How can you make sure they do? _____

_____

Continued on next page..

Yes No

❑ ❑ Do you give customers an easy way to make complaints? How can you make it easier for customers to complain? _____
_____

❑ ❑ Does everyone in your business who deals with customers have in-depth product knowledge? What do your customer-contact people need to know to be most helpful? _____
_____
_____

❑ ❑ Is your business listed in the white pages of the telephone directories in the area your business serves? Which ones? _____
_____

❑ ❑ Is your business listed under the appropriate subject heading(s) in the yellow pages of the telephone directories in the area your business serves? Which directories? _____
Which subject headings? _____

❑ ❑ Do you use an answering machine or answering service for messages after business hours? If not, why not? _____
_____

❑ ❑ Do you use a toll-free 800 number to make it easier for customers to contact your business? If not, why not? ___
_____
_____

❑ ❑ Do your business name, address, and phone number appear on all printed materials? If not, what should you add them to? _____
_____

❑ ❑ Do you include a map showing your location on your printed materials? If not, what should you add maps to?
_____

❑ ❑ Does your business have an easy-to-see, easy-to-read sign? If not, why not? _____
_____

❑ ❑ Do you have convenient parking for your customers? If not, what can you do about it? _____
_____

❑ ❑ Are your business hours convenient for your customers? If not, what can you change them to? _____
_____
_____

Successful businesses make it easy and enjoyable for customers to keep coming back again and again. It's up to you to make sure your customers' impressions of your business are accurate and favorable. You can help do this by answering the following questions. The more "yes" answers you have, the better your business will be perceived. Each "no" answer indicates an area that can be improved.

Facilities:

Yes No

- ☐ ☐ Do you have an attractive, easy-to-see, and easy-to-read sign?
- ☐ ☐ Do you have an attractive, eye-catching window display?
- ☐ ☐ Is the outside of your business neat and clean?
- ☐ ☐ Is your business located in an area that people enjoy coming to?
- ☐ ☐ Is the inside of your business clean and attractive?
- ☐ ☐ Is your place of business free of clutter?
- ☐ ☐ Is your place of business free of hazards?
- ☐ ☐ Does your place of business have ample lighting?
- ☐ ☐ Is your place of business free of unpleasant smells?

Merchandise/Product:

Yes No

- ☐ ☐ Do you have an ample amount of inventory on hand?
- ☐ ☐ Is it arranged attractively?
- ☐ ☐ Is all merchandise clearly marked with price tags?
- ☐ ☐ Are your products or merchandise labeled?

You:

Yes No

- ☐ ☐ Are you polite to customers?
- ☐ ☐ Do you attend to customers promptly?
- ☐ ☐ Are you clean and dressed appropriately?

Employees:

Yes No

- ☐ ☐ Are your customer-contact people polite?
- ☐ ☐ Do your employees attend to customers promptly?
- ☐ ☐ Are all customer-contact people clean and dressed appropriately?

Printed materials:

Yes No

- ☐ ☐ Do your printed materials answer your customers' questions and/or tell them what they need to know about your product or service?
- ☐ ☐ Are all your printed materials easy to understand?
- ☐ ☐ Are your printed materials uncluttered and inviting to look at?
- ☐ ☐ Are your printed materials done in standard sizes for easy use?

PURCHASING

Straight to the Bottom Line

The importance of skillful purchasing is illustrated by the old adage that the secret to business success is to "buy low and sell high." While this is an obvious oversimplification, the fact remains that if you pay too much for supplies or inventory, it comes out of your profits. A one-and-a-half percent savings on purchasing, for instance, can result in as much profit as a seven percent or greater increase in sales. That's because the savings from purchases goes straight to the bottom line, while profits resulting from additional sales involve incurring added costs.

When you start a new business, you may do all the purchasing yourself. As you add employees, however, you may begin to delegate some of this responsibility. But sloppy buying habits can develop when several people have purchasing authority. This can result in a great deal of costly waste and even dishonesty. With a number of people ordering things, it's easy to lose track of what has already been purchased and what else should be ordered. To prevent these problems, one person should be selected to have ultimate responsibility for purchasing.

Price Considerations

When making purchasing decisions business owners are often tempted by a seemingly low price. While price is important, the lowest priced item is not always the best buy. The other factors that need to be evaluated along with price include:

- **Quality.** Regardless of the price, no deal is good if the materials don't suit your needs. Inferior quality materials and merchandise can cause problems leading to lost customers. Be clear about the level of quality you need and insist that vendor prices are based on providing that level of quality.

- **Delivery time.** In some instances delivery can be as important as price. If you need delivery within two weeks and one vendor quotes you $1200 and 6 to 8 weeks for delivery, and another quotes $1700 but promises delivery in five days, you may want to pay the higher price to get the materials on time.

- **Terms.** If you're short of cash, using a vendor that will give you generous terms may be better than getting a lower price, particularly if you would have had to put up a large amount of cash as a down payment to get the lower price.

- **Supplier stability.** Because the best vendor relationships are built up over time, a vendor's reputation and history are important. You can count on the most stable suppliers to have adequate inventory levels and to ship according to schedule.

- **Order quantity.** Often the best prices are for the highest quantities. Even though you may want the lowest price, don't order more materials than you can use just to get it. The excess could end up as unsold inventory.

Another thing to consider is hidden costs. You may get a lower price from a supplier over a thousand miles away, but when you add in the extra shipping costs, their total cost may be higher. Sales taxes can be a hidden cost when purchasing supplies or materials for your own use, such as catalogs or other printed materials. If sales taxes apply to your purchase, it could raise these costs another 5% or more.

vendors, you should establish relationships with auxiliary suppliers for less essential inventory items, and to use as backups in case of a problem with a major supplier.

> ## "Goods well bought are half sold."
> Proverb

How to Choose Your Suppliers

Regardless of the type of business you're in, you'll probably be dealing with a number of suppliers. Your relationship with them is very important to the growth and prosperity of your business. Good vendors are an extremely valuable asset to any business. It's not an exaggeration to say that in many instances vendors can make or break a business, so it's important to cultivate good vendor relations.

When looking for suppliers, ask other people in your field which vendors have the best reputation. You can also refer to directories such as Thomas' Register of American Manufacturers and the U.S. Industrial Directory, which are found in most libraries. These directories list available products in alphabetical order, along with the names and addresses of the manufacturers. Attending trade shows is also an excellent way to meet suppliers.

After contacting a supplier, you may find that they won't sell to you directly. In that case ask for the distributor nearest you and contact them. Ask suppliers for references and samples of their work, if appropriate. Make sure you feel comfortable dealing with them.

A small business should have enough sources of supply that it's not totally dependent on one vendor, while at the same time limiting the number of suppliers in order to establish close working relationships with them. Vendors will favor larger and more loyal accounts, particularly those with whom they have a personal relationship. As a preferred customer, you may receive favorable treatment in the form of faster service and quicker resolution of problems. In addition to your major

Treat suppliers with the same respect you expect from your customers. Don't try to drive hard bargains or press for unreasonable delivery schedules. And be sure to pay your bills on time. When you've decided on the major suppliers for your business, use the "Major Vendor List" at the end of this section to record the pertinent information about them.

By establishing good relationships with your vendors, you'll be in a position to ask for special treatment at the time a real emergency occurs. When your customers make difficult demands on you, a vendor can often save the day by speeding up delivery or shaving the prices a little so you can get the order. But these accommodations are more likely to be granted the less they're used. When asking for favorable treatment, it's good to remember that the supplier, like you, is in business to make money. And as soon as your demands begin to outweigh your value as a customer, you can expect to be given less than preferential treatment.

Obtaining Bids

Before placing an order for anything, contact several suppliers to compare prices and delivery terms. Use the "Supplier Comparison Form" at the end of this section to record the information on various suppliers. You may be surprised at the wide variety in the prices and terms of different vendors for the same item. One supplier may charge twice as much as another. But don't choose a vendor on price alone. There's a sound reason behind the saying "You get what you pay for."

It's a good idea to make sure all your price quotes from suppliers are based on the same specifications, so you have an accurate basis for comparison. To reduce the possibility of confusion, send each vendor a request for quotation clearly outlining your specifications. All the quotes should be for the same quantity and be computed on a common basis, e.g. units, dozens, lots, etc. Ask if any other costs, such as packaging and shipping, are excluded from the quote. If so, ask the vendors for estimates of these costs so you can make an accurate comparison between quotes.

Negotiating the Best Deal

In order to get the best deals when purchasing goods and services, it's usually necessary to negotiate improvements in prices and terms. Here are a few tips:

■ Remember that in business, just about everything is negotiable. It doesn't hurt to ask for better prices and terms, you just might get them.

■ Prior to any negotiation, know which terms and conditions are most important to you and which you're willing to give up. For example, could you wait an additional two weeks for delivery if the vendor paid freight costs?

■ When getting prices over the phone or in person, it's a good idea to ask, "Is that the best you can do?" This simple question by itself can often lead to a better deal.

■ After you've gotten the best price you can, there's still more room for bargaining. Ask if they'll pay the freight. If not, offer to split it.

■ There's even more room to deal with regard to payment. Try to get a cash discount for prepayment or early payment, say within ten days. Or you can ask for extended terms, forty-five days to pay instead of thirty, for instance.

> *"In business you don't get what you deserve, you get what you negotiate."*
>
> Chester Karrass, Author
> *The Negotiating Game*

■ The secret in getting good deals is in asking for them, then being quiet and listening to what the other person says. The more you listen, the more you'll find out about the other person's position, and the less you'll reveal about your own.

■ The best deals are "win-win," where each party gets something they want. Remember that your suppliers have to make a living too, so treat them the way you'd want to be treated. If you try to drive too hard a bargain, the supplier may want to "get you" the next time, or the supplier may decide not to deal with you any longer.

Tips for Saving Money on Purchases

■ Continually search for new suppliers and products that can meet your needs at lower costs.

■ Always have back-up suppliers to protect yourself against a sole supplier raising prices or reducing output.

■ Buy in large quantities when discounts are available if you're certain you'll be able to use or resell the entire amount purchased.

■ Periodically review which items, if any, you can make for less cost than purchasing them in finished form.

■ Constantly try to improve the terms and conditions of your purchases.

How to Obtain Trade Credit

Since most business transactions are done on credit, you'll need to establish credit for your business. If you've been in business for some time, simply type up a list of trade references and your bank reference on a sheet of your letterhead.

If you're just starting out in business, you may be asked to submit a personal financial history. Don't inflate your financial position to compensate for not having trade references. If your personal credit isn't good, look for ways to straighten it out, rather than trying to obtain credit fraudulently.

A personal visit to the vendor's place of business can help reassure a new supplier about opening a line of credit for you. While there tell the vendor about your business's prospects for success. You might also say something reassuring: "I honor my obligations and any time you want to talk with me, feel free to call me either at work or home."

Some vendors may ask you to take your first few orders C.O.D. (Cash On Delivery). That's OK because once you establish credit with them, you'll have a trade reference. Once your business has established credit, keep it good by paying your bills on time. Even if you have enough cash on hand to get your business started, it's still a good idea to make some credit purchases to establish a business credit history.

Receiving Shipments

In many instances, the materials you order will be shipped to you. Since much can happen to a shipment between the time it leaves the shipper's loading dock and the time it arrives at your location, you should know how to minimize freight problems.

At the time of delivery, verify the count to make sure you have received the same number of cartons as are listed on the delivery receipt. Carefully examine the outside of each carton for damage. If you see evidence of damage, note it on the delivery receipt and have the driver sign your copy.

Immediately after delivery, open all cartons and inspect for damage to the contents. Retain any damaged items and call the carrier to report the damage and request an inspection. For your own protection, write a letter confirming the call.

After the carrier's inspection, read the damage report before you sign it. Continue to retain the damaged items. Don't return them to the shipper until you have written authorization to do so from either the shipper or the carrier.

> *"Caveat Emptor."*
> *(Let the buyer beware.)*
>
> Traditional saying

Resale Permits

Most states require sellers to have resale permits (see the section on *Taxes* in **Finance**). These permits allow a business to purchase merchandise or materials for resale without having to pay sales tax. The sales tax for those items is collected by the seller upon sale to the final consumer.

Contrary to a popular misconception, a resale permit does not allow a business to avoid paying sales tax on business-related items purchased for its own use. All such purchases are fully taxable. Neither does a resale permit automatically entitle the holder to make purchases at wholesale prices; manufacturers and wholesalers set their own terms and conditions.

Vendor Records

Set up a separate file for each of your most important vendors. Use it to store their catalogs, price lists, quotes, and correspondence for easy reference. It's also a good idea to keep information on backup suppliers handy too, in case your primary vendors can't supply you for one reason or another.

Tips for Using the Following Form:

Note: You are encouraged to copy this form for your own use. Keep the unmarked original in a safe place and make copies of it to work from.

Supplier Comparison Form – For each major item you need for your business, fill in its description where indicated. Fill in the names of various suppliers and call each of them for quotes. Enter the price, delivery time, sales terms, and credit terms in the spaces provided under each of those headings. Using this form gives you a handy way to compare competing suppliers with each other. If you're going to be getting quotes for more than five items, make additional copies of the form. Some of the information on this form will be used in your business plan.

SUPPLIER COMPARISON FORM

Item Description:

Supplier	Price	Delivery Time	Sales Terms	Credit Terms	Comments

Item Description:

Supplier	Price	Delivery Time	Sales Terms	Credit Terms	Comments

Item Description:

Supplier	Price	Delivery Time	Sales Terms	Credit Terms	Comments

Item Description:

Supplier	Price	Delivery Time	Sales Terms	Credit Terms	Comments

Item Description:

Supplier	Price	Delivery Time	Sales Terms	Credit Terms	Comments

INVENTORY

Your Money Sitting on a Shelf

Inventory refers to anything you have to stock in order to do business, including raw materials, goods in process, and finished goods. What makes inventory so important is that until it is sold, it represents your money sitting on a shelf.

Since inventory can often represent a sizable portion of your business investment, how it is managed can have a substantial impact on your profits. Successful inventory management involves balancing the costs and benefits of inventory. Without adequate control, inventories become unreliable, inefficient, and costly.

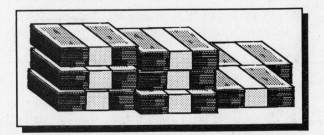

Many small business owners don't realize the true cost of carrying inventory. In addition to the direct costs of storage, insurance, taxes, and the like, there is also the cost of the money that went into purchasing the inventory. For manufactured and assembled products, the cost of production labor must also be added.

Further raising the cost of inventory is that, in most cases, the cost of your inventory is not deductible from your tax return until the year it is actually sold. Let's say you purchase $2,500 worth of merchandise or materials in December of this year. If half is sold in December and half in January, $1,250 will be deductible on this year's tax return and the remaining $1,250 on next year's. This is because until it is sold, inventory is considered an asset of the business, not an expense.

Because inventory can tie up so much capital in the ways described above, it can lead to a severe financial crisis if it isn't managed properly.

Inventory Management

One of the main purposes of inventory management, or control, is to incur the minimum possible annual cost of ordering and stocking each item. This is done by determining both the proper size and frequency of orders, and the reorder point, which is the inventory level at which reorders are made. These decisions should take into account the cost of placing an order, the annual sales rate of the item, its unit cost, and the cost of carrying the inventory.

There are two widely used methods of inventory management. The first, called the "maximum/minimum system," can be used effectively in a small business. This method has two parts: establishing a standard order amount and a reorder point. The standard order is based on finding the most economical price by ordering the maximum amount possible, to get the highest quantity discount, but without purchasing more inventory than can be sold in a reasonable period. Then by considering sales rates and delivery times, a minimum inventory level is set, and whenever inventory falls to this point, a reorder is automatically placed for the standard order quantity. If the standard order begins to result in overstocks or shortages, it should be adjusted.

For example here's how the Clubhouse Connection figured the "maximum/minimum" for a popular basketball it sells:

Item: Basketball

Monthly sales: 68 (17 per week)

Pricing:

Quantity Ordered	Cost, Delivered
1-36	$10.00
37-72	9.00
73-144	8.00
145+	7.00

Delivery time: 2 weeks

Minimum inventory level: 51 units
(delivery time + a one week buffer x weekly sales)

Order amount: 145 units
(provides over 2 months supply, an inventory turnover of over 9 times, and a $3 or 30% savings over the minimum order price)

By ordering according to the above, the Clubhouse Connection will maintain inventory levels as shown on the following graph:

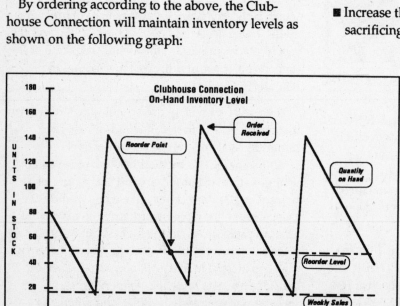

The other technique is called the "Just-In-Time" method. It involves ordering only what is needed for current activities rather than ordering to stock inventory. This method is primarily used by large manufacturers, who can still obtain low unit costs because of the purchasing clout their enormous volumes give them. Most small businesses don't have enough purchasing clout to use this system. The higher unit costs they have to pay for small orders more than offsets any potential inventory management savings.

Effective inventory management is a balancing act between having enough inventory on hand so that sales revenues aren't lost and keeping the investment in inventory as low as possible. Here are some tips that show the contradictory nature of inventory management:

- Keep as many different items on hand as necessary, while at the same time maintaining high enough levels of your fastest moving stock

- Keep inventory levels as low as possible, but without inconveniencing your customers

- Buy in volume to get lower prices, but only if you can sell the larger quantity in a reasonable time

- Keep an adequate inventory on hand, but don't hold on to items that aren't selling

- Increase the inventory turnover rate, without sacrificing good service.

To see how these tips apply in practice let's first look at a retail store. It needs to have enough merchandise on hand to be able to supply whatever customers ask for, but not so much that the inventory investment is so great that other areas of the business suffer. Not having requested merchandise available can mean lost customers but having excessive inventory can result in a serious cash flow crisis.

Manufacturers and other product-based businesses have an even more complicated task

The Old Pro says:

"Out of control inventories are often the biggest threat to a healthly cash flow."

because they have two inventories to maintain, one for their raw materials and the other for their finished products. They have to keep enough materials on hand so that production stoppages don't occur, but this has to be balanced by how much money the business can afford to have tied up raw materials. Similarly, there have to be enough finished products so that orders can be shipped promptly, but there shouldn't be so many sitting around gathering dust that they become a financial drain on the company.

In any business, "dead inventory" (obsolete and slow moving, non-seasonal items) should be written down after a couple of months to reflect their current market value. The paper loss will be offset by the tax deduction. You don't have to throw these items away; you can sell them at a later date, discount them to a dealer in excess inventories, or donate them to charity.

While no rule of thumb applies in all cases, one rule of inventory management to remember is "Don't overstock." Small businesses that start out with their inventories at too high a level limit the amount of operating capital at their disposal. This often results in cash flow problems – one of the leading reasons new businesses fail. Use the "Start-Up Inventory Planner" at the end of the section to determine your initial inventory.

Inventory Tracking

Keeping inventory records is fairly simple. Accurate inventory records can tell you how various items are moving, giving you a way to determine which items to stock in greater quantities and which to drop. Inventory records also tell you what is currently on order and alert you to profit-draining shortages.

Most new businesses can use inventory control cards, like the "Inventory Control Card" at the end of this section, to keep track of their inventory manually. As your inventory grows, you may find it beneficial to computerize your inventory records to save time and labor. Here's an example of a simplified inventory control card:

Item # 103		Description: Tennisball Sets				
Cost: $4.88		Supplier: Worldwide Sports				
Ordered		Received		Sold		
Date	Quantity	Date	Quantity	Date	Quantity	On Hand
5/4	100					0
		5/17	100			100
				5/19	11	89
				5/26	17	72
				6/2	23	49
				6/9	18	31
6/10	50					31
				6/16	20	11
		6/19	50			61

Inventory Control Card

Physical Inventory

At least once a year you'll need to take a physical inventory and count each item in stock. The actual quantities on hand should be compared with the inventory records and any differences noted. Shortages can indicate employee theft, shoplifting, poor recordkeeping, undershipments by suppliers, or unbilled sales to customers. Regardless of the reasons for shortages, they are losses that cut into profitability, so they should be minimized by improved procedures for security, receiving, and billing.

At least once a year, count each item in stock.

Inventory Turnover Rate

The turnover rate, also called turnover ratio, indicates how many times an average inventory is sold during a year. The higher your turnover rate, the more sales volume is being produced from a given investment in inventory. This ratio is computed by dividing the cost of goods sold in a period by the average inventory for the same period (which is found by adding the inventory at the beginning of the period to the ending inventory, and then using half that figure as an average). For example, last year Caren Savage's Florida store, Caren's Cotton Casuals, had a cost of goods sold of $196,699 and an average inventory (at cost) of $22,872, her calculation would be as follows:

Cost of Goods Sold + Average Inventory = Inventory Turnover

$196,699 + $22,872 = 8.6 times

For her kind of store, 8.6 is a good turnover rate. It means, that on the whole, she replaced her inventory between eight and nine times last year. Though it is most often used as a measure of how well a business is managing its inventory, turnover rate can be used to indicate which individual items have the fastest turnover. Caren can also perform the same calculations for each inventory item to determine which had the highest turnover rates. This gives her the information she needs to know which are the faster selling items and which are the slower moving ones. Based on this knowledge,

she can order more of the fastest moving items, and fewer of the slower moving ones.

The turnover rate provides a rough guideline only, its significance depends on the type of business and the function of the inventory. Some businesses have an average turnover rate of 2.0, for others it can be 8.0. Trade associations can provide industry average turnover rates so you can compare your figures to find out how well your figures compare with others in your field. Once you know what the industry averages are, make it a goal to outperform them.

Valuing Inventories

How you value your inventory is an accounting convention that doesn't affect how you actually stock and ship your inventory on a day-to-day basis, nor how you pay for it. Nevertheless, because it can have a financial impact on your business, it's important that you be aware of it.

There are two primary ways to value inventory for accounting and tax purposes, they're called FIFO (first in, first out), and LIFO (last in, first out). FIFO assumes that your inventory sells in the same order it was acquired or produced, with the oldest stock being subtracted from the inventory first, leaving the most recently purchased items in inventory. FIFO is considered to give the most realistic view of the actual flow of inventory.

LIFO, on the other hand, takes the opposite approach. In this method, the inventory acquired or produced last is assumed to have been sold first, leaving the older items still in inventory. LIFO is said to give a more accurate view of net income because it relates your most recent costs to your current revenues.

Here's an example of the difference this can make. Let's say you have 10 widgets in stock that cost you $10 each and you order 10 more at a price of $15 each. Your inventory is then worth $250 (10 @ $10 plus 10 @ $15). Then let's suppose you sell 15 widgets.

Using the FIFO method, you'd first deplete all the early stock and half the new stock (10 @ $10 plus 5 @ $15 = $175) to give you an inventory value of $75 ($250 - 175).

Using the LIFO method, you'd first deplete all the latest stock and half the older stock (10 @ $15 plus 5 @ $10 = $200) to give you an inventory value of $50 ($250 - 200).

	FIFO	LIFO
Beginning inventory value:	$250.	$250.
Cost of 15 items sold:	$175.	$200.
Ending inventory value:	$ 75.	$ 50.
Tax deduction for cost of goods sold:	$175.	$200.

In this example the FIFO method values the final inventory $25, or 33%, higher than the LIFO method does. In addition, the LIFO method provided a $25, or over 14%, greater tax deduction for cost of goods sold. As this example shows, generally speaking, LIFO will be the desired method of inventory valuation during periods when prices are rising. It is also preferred when inventory levels are increasing.

The FIFO method improves your balance sheet, while LIFO improves your cash flow by generating larger tax deductions. Of course, increased tax deductions only mean something if your business is profitable. The IRS allows your business to operate using either method, but after choosing one of the methods, you must get IRS approval if you want to switch.

There are other inventory valuation methods, besides FIFO and LIFO, that have applicability to specific types of business. Your accountant can advise you on which method is most financially beneficial to your business.

Notes:

Tips for Using the Following Forms:

Note: You are encouraged to copy these forms for your own use. Keep the unmarked originals in a safe place and make copies of them to work from.

Start-Up Inventory Planner – List all the merchandise and materials you'll need to start your business along with how much they'll cost. When these costs are added up, you'll know how much you'll need to spend for start-up inventory. Making sure you have identified sources of supply and actual costs for each item before you open for business helps eliminate potential supply problems.

Inventory Control Card – This form is suitable for beginning and maintaining an inventory management system for just about any business. At the top of the form, fill in the item number and description of the inventory item. Next enter the supplier and unit cost (at the reorder quantity). Then enter the delivery time, reorder point, and reorder quantity. Each time you order this item, put the date and quantity in the first two columns. When the item is received, place the date and quantity received in the third and fourth columns. On a weekly basis, enter the sales of the item in the fifth and sixth columns. Make adjustments to the Balance On Hand column each time items are received or sold.

	Item Description	Quantity	Unit Cost	$ Total Cost	Supplier	Comments
1						
2						
3						
4						
5						
6						
7						
8						
9						
10						
11						
12						
13						
14						
15						
16						
17						
18						
19						
20						
21						
22						
23						
24						
25						
26						
27						

Subtotal	$	
Previous Page Total	$	
Total Cost	$	

Inventory Control Card

Item #:	Description:		
Cost:	Supplier:		
Delivery Time:	Reorder Point:	Reorder Quantity:	

Ordered		Received		Sold		Balance
Date	Quantity	Date	Quantity	Date	Quantity	On Hand

Inventory Control Card

Item #:	Description:		
Cost:	Supplier:		
Delivery Time:	Reorder Point:	Reorder Quantity:	

Ordered		Received		Sold		Balance
Date	Quantity	Date	Quantity	Date	Quantity	On Hand

PROCEDURES

Normal Business Operations

Every business needs a certain consistency of operations to become successful. Without it, inefficiency, confusion, waste, and losses are inevitable. Even though customers, suppliers, and employees all appreciate consistency, not all business owners realize the importance of predictable business operations.

For the most efficient and trouble-free operations, certain areas of your business should be a matter of routine. Basic considerations like having set hours of business and someone to answer the phones are obviously important. If someone comes to your location during normal business hours and finds the door locked, or calls and the phone isn't answered, you've risked losing a customer.

Developing a set of policies and procedures will give your business the stability others expect from it. Having firm policies and procedures eliminate the need to make the same decisions over and over again. Of course, policies can always be changed to reflect new circumstances.

The considerations involved with routine operations are common to most businesses, but procedures are also needed for those tasks peculiar to your specific business. Use the "Operations Planning Guide" at the end of this section to remind yourself of the areas that should addressed as part of your normal business operations.

Know What You're Doing and Why

Mark Twain once said "It's not so much what we don't know that gets us into trouble, but what we know that isn't so." This quotation holds a special meaning for small businesses owners, most of whom know their fields well.

> *"Nothing is particularly hard if you divide it into small jobs."*
>
> Henry Ford

A high level of knowledge and experience in a particular field, though a key element of business success, may give a business owner a false sense of security. Very few people are so expert that their performance can't be improved, often dramatically, by taking a careful look at what they're doing and why they're doing it, as the following story illustrates:

Some time ago, a young girl asked her mother why she always cut a third of the roast off and placed it in a separate pan before cooking it. The mother said she didn't know why exactly, but said that she'd been doing it that way for years because that's how her mother had always done it. Curious, the young girl called her grandmother to ask her why she went through the extra work of cutting the roast into two pieces before cooking it. "Because I didn't have a pan large enough for the whole roast," was her answer.

We can all be like that sometimes: falling into routine ways of doing things, getting used to them, and never questioning why we're doing them that way. This can be especially dangerous in business where it is important to be doing the things that give your business a competitive edge today, rather than what worked five or ten years ago.

That's why understanding the specific steps you take in each aspect of your business is so important. Regardless of whether you provide a product or a service, you have to understand what is essential to what you're doing and what is unnecessary. One of the best ways to get this understanding is by thinking through and writing out each step of every major task in the operation of your business.

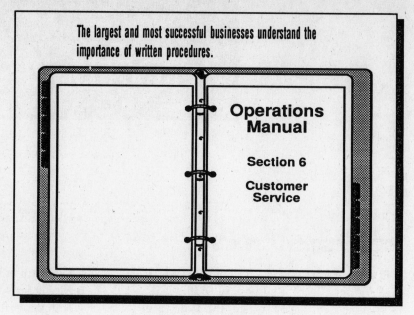

The largest and most successful businesses understand the importance of written procedures.

Operations Manual

Section 6

Customer Service

The Importance of Written Procedures

The largest and most successful businesses understand the importance of written procedures and have operations manuals that clearly outline all the steps required for each job. These companies know that their continued success depends on doing things consistently and not leaving anything to chance. Written procedures are a good idea for small businesses too. Here's why:

■ How will everything get done if for some reason you're unable to do it? If you're the only one who knows how to do everything in your business, you're taking an enormous risk by having the business be totally dependent on you. Written procedures provide a clear set of instructions on how to do what needs to be done so someone else can fill in for you if necessary.

■ Procedures form a pattern of consistency so that customers know what to expect each and every time they deal with you. Customers appreciate transactions that go smoothly, and they feel more comfortable dealing with a business that gives them what they expect. One of the chief reasons customers give for their continued patronage at huge national chains like McDonald's is that they know

what to expect. In other words, procedures can help eliminate inconsistencies that could harm your business.

■ Writing out procedures also requires you to think about what you're doing and allows you to see where time- and money-saving improvements can be made in your operations. Once a business procedure is established, it tends to continue out of habit, regardless of whether it is efficient or not. By having the procedures down on paper, you'll be able to see beyond the old habits and find new ways to increase productivity, improve service, and reduce costs.

■ Having procedures allows you to hire less skilled employees (who are much easier to find and less expensive to hire than highly skilled workers). Procedures give these workers a structure within which they can work comfortably, knowing what is expected of them and how they are expected to perform. Procedures also minimize the expense and frustration of mistakes arising from poor decisions by inexperienced employees.

You Need Procedures for Every Part of Your Business

To get you thinking about your procedures, here are a few examples of how a small business can start formalizing its procedures. Blaine Concannon has a mail order business called Earthsaver Products. She sells environmentally sensitive products through a catalog and receives orders by phone and by mail. When she began operations, she put together a written guide to orient her newly hired assistant on how to process orders. The first steps looked like this:

1. Pick up mail at post office

2. Open mail and put all orders together

3. Check orders to make sure math is correct and that payment is enclosed

4. Put problem orders aside temporarily

5. Stamp checks on back with deposit stamp and place in deposit folder

6. Enter "clean" orders in computer

7. Send "Payment Not Enclosed" form letters for each order without a check

8. Separate orders with errors in math as follows:

   a. If error is less than $5, process order and send "Payment due" form letter with invoice

   b. If error is more than $5, send order and check back to customer with "We're sorry, but ..." form letter.

9. Etc.

Trina Ross-Bell's The Write Stuff, a word processing firm that employs part-timers during peak periods, uses a style manual showing exactly how to abbreviate common words, the punctuation to use in specific situations, and preferred forms of address. She also has an instruction sheet to acquaint her employees with her operating procedures, such as directing them to back up their work to a disk every fifteen minutes as part of their work routine.

Each aspect of your business operations should be broken down into its individual steps in the same way. No matter what your business is, you will benefit from developing procedures for processing orders, for billing and collections, for shipping and receiving, for handling customer inquiries and complaints, for securing your business from crime, and every other function that is a regular part of your business.

Next take the time to get all these procedures down in black and white. While your written procedures do not need to be elaborate, they should cover the most important elements of a task. Your efforts will be rewarded in many ways. You're likely to uncover inefficiencies that can be eliminated. You may even discover new ways to do things that save time and money. And if you have employees, they be able to do their jobs efficiently without you having to personally direct their efforts.

Franchised businesses have a survival rate five times that of independent businesses, to a large extent because the parent companies insist that franchisees follow the procedures that have proved successful through experience. You can increase your chances of business success by following their example – put your procedures in writing.

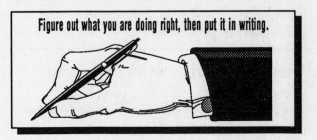

Figure out what you are doing right, then put it in writing.

How to Establish Procedures

Establishing procedures is a matter of using common sense to think things through. The first step is to be clear about what each task is meant to accomplish and then look at each step closely to determine if it is necessary for the achievement of that task. If it isn't, it can be discarded. Even if it seems necessary, you should still ask yourself if there is a better way to accomplish the same end.

If you've previously worked in a similar business, then you've already been exposed to one way that type of business can be run. While employed there, you may have thought of ways things could be improved. But even if the business seemed to run well, that doesn't mean that it was run as well as it could be. Don't make the mistake of following the former procedures blindly or you could end up "cooking your roast in two pans" without knowing why.

Motivated, satisfied employees are the key to high productivity.

When you have employees, encourage them to look for ways to improve your business procedures and remain open to their suggestions. The person who does a particular job every day is in an excellent position to know where improvements can be made. Most employees want to contribute; if you give them the chance they will feel more a part of the business, and your business will be better for it.

Always aim to simplify your procedures. The simpler it is to do something, the more likely it is to be done correctly, and the better chance it can save you money. When Recliner World, a specialty furniture store in Ohio, found its profits declining, owner George Olsen looked for ways to improve operations.

With the help of its employees, Recliner World was able to streamline billing, warehousing, and shipping procedures enough to save $3000 a year. This amount represented the profit equivalent of $15,000 in additional sales, without having to sell one additional recliner. And these savings went straight to the bottom line.

As this example shows, procedures will change over time as your business outgrows them or you find better ways to do things. Don't fall into the trap of thinking procedures are "carved in stone." Procedures are meant to be guidelines, not commandments. Design your procedures to ensure the most efficient operation possible, but don't lose sight of the need to allow for flexibility, changing conditions, special circumstances, and employee initiative.

Productivity

A business with fewer employees can sometimes outperform another business with more, and better paid, employees. The difference is how much work the employees actually do – how productive they are. The best procedures in the world won't guarantee success if disgruntled, low-output employees are performing them.

The key to high productivity in any business is motivated, satisfied employees. Employees work best when they're paid fairly, have a good work environment, and get to participate in decisions that affect their jobs (see *Personnel* for information on how to hire and retain good employees).

Productivity is often defined as output divided by input, and it can be measured in many ways. One of the most common ways is to divide total sales by the total cost of employee compensation (wages and benefits). If a business has yearly sales of $280,000 and compensation costs of $70,000, that business has a productivity ratio of 4, in that it produces $4 in sales for each $1 of compensation. Another measure is to divide total sales by the total number of hours worked, which provides a measure of the amount of sales generated by an hour of work.

But regardless of how it is measured, increased productivity is one of the best ways to increase profits without additional sales. Increased profits from productivity gains and improved procedures are the closest thing to "found money" in the business world.

Checklists

Procedures are intended to ensure that everything that needs to be done, gets done – that all the bases are covered. For particularly important tasks, it's a good idea to have a checklist that includes all the most important details. This is why checklists have been included in several sections of this manual. Pilots and others engaged in activities where errors have serious repercussions routinely use checklists to monitor their actions, even after they're thoroughly familiar with the necessary procedures.

Astute business owners who want to prevent problems from occurring, use checklists for the same reason. Take a simple task like ordering a mailing list. To ensure that all the things that can affect this task are handled properly, each step is a separate item on the checklist, as is shown in the following example:

❏ **Order date:** 3/1/90

❏ **Description of list:** New home buyers, Homeowner Magazine subscribers

❏ **Source of list:** ABC List Co.

❏ **Format:** 4-across Cheshire labels

❏ **Price:** $65 per thousand + $1 per thousand for key code

❏ **Quantity:** 10,000

❏ **Selection:** Every nth name, zip code order

❏ **Title address:** none, list includes homeowner names

❏ **Key code:** HM490

❏ **Date needed:** 4/2/90

❏ **Shipping instructions:** Ship labels by 2nd day air

In the rush and pressure of everyday business activities, it's easy to forget a small detail. If, for instance, the title address is left off when it should be included, the mailing may not reach the intended prospects and the response will be lower than anticipated; if the key code is omitted, then there won't be any way to track the response; if the shipping instructions aren't explicit, slow delivery of the labels could delay the entire mailing. Missing or incomplete information leads to costly, time-consuming mistakes. By using checklists like the one shown above, it's much less likely that mistakes will be made.

Production Records

Just about everybody hates paperwork – that's a given. Yet to be successful in business, it is necessary to keep track of what you're doing. Whether you make a product or provide a service, you have to know how long it takes and how much it costs. Knowing these things will determine your pricing, and ultimately your profitability.

Keeping Track of Production

If your main activity is producing some kind of product, whether it is pottery, belts, wreaths, jewelry, or whatever, you need to know how long it takes to produce a given amount of your product and what quantity of raw materials are needed.

To compute time and cost you can use a form that serves the same purpose as that an auto mechanic uses to keep track of the charges for the repair work on a car. Each part used is itemized and the time needed to do the job is carefully recorded.

Many new business owners forget that their time is valuable – and an integral part of the cost of any job. Let's say you're making belts. Each leather strip costs you so much and each buckle also costs you a certain amount, as do any labels or packaging you might use. In addition to these obvious material costs there are also the labor costs involved in cutting, punching, tooling, staining, and assembling each belt. The expense of all this labor has to be added to the cost of the raw materials in order to determine the true cost of making each the belt.

To keep track of how much your raw materials and labor cost to make each piece, use the "Product Cost Worksheet" (see *Product Development*). Then you'll be assured of knowing your true costs. This is vitally important because each increase in the cost of your materials, and each increase in the time it takes to make the product, cuts into your profit margin. If either material or labor costs rise significantly, then your profit can evaporate completely.

Keeping Track of Time

Many service businesses charge an hourly rate for their services, and often work on several projects at once. To ensure accurate billings, they find it necessary to keep track of how much of their day is spent on each client's work. To do this they may use a standard timesheet (like the "Professional Time Record" at the end of this section) or create one that is designed just for their business. For your own time sheet you may want to include another column for hourly rates if you charge different rates for different services.

Anita DeLouche, a New York graphic designer, uses a simple timesheet, a sample of which is

> *"It takes more than money to make a business succeed. You must also know what you are doing."*
>
> Mary Kay Ash, Founder
> Mary Kay Cosmetics

shown below. The only notations she makes are for time spent working for a client. Time spent getting new business, invoicing, lunch, and other things not billable to clients isn't indicated except as gaps between the billable work:

Date	Start	End	Hours	Job#/Client	Description
2/14	8:00	9:45	1.75	Echo Ind.	Rough layouts/stationery
	9:45	11:15	1.5	Jones Auto	Design/Yellow Pages ad
	11:30	12:30	1.0	Echo Ind.	Spec type/stationery
	1:30	3:30	2.0	"	Paste up/stationery
	3:45	5:30	1.5	Lotus Rest.	Illustration/menu
2/15	7:45	9:30	1.75	Echo Ind.	Design/brochure
	10:00	12:15	2.25	Ames Prtg.	Set type/flyer
	1:30	2:00	.5	D'Arcy	Thumbnails/bus. card
	3:30	4:45	1.25	Western	Consultation
	5:15	6:30	1.25	Echo Ind.	Paste up/brochure

Professional Time Record

Tips for Using the Following Forms:

Note: You are encouraged to copy these forms for your own use. Keep the unmarked originals in a safe place and make copies of them to work from.

Operations Planning Guide – Use this form to develop the standard business policies for your normal business operations. Answer the questions you can and cross off the ones that don't apply to your business. If you're already in business you can enter your actual procedures, and if you haven't started your business yet, just write in your planned operations. The questions you can't answer indicate the areas where you need to develop a policy. Some of your answers on this form can also be used for developing your business plan. These questions are clearly indicated, along with instructions on where to insert them in the business plan.

Professional Time Record – This form is suitable for most simple time tracking purposes, particularly for service businesses, but it can also be used by other businesses who want to track how long it takes to produce or assemble products. The week the timesheet covers goes at the top of the form. For each task, put the date in the first column, then the starting time in the second. Enter the job number, if there is one, in the fifth column, then fill in the client's name, description of the task and any comments in the appropriate columns. When stopping work on that task, place the ending time in the End Time column and then subtract the Start Time from it to get the hours worked, which is entered in the Hours column as a decimal (e.g. 2.25, 3.5). At the end of the week, add up the hours for each job number or client for billing purposes.

*1. How many days per week are you open for business? _____

*2. What are your daily hours of operation? _____

3. Is someone available at all times during business hours? _____

4. What do you say to callers when you answer the telephone? _____
_____

5. How do you greet people coming into your place of business? _____
_____

6. What forms of payment do you accept?

❏ Cash ❏ Check ❏ Credit ❏ VISA ❏ MasterCard ❏ American Express ❏ Other _____

7. If you extend credit, what are your credit terms? _____
_____

8. Is your business closed for any holidays? _____
Which ones? _____
_____

9. Is your business closed for vacation, inventory, or maintenance? _____
When? _____
_____

10. Will customers come to you or do you have to go to the customer's location? _____
_____

*11. a. How will you provide repairs and service to customers? (if applicable):

❏ At their location   ❏ At your location ❏ Through a third party

b. Who will pay for repairs and service? (if applicable):

❏ Service contract   ❏ The customer   ❏ You   ❏ Warranty

*12. How will your product be produced? (if applicable):

❏ Your factory   ❏ Third party factory

†13. Where will you maintain your inventory? (if applicable)

❏ On-site   ❏ Remote warehouse   ❏ Third party (fulfillment service)

* This information will be used in the Ordinary Operations subsection of the Production/Operating Plan of Business Plan

† This information will be used in the Inventory subsection of the Production/Operating Plan of Business Plan

PROFESSIONAL TIME RECORD

WEEK ENDING:

Date	Start Time	End Time	Hours	Job #	Client	Description/Activity	Comments

EQUIPMENT

Your Mechanical and Electronic Assistants

Just about every business requires equipment of some kind. Companies that do manufacturing may require a number of specialized, often expensive, machines. But even companies that don't produce anything – either because they provide a service or sell an already existing product – still need a wide variety of office machines. In today's small business, office equipment isn't a luxury, it's often the only way a business owner can get the work done.

The proper equipment can leverage your time, allowing you to do more, and do it more professionally than you'd be able to otherwise. The wide variety of affordable equipment available today lets small businesses appear as professional as firms many times their size. And, more importantly, allows them to compete effectively with these larger companies.

Your type of business will dictate the kind of equipment you will need and when you'll need it. While it's good to know what kind of equipment is available, few businesses, particularly when starting out, will need every piece of equipment listed below. But you should know enough about the options available to be able to make an informed choice when your business needs any of the following equipment:

- **Telephone system.** The telephone is an essential tool for any business. That's why it's so important to have a separate business phone, even if you're working out of your home. In the first place, a business phone enhances your professional image. And in many states using a residential phone for business violates telephone regulations.

Because the telephone is a vital link that keeps your business connected with the world, it's important that your phone system be capable of growing with you and have all the features you need. But don't get so carried away with all the "bells and whistles" that you waste money on capabilities that aren't truly needed. Three handy features you might want your telephone to have are a hold button, storage and recall of frequently called numbers with speed dialing, and automatic re-dialing. If you only have one or two incoming lines and you plan to receive many calls, call waiting could help assure that your customers don't get busy signals when they call. Your business might also benefit from a toll free number. In many areas you can obtain a toll free number for an area as small as your area code. Instead of tying up capital purchasing a telephone system, you may want to use the business telephone services (such as Centrex) offered by your local phone company, and let them be responsible for maintaining the system.

- **Telephone answering.** Lost calls can mean lost business. To avoid missing calls, you can use a telephone answering machine or a voice mail system. Your outgoing message can give answers to the most often asked questions about your business, such as your normal business hours and whether you take credit cards, or it could include announcements about special offers or sales. One important feature you should look for in an answering machine or voice mail is variable length message recording so a caller can leave as detailed a message as they need to. If you're often away from you place of business, you may want the remote feature, which allows you to retrieve your messages from any phone. Voice mail is often available through your local telephone company.

Fax Machine

■ **Computer.** Of all the tools a small business person can own, a computer can have the greatest impact. For some types of business, such as secretarial or accounting services, a computer is a virtual necessity. But for many other businesses, while not an absolute necessity, a computer can improve productivity by eliminating much of the drudgery involved with common business tasks, such as inventory tracking and billing. On the other hand, if you buy a computer without having a specific task in mind, it can easily become a very expensive paperweight. As you read the discussion on computers later in this section, be sure to remember that your specific needs, not technology, should be the primary consideration when choosing a computer for your business.

■ **Copy machine.** Now that the days of carbon paper are becoming an increasingly dim memory, copy machines are the workhorses of today's offices. There are models in every price range, starting at about $500, up to machines with the most advanced features (collating, reduction, enlargement, two-sided copying, etc.) costing thousands of dollars. The use of plain paper, copy quality and speed are typically the most important features to look for in any copy machine.

■ **Facsimile machine.** When next day delivery either isn't fast enough or costs too much, use a facsimile machine to send your documents anywhere in the world instantly. Businesses which send time-sensitive documents, such as letters, orders, contracts, estimates, drafts, or proofs, by overnight delivery services or same-day messenger

services, can save money by faxing them instead. If you buy a fax machine, make sure it is compatible with the industry standard (Group III) machines. Most small businesses, which have no more than an occasional need for faxing, can save money by finding a local service that sends and receives faxes. Copy shops, instant printers, and mail box rental shops often provide facsimile service.

■ **Postage meter.** You can avoid the inconvenience of dealing with postage stamps by renting a postage meter, which a business can rent but not own. Not only do you have the exact postage when you need it, but the imprint of a postage meter on your mail enhances your business professionalism. For most small businesses, the least expensive model is adequate. If you start sending out large numbers of packages, you may consider upgrading to a postage meter with a built-in scale and automatic computation of the postage.

■ **Calculators.** An invaluable tool for any business, calculators are available in a wide range of models and prices. Whichever calculator you choose, make sure it is a ten-key model, prints out a tape, has at least an eight digit capacity, and is able to handle negative numbers.

■ **Cash Registers.** Most retail stores need a cash register for transacting and recording daily cash sales. The newer electronic cash registers not only give daily totals, but can also generate reports on the types of items sold, amounts rung up by different sales clerks, and other information useful for tax purposes. Bar coding technology is now allowing small retail shops to track each individual sale by item, making inventory control far more precise.

When considering the purchase of equipment, avoid buying more than your business actually needs. Unnecessary equipment purchases can tie up your cash, causing severe financial problems. Use the "Equipment & Supplies Needed Worksheet" at the end of this section to determine your initial equipment needs, then list any equipment you purchase on the "Equipment List." When starting out, it's often wise to keep your equipment purchases to a minimum. Consider using copying, fax, and computer services available on an as-needed basis from some instant printers and private "mailbox" services.

Computers: The Inside Story

A computer system is made up of "hardware," the computer and related pieces of equipment, and "software," the programs that instruct the computer on how to do various tasks. Computer hardware consists of a number components:

- The **CPU** (Central Processing Unit) is the brain of the computer and controls the speed at which the computer can process information. This speed is determined by the type of processing chip used, usually designated by a number, such as 386 or 030; and the amount of random access memory (RAM), measured in kilobytes (K) or megabytes, which determines how much information the computer can process at one time. RAM is where your work and currently active programs are stored. When the computer is turned off, RAM is emptied of all contents. In most computers the CPU is housed in a separate case, and is connected by cables to the monitor, keyboard, and printer.

- The **monitor** is a screen, similar to a TV, that enables you to view your work. Also like TVs, they come in either color or black and white and a variety of sizes.

- The **keyboard** looks like a typewriter keyboard. It's used to enter work into the

computer and give commands to the software programs. Many systems also use a pointing device called a "mouse" to enter instructions.

- A **disk drive** is a mechanism for reading disks and writing to them. The diskettes are removed from the drive for storage or transport.

- **Diskettes** are portable plastic devices, whose internal magnetic coatings will hold instructions to the computer and information. The most common ones are 3.5" square, although many computers use a 5.25" floppy diskette.

- A **hard disk** is a device for storing large amounts of data, often located in the same case as the CPU. The hard disk serves the same function as a diskette for storing programs and information, but unlike the diskettes, it usually isn't portable. The hard disk's contents remain intact even after the computer is turned off. Hard disks can store from twenty to over a hundred times as much information as diskettes. The capacity of a hard disk drive is measured in megabytes, typically 20 to 80 MB. For applications, such as graphics and sound, which require large amounts of memory, CD-ROM storage devices are available that have even greater storage capability.

- A **printer** is an output device that creates printed versions of your work on paper, labels, envelopes, or overhead film. There are three major kinds of printers: laser, the highest quality and most expensive type; impact, which produces typewriter-like output; and dot-matrix, the lowest quality and least expensive type.

Even with all this hardware in place, you still won't have a computer system without two kinds of software: an operating system and application programs. The operating system provides an environment inside the computer allowing the application programs to communicate the instructions necessary for performing their functions to the computer. The application programs provide all the instructions the computer needs to accomplish the tasks you bought it for.

Choosing the Right Computer for Your Business

The first thing to consider when thinking about a computer is what you intend to use it for. Then you'll want to look at which software programs will do those jobs. As you read the section below that describes the kinds of computer programs you may need for your business, write down the applications that are most important to you, the ones you'll use the most. Then review the discussion on software below for the names of the most popular software programs in those categories.

In most cases, your choice of a computer will be between an IBM personal computer or "clone" (PC), and an Apple Macintosh computer (Mac). While it's true that some medium-size businesses may need the power of a minicomputer, virtually all small businesses will select either a PC or a Mac as their first computer.

When you do purchase one of these computers, you'll have to purchase the software separately, and perhaps some of the peripherals such as a printer, hard disk, cables, etc., which aren't always included in the price of the computer.

Here are some factors to consider when choosing a computer:

■ **Ease of Use.** The PC has gotten a lot easier to use in the last couple of years, but it still doesn't compare with the Mac in terms of operational simplicity. However, the wide acceptance of Windows 3.0/3.1, has narrowed the gap considerably. On the Mac, pictures, or "icons" are used to represent different operations. When you want to do something, you just use the mouse to point the cursor at the appropriate icon. A PC that isn't operating under Windows, uses keyboard entries as the primary way to enter commands to the application programs.

Keyboard entries aren't as easy to use in the beginning as the Mac's icons, but once learned, can be faster to use. A PC with Windows uses an icon-based system similar to the Mac's.

■ **Cost.** PC "clones," systems using IBM design but manufactured by a variety of companies, are relatively inexpensive, some selling for under $1000. The Macs priced that low won't have the features you'll need to run your business. Expect to pay between $1500 and $2000 for a Mac, although lower priced Macs are available. Like most electronic equipment, computers are often sold at prices substantially below manufacturer's list. The lowest prices are generally available from discount chains and reputable mail order companies. But if you're buying your first computer, it may be worthwhile to buy from a computer store that can help you get set up and running.

■ **Configuration.** PCs should come equipped with 3-5K (kilobyte) RAM (random access memory) if you plan to rum Windows, and at least a 40 to 80 MB (megabyte) hard disk drive. A Mac will come with 2-4 MB RAM and at least a 40 to 80 MB hard drive. It's generally a good idea to expand the RAM to 5-8 MB if you intend to use graphics or desktop publishing programs extensively. Both machines will come with at least one internal 3.5" floppy disk drive.

■ **Learning.** All computers require you to do some learning. For most people the Mac is an easier, less confusing machine to learn. And most Mac software packages, unlike those for the PC, use similar commands, so they are often simpler to learn also.

■ **Availability of software.** More programs are available for the PC than for any other kind of computer. While there are a number of good programs for the Mac in each of the major categories, there is a far wider selection for PCs because there are so many more of them in use. If you need a specific application for your particular business, be sure to find the application before selecting a computer.

Regardless of which computer you choose for your business it will probably take more time than you think to get up to speed on it, so plan on ample learning time. Another important thing to remember is that computers won't compensate for poor manual systems. Before you try to computerize any procedure, be sure it's working the way you want it to manually. If you computerize a sloppy procedure, you won't be correcting the procedure's faults, you'll only be making them automatic.

> *"If it keeps up, man will atrophy all his limbs but the pushbutton finger."*
>
> Frank Lloyd Wright

Selecting the Right Software for Your Business

Software is the part of a computer system that performs the functions, like word processing or database management, you wanted to accomplish by buying the computer. Generally, each separate function requires a separate software program, but there are some "integrated," or combined function programs.

For many small businesses an integrated program that combines word processing, spreadsheet, and database capability is often sufficient for most of their business needs. Programs like Q and A, and PFS:First Choice for the PC and Microsoft Works for the Mac supply all the software functionality many business owners need.

In order to acquaint you with the basic functions, and best sellers, of the most commonly used applications, here is an overview of business software:

- **Word processing.** Anyone whose work involves extensive writing or correspondence, will appreciate not having to retype entire documents to change a few words or lines. With a word processing program, you write and edit on the screen first, and print

out the final draft when you're satisfied with it. Some programs have built-in spell checkers and separate programs are available for grammar checking. Merging capabilities allow you to automatically combine a form letter with a list of names to automatically produce a letter that appears to be personally typed to each name on the list. This is a handy feature for sending out marketing letters, or to meet any other need you have for communicating with large numbers of people using semi-personalized letters. Two important features to look for in word processing programs are ease of use and compatibility, which means that the documents it creates can be moved into, and modified by, other programs.

The best selling word processing programs are Microsoft Word and WordPerfect, both of which offer PC and Mac versions. Other popular programs are PC-Write for the PC and WriteNow and MacWrite for the Mac.

- **Spreadsheet.** Financial management is much easier with spreadsheet programs than it is with pencil and paper. Using spreadsheet programs allows you to create financial statements, sales and profit projections, and many other financial documents. With a spreadsheet program you can easily change one or more numbers and all the related numbers on the spreadsheet automatically change to reflect the new figures, allowing you to do "what if" projections quickly and easily. Some small businesses also use spreadsheet programs to keep track of their accounts receivable, accounts payable, inventory, and payroll. Ease of use and flexibility in formatting are probably the most important features of spreadsheets.

The most popular spreadsheet program is Lotus 1-2-3 for the PC, the next most popular is Microsoft Excel for both the PC and the Mac. Wingz is another popular spreadsheet for the Mac, and Lucid 3-D is available for the PC.

■ **Database management**. For storing and updating customer records and other large groupings of information, you'll find database programs invaluable. Not only can you store and manipulate large amounts of information, but you can sort based upon whatever criteria you choose. Let's say you want to contact only your best customers. You can sort your entire customer list and select only those customers who have spent at least $500 in the past year. The larger programs allow you to create an entire business operations system, including order processing, invoicing, customer history, accounts receivable, and inventory management all connected together and derived from the same data. Such a full-featured database program is called relational, so-called because when you change something on one record, every related record reflects that change automatically. Not all small businesses need such elaborate capability, for many a simple file manager program, or even a mailing list program is sufficient. To be most useful, a full-featured database management program should be relational and easy to use. The simpler programs won't be relational, but they should still be easy to use.

Software often requires considerable learning time.

The most widely used database management program is dBase, which is relational and available for both the PC and the Mac. Other popular PC database programs are Reflex, Paradox, PFS: Professional File, and PC-File. For the Mac there is FileMaker Pro, 4th Dimension, and FoxBase+.

■ **Bookkeeping/Accounting**. Many small business owners choose to buy off-the-shelf bookkeeping programs instead of using a sophisticated database management program to create a bookkeeping system from scratch. Some accounting packages perform several functions, e.g. accounts receivable, accounts payable, payroll, etc. Others offer each of these functions as a separate module. Accounting programs should be chosen on the basis of your particular needs. It doesn't

matter how many features a program has if it doesn't do what you need it to do. Make sure any accounting program you buy is compatible with the way you do business, otherwise you could end up changing the way your do business to accommodate the program.

In-House Accountant and the Great Plains Accounting Series are available for both the PC and the Mac. ACT 1 & ACT 2, Money Counts and the CYMA Accounting Series are designed for the PC, while Quicken, At Once! and MYOB are available for the Mac. If you bill by the hour, you should look into Timeslips, which was designed specifically for this type of billing.

■ **Desktop publishing**. Now professional-looking business communications can be produced quickly and economically with desktop publishing software. You can create your own forms, brochures, newsletters, and other materials to help organize and promote your business. While it's true that desktop publishing programs can produce near-typeset quality camera-ready art at a fraction on the price it would cost to obtain from a traditional typesetter, there are two important things to bear in mind. The first is that these programs require a considerable amount of learning time. And the other thing is that good design requires skill, and that use of computer to produce a form or a brochure without this skill can lead to illegible, unattractive, and ineffective results. Even so, if you're willing to learn how to use desktop publishing programs and equipment, you'll be giving your business a tremendous amount of flexibility and power. Besides ease of use, the most important feature is the quality of the final image. Some of the best image quality comes from programs that can be output on a Linotronic typesetting machine, which can be found at computer service bureaus and typesetting shops.

The most popular desktop publishing program for the Mac is PageMaker, which also comes in a PC version. Ventura Publisher is popular for the PC. Publish-It! is available for both the PC and the Mac, and Quark is another popular Mac desktop publishing program.

Besides these main categories of programs there are numerous other utility and special purpose programs you may want to investigate. Communications programs allow computers to "talk" with each other over telephone lines with the aid of a modem. There are also drawing programs, presentation software, outliners, and a host of other applications. There is also a wide variety of software designed for specific businesses, such as video rental stores or dental practices. Whatever your needs, there's probably a program available to help you.

Before buying any software, talk to people who use it regularly and try to get a demo at a computer store. Don't buy a program because of what its ads say or because of what it says on the package. Make sure that the software you buy will do what you need it to do before you buy it.

Getting the Equipment You Need

As your business grows and the need for more equipment becomes apparent, you'll probably start looking around to see how you can acquire this equipment. So let's look at the three basic ways you can get the equipment you need for your business:

■ **Purchase**. You can buy new or used equipment from a variety of sources. When you buy, you own the equipment and it becomes an asset of your business. At the same time, you're depleting capital that could be put to other uses. You can, however, deduct the depreciation of your equipment from your business income taxes.

■ **Leasing**. You can lease new or used equipment for certain period of time at a set monthly fee. While the leasing company owns the equipment, you can deduct your monthly payments as a business expense.

Some leases have a purchase option, so that with a final payment at the end of the lease, you take ownership of the equipment. The total payments over the life of the lease plus the buy-out payment can work out to twice the original purchase price. Even so, it often makes good sense from a cash flow perspective to lease rather than buy. When shopping for equipment, ask the seller or manufacturer if they offer a competitive lease option; if not, contact one of the many independent leasing companies who deal with small business.

■ **Rental**. Many types of office equipment can be rented on a weekly or monthly basis. The fee can be rather high, and a steep deposit is almost always required. You can deduct the rental payments as a business expense. Rentals are good for temporary replacements, or to test out a piece of equipment before purchasing something similar. Renting is a short-term rather than a long-term solution for acquiring equipment.

Notes:

Tips for Using the Following Forms:

Note: You are encouraged to copy these forms for your own use. Keep the unmarked originals in a safe place and make copies of them to work from.

Equipment & Supplies Needed Worksheet – This form gives a convenient place to keep track of the equipment you'll need to start your business. It also contains information that's part of your business plan (see "Business Plan Guide" in **Business Plan**). Write in the type of equipment you need in the first column, the supplier you have selected in the second column, and its cost in the third column. Note whether it will be leased or purchased in the fourth column, and how long it will take for delivery in the fifth column. When all the equipment has been put on the form, add up the total costs for the equipment listed under A, B and C enter them into the Capital Expenditures portion of the "Projected Expense Budget & Capital Expenditures."

Equipment List – After you've obtained a piece of equipment, use this form make a record of it. In the first column enter a description of the item (e.g. electric typewriter). In the second column enter the brand name, and in the third the serial number. Next enter the purchase date and the cost. Store the completed form in a safe place, it could be helpful to you in case of fire or theft, as well as provide the basis for your depreciation calculations.

EQUIPMENT & SUPPLIES NEEDED WORKSHEET

Item	Supplier	Cost	Lease/Buy	Date Needed	Comments
A. Production Equipment		$			
B. Office Equipment					
Telephone system					
Answering machine					
Copy machine(s)					
Computer(s)					
Computer printer(s)					
Computer software					
Computer software					
Computer software					
Postage meter					
Fax machine(s)					
C. Supplies & Miscellaneous					
Business stationery					
Business cards					
Total Cost		$			

EQUIPMENT LIST

	Item Description	Manufacturer/Model	Serial #	Date Purchased	Cost
1					
2					
3					
4					
5					
6					
7					
8					
9					
10					
11					
12					
13					
14					
15					
16					
17					
18					
19					
20					
21					
22					
23					
24					
25					
26					
27					
28					
29					
30					
	Total				

EQUIPMENT
FORMS

OPERATIONS

ADMINISTRATION

FACILITIES

INSURANCE

LEGAL

PERSONNEL

FILING &
RECORDKEEPING

FACILITIES

Business Location

For most new businesses, where to locate should be an early consideration. Where you locate will depend on your type of business as well as who and where your customers are. Retail stores and restaurants (where location, location, and location have been called the three most critical factors for success) have to be located very near to their customers, but other types of business may have more flexibility in choosing a location.

For service businesses, such as exterminators and carpet cleaners, who perform their services at the client's place of business or home, the location of their facility isn't that important. They, along with mail order businesses and other businesses whose customers don't visit their facilities, can be very flexible in choosing a location. Manufacturers, on the other hand, may need to locate close to suppliers or customers and have to consider transportation, labor, power, taxes, and regulations before they choose a location.

The first thing to consider is whether where you intend to locate is right for your type of business. A business that is successful in one community, may not be successful in another, particularly if the two communities are fairly dissimilar. A store selling only beach supplies might work well in Los Angeles or Miami, but probably not in Cleveland or Pittsburgh.

But assuming the population trends, purchasing power, competitive situation, and potential of the community are all favorable, then the next thing you'll want to look at are specific areas within the community you've chosen.

Retail stores will generally want to locate near their clientele. How near depends on the frequency of a customer's visits, which is a function of the type of merchandise being sold:

- **Convenience goods** that are widely available, like candy and milk, have to be located very close to customers and be very easy to get to. Corner locations are generally best because of their visibility to traffic going in both directions. Unless there is heavy foot traffic, adequate parking has to be provided, which is why "strip shopping centers" are often desirable locations.

- **Shopping goods**, like clothes, cars, and furniture, should be convenient to the specific consumers of that particular merchandise. The best sites are located within a large concentration of the target market. Often these stores will cluster in areas that buyers will travel to when looking for a particular item.

- **Specialty goods** are high-priced items, such as fine jewelry, expensive perfume, exclusive designer clothing, and similar merchandise. They don't have to be as close to their customers as other retailers, but they do have to be located in an area compatible with what they're selling. Luxury stores tend to congregate in upscale shopping districts like Rodeo Drive in Beverly Hills or Fifth Avenue in New York City.

Service businesses operating out of storefronts, like dry cleaners and shoe repair shops, depend on foot or drive-by traffic and have to be located where their customers are going to pass them on a regular basis. Other personal service businesses which are visited less frequently, like beauty parlors and barbershops, can cultivate a base of steady clients who are more willing to go out of their way. Many retailers and service businesses will want to locate near a large department store or mall that attracts large numbers of shoppers.

Besides customer proximity, the area you select will be affected by the cost of rents in that area and the compatibility of the area's prestige with your product or service. You'll also want to take zoning laws and local regulations into consideration before choosing the specific area for locating your business.

Non-residential Business Site

Once you've settled on the geographic area, the next step is to choose the specific location. Here are the major considerations that go into choosing a business site:

- **Personal convenience.** If the location is too far from your residence, you're going to spend a lot of time commuting.

- **Customer proximity.** If your business needs to be geographically close to its customers, then locate where the bulk of the customers are. And remember that the more often your customers need to visit you, the closer you should be to them.

- **Supplier proximity.** If certain raw materials or supplies are crucial to your business, you may need to locate close to your sources of supply in order to reduce freight costs and delivery times.

- **Competitor proximity.** Some types of business, like women's clothing shops and auto dealerships, tend to locate in clusters because customers like to shop extensively before purchasing, and so these businesses draw customers to each other. Other types of business, like convenience stores or dry cleaners for example, should not locate near competitors since they will take business away from each other as customers patronize one shop or the other.

- **Physical suitability of the building.** Find a building or space appropriate for your kind of business; one that is already, or could easily become, just what you need to be successful.

- **Type and cost of lease.** How much the rent is and how long of a lease term you can get are important factors, as well as what options you can get in the leasing agreement (see discussion of leases below).

- **Possibilities for expansion.** Growth is virtually always a part of business success. Can this location accommodate your business's needs for space to accommodate additional employees, supplies, and inventory as it grows?

- **Transportation and parking.** For the convenience of both customers and employees, the availability of accessible roadways, public transportation, and ample parking is an important factor to consider.

- **Availability of qualified employees.** As your business grows, it becomes increasingly important to have a pool of qualified potential employees.

Use the "Facility Planner" below to determine the requirements for your business location and the "Site Selection Worksheet" at the end of this section to help you evaluate your options and choose the right location for your business.

Facility Planner

By answering the questions below, you can determine the requirements for your ideal business location:

What kind of facility does your business need?

❑ Home ❑ Office ❑ Store

❑ Factory ❑ Warehouse ❑ Other

Do you intend to lease or purchase your business facility? _____

How much are you willing to pay per month? _____

How many square feet do you need? _____

Do you need additional space for future growth? How much? _____

What special requirements does your business have?

❑ Electrical _____ ❑ Plumbing _____

❑ Heating _____ ❑ Air Conditioning _____

❑ Ventilation _____ ❑ Refrigeration _____

❑ Water _____ ❑ Storage _____

❑ Access _____ ❑ Other _____

Rank the following (from 1 to 5) in terms of their importance to your business:

____ Customer convenience

____ Supplier proximity

____ Employee proximity

____ Competitor proximity

____ Personal preference

Where could you locate your business to satisfy the two most important considerations above?

_____

Leases

Since most business locations are leased, there's a good chance you'll sign a lease agreement some day. A lease is a binding, legal agreement between the landlord (the lessor) and the tenant (the lessee). It spells out the rights and obligations of each party. Since the lessee is obligated to pay the full amount of the monthly payments for the entire term of the lease, signing a lease is a serious financial transaction. As with any contract, have an attorney review the lease agreement before you sign it.

Here are some of the major considerations that should be resolved to your satisfaction before signing a lease:

■ **Rent.** How much is the rent payment? How does this compare to other sites in this area and with that of other firms like yours? Which of the following methods will be used to determine your monthly payment:

  (1) Flat monthly payment

  (2) A set percentage of your gross sales, 5% for example.

  (3) Sliding percentage of your gross sales, where the percentage varies at different sales volumes

  (4) Some combination of a minimum payment and a percentage of your gross sales.

■ **Term.** What is the total lease term? What renewal provisions does the tenant have? If you're just starting your business, it's best to get a short-term lease with a long-term renewal option, e.g. a two year lease with an option to renew for eight years. Do you have the option to obtain additional space in the building at the same rental rate?

■ **Improvements.** Who is responsible for painting, remodeling and other initial improvements? Who owns the improvements you make? Often a tenant can reduce the monthly rent payment by agreeing to make some improvements on the property. Extensive landlord improvements usually mean higher rents.

■ **Insurance.** What insurance does the landlord hold? What insurance coverage are you required to have? The landlord should at least have coverage for any accidents occurring in the common areas, while the tenant may be required to have insurance covering accidents and fire damage occurring in the leased area.

■ **Sublet.** Does you have the right to sublease all or part of your space to another party? This is a valuable right for a tenant to have. If you find out you've leased too much space, it helps to be able to sublet the part

you're not using. And if you have to leave that location before the lease is up, subletting allows you to bring in a new tenant to finish out your lease.

■ **Restrictions.** Are there any restrictions on the use the property? There shouldn't be any restrictions against using the leased property for any legitimate business purpose. Many leases prohibit anyone living on the property and some prohibit certain businesses that create excessive noise, smells, or other disturbances.

■ **Termination.** Does either party have the right to terminate the lease? Under what conditions? Leases generally aren't terminated, except under extraordinary circumstances, such as gross non-compliance with lease provisions or criminal activity. Many leases contain a provision that instead of terminating the lease in the event of a dispute, one of the parties may bring the case to arbitration, with the losing party paying the costs.

Nearly 20 million people now operate homebased businesses.

Operating Your Business from Home

Operating a business from home has become an increasingly popular trend among new business owners. At one time there was a stigma attached to homebased businesses, but now they are widely accepted, and often envied. Currently, there are nearly twenty million full- or part-time homebased businesses operating across the nation. Because homebased businesses have become so popular, let's look at some of the advantages they offer:

- **Lower start-up costs.** There are no moving expenses, and the extent of renovations is completely up to you.

- **Lower overhead.** Only your regular rent or mortgage payment is due every month, and you're already accustomed to handling that.

- **Tax benefits.** Homebased business owners can receive tax deductions for the portion of their homes used exclusively for the business (see *Taxes* in **Finance**).

- **Lifestyle flexibility.** You can dress as you please, work according to your own schedule, and even take care of your children while you work.

There are also disadvantages to homebased businesses, here are some of them:

- **Isolation.** Because you're off in your own isolated world you may miss opportunities, your view of what's happening may become limited, and you may begin to feel like it's you against the world.

- **Space limitations.** As time goes by, the business may start to overflow into the living areas of your home, and if the business takes off very quickly, there may be no room at all for expansion.

- **Zoning laws.** In some areas the zoning laws are very strict and prohibit certain businesses (and in some cases, any business) from operating out of a residence.

- **Security concerns.** The office equipment and inventory you have on hand may attract thieves.

- **Household interference.** The possible resentment of family members, distractions, and interruptions can all make working at home difficult.

The main question about working from home is self-discipline. Can you be diligent enough to stick to your work while avoiding distractions from children, television, and personal telephone calls? If so, and provided the advantages outweigh the disadvantages, then a homebased business may be for you.

Alternative Business Sites

For non-retail business owners who can't quite afford commercial rents, don't need much space, or can't operate from home, but who still want to operate in a business-like fashion, there are other alternatives:

- **Shared space.** As a way to reduce costs, a group of similar small business people, such as graphic designers, may rent a space together, and share the costs of rent, maintenance, and perhaps some support staff. They may also lease and share office equipment.

- **Executive suites.** In many areas there are businesses that rent office space, offering two distinct kinds of service: individual offices and shared offices. With the individual office rental, the space is for your exclusive use during the duration of your rental agreement. The shared offices are more suited for those who do the bulk of their work at home or at a client's location, but still want a business setting for meetings with clients and prospects. These well-appointed offices are used by several business people who reserve them at different times for various business purposes, for which they pay a fee commensurate with their usage. With both the individual and shared office rentals, a wide variety of services, such as telephone answering, office equipment usage, and support personnel is also available. Since payment for these services is based on actual usage, the tenants have the convenience of a large office without the burden of overhead. You'll find listings for these types of rentals in the Yellow Pages Directory under "Executive Suites."

Business incubators are a new alternative designed to foster the growth of new businesses. In over 430 locations across the country, business incubators provide inexpensive space and shared services to a number of new businesses. These incubators are sponsored by government agencies, universities, or private investors. Their services and fees vary, but most of them offer a full-service business facility at below-market rates. Most also include on-premises consulting services. One of their greatest benefits is that they allow entrepreneurs to interact with each other, share experiences, and encourage each other. For more information contact the National Business Incubation Association listed in the **Resources** section.

Security Worksheet

Each year burglary, robbery, employee theft, shoplifting, and bad checks cost businesses billions of dollars. And while it's not possible to eliminate these losses entirely, there is much you can do to keep them at a minimum. The following questions will get you started thinking about what you can do to protect your business from crime. Under each question, check the security measures that apply to your business. Any questions you can't answer may indicate a potential security problem.

How will you ensure the honesty of your employees?

❏ Bonding

❏ Limited access to cash

❏ Other _____

❏ Reference checks

❏ Monitoring systems

What methods are you going to use to handle computer security?

❏ Limited or password access

❏ Tracking software

❏ Cable locks

❏ Other _____

What steps are you taking to prevent shoplifting?

❏ Vigilant employees

❏ Sensors at exits

❏ Security guards

❏ Extra security for high-ticket items

❏ Cameras

❏ Other _____

What are your procedures for handling cash?

❏ Limit number of employees handling cash

❏ Make daily deposits

❏ Accept no bill larger than $20

❏ Limit cash on hand

❏ Locate cash register away from door

❏ Other _____

What are your procedures for accepting checks?

❏ With drivers license and credit card only

❏ Upon authorization of check approval service

❏ Drawn on local bank only

❏ Other _____

What are your procedures for accepting credit cards?

❏ Check "hot" list

❏ Through electronic data capture

❏ Call for authorization

❏ Other _____

Do you need an alarm? What kind?

❏ Site bell only

❏ Doors and windows

❏ Other _____

❏ Ring to central station

❏ Interior movement

What other security measures does your business need? _____

_____

Tips for Using the Following Form:

Note: You are encouraged to copy this form for your own use. Keep the unmarked original in a safe place and make copies of it to work from.

Site Selection Worksheet – Use the Location columns near the top of the form to list the different sites you're comparing. In the upper section of the form, enter the cost of each factor in the appropriate space beneath each prospective location. Under desirability factors in the lower section of the form, enter the value, or weight, from 1 to 10, with 10 being the highest, based on how important each of these factors is to your business. Then, based on your assessment of each location's desirability, enter a grade from 1 to 10 in the spaces opposite the various factors. When each of the locations is graded for the weighted desirability factors, multiply the value you've assigned to each factor by the grade you've given to each location. The resulting scores are a numerical indication of how the sites compare with each other, and give you a quantitative way of determining which is the best location for your business.

SITE SELECTION WORKSHEET

Key Considerations		Location 1	Location 2	Location 3
Cost factors				
Monthly rent				
Deposit required				
Usable square footage				
Cost of improvements				
Allowance for improvements				
Telephone equipment				
Operating expenses				
Electric use				
Gas use				
Water use				
Special assessments				
City/Local tax amount				
Insurance requirements				
Common area fee or load factor				
Personal guarantee				

Desirability Factors	Value	Grade	Score	Grade	Score	Grade	Score
Personal convenience							
Customer convenience							
Building suitability							
Expansion potential							
Transportation / parking							
Availability of employees							
Attractiveness							
Utility/Use restrictions							
Competition							
Total Score							

INSURANCE

Managing Risk

Being in business involves some degree of risk. Many common risks, such as fire and accidents, can have serious financial effects on the day-to-day operations of a business. While it isn't possible to avoid risks completely, with the proper insurance coverage you can protect your business from the severe financial losses resulting from these risks.

Because insurance can shield your business from financial disaster, you should begin thinking about insurance coverage before starting your business. Insurance is a necessary business expense and postponing it can lead to catastrophic losses in the event of an accident or natural disaster.

Large companies employ risk managers, whose job it is to obtain the proper insurance and take other steps to protect the company against accidental and preventable losses, and to minimize the financial consequences of unavoidable losses. As a small business owner, however, you'll probably have to take on this responsibility yourself. So it is important that you understand insurance coverage, how it can benefit your business, and what you stand to lose if you're not adequately covered.

Types of Coverage

The first step in risk management is to identify the kinds of risks your business faces. Next you have to analyze the potential losses and come up with strategy for protecting your business against them. You can use the "Insurance Worksheet" at the end of this section to help you understand your insurance needs. Here are some of the main risks you may want to consider insuring your business against:

■ **Property Damage** most commonly covers damage from fire. Other common perils are windstorm, lightning, and vandalism. Retail stores often carry glass insurance as well. Insurance is also available to protect the contents of a business, such as raw materials, finished goods, inventory ready to ship, employee property, accounting records, equipment, and machinery.

■ **General Liability** protects a business from claims of personal injury or property damage due to general business operations. For example, a customer who trips and falls, sustaining an injury serious enough to prevent them from working for some time, may hold the business liable for medical expenses and lost income.

■ **Product Liability** protects against claims for damages or injuries related to defects in the products a business produces or sells. Generally speaking, if someone is injured due to a defect in a product, both the maker and seller of the product are liable for damages. Many of these cases result in multi-million dollar judgements. Regardless of who wins a liability suit, litigation is time-consuming and expensive. No matter how ridiculous or unfounded a lawsuit may be, productive business hours are lost, lawyers still have to be paid, and other related costs have to be met.

- **Disability** provides income replacement in the case of missed work due to injury or illness. If you're the major source of income for your family, you may want to consider having enough disability insurance to cover your family's living expenses in the event you are unable to work for an extended period of time.

- **Worker's Compensation** covers employees for loss of income and medical expenses resulting from a job-related accident or illness. Every state has some sort of worker's compensation act. Many states require this coverage for most businesses, and some states even require companies to pay benefits to employees of contractors who have failed to provide coverage themselves. When hiring any kind of contract labor, be sure to ask for a certificate of insurance. When you become an employer, federal law requires that you (1) provide a safe place to work, (2) hire competent fellow employees, (3) provide safe tools, and (4) warn employees of existing dangers. Failure to do so makes you, as an employer, liable for damage suits brought by employees as well as fines and possible prosecution by the government.

- **Business Interruption** provides coverage in the event business activity is stopped by some unforeseen event, such as a fire. It covers lost income and the extra expenses necessitated by the event that caused the interruption. These extra expenses may include additional payroll, temporary rented quarters, and leased furniture and equipment. Business interruption insurance defines lost income as the difference between normal income and whatever income is earned during the interruption of normal business activities.

- **Key Person** provides financial protection in case of the death or disability of an owner, partner, or key employee. A new business depends heavily on its founders. If one of them dies, the business could be devastated. Key Person Insurance provides a means to reduce the resulting financial losses, and to recruit and train a replacement.

- **Health or Medical** protects against the high costs of major medical expenses. Health care is expensive – even a short hospital stay costs thousands of dollars. Many people have been financially drained, even bankrupted, by medical expenses. That's why it makes sense to protect yourself and your family with health insurance. If you have employees, group health insurance may cost less and provide more benefits than individual policies.

The types of insurance your business needs depends on the risks you are juggling.

Other Types of Insurance

Depending on your type of business, you may need to investigate other forms of coverage, such as automobile, crime, computer, life, errors and omissions, and malpractice. In addition there is also Sole Proprietor Insurance, Partnership Insurance, and Shareholder Insurance. Fidelity bonds for employees with access to company funds guarantee against loss from embezzlement. Insurance can also be useful as a tax and estate planning tool. Your agent can provide additional information about the types and uses of insurance.

Insurance Tips

- If you are working out of your home, you should be aware that your homeowner's or renter's insurance policies will not cover all of your business equipment, supplies, or inventory. If the total value of your business property isn't very large, you may be able to cover it with a "Business Pursuits Endorsement."

- Make sure your policy pays replacement-value on stolen or damaged property. That way you'll get enough to replace the item, as opposed to being reimbursed for current depreciated value, which is almost always a far lower amount.

- Be sure to keep a record of all insured property, including photographs of each item, in case you have to substantiate any losses. Store these lists and photos in a safe place, such as a safe deposit box, or make two copies and store them at different locations.

- Some insurance companies offer "standard" business insurance packages at low rates. These cover the most common risks and satisfy most standard insurance requirements. There are also special "packages" for different types of business, retail stores for instance. Also ask your insurance agent or broker about an "umbrella policy" that can provide substantially increased liability coverage for a relatively modest increase in premiums.

- If your business is short of cash, request a monthly payment schedule instead of quarterly or semi-annual premium payments. You may have to pay a small service charge for the extra paperwork necessitated by monthly payments, but conserving your cash may be worth this nominal charge.

Dealing with Insurance Brokers & Agents

While insurance is sometimes purchased directly from an insurer, most often it is purchased through agents or brokers. Traditionally an agent represents a single insurer and offers its lines only, while a broker, who represents several insurers, can offer a wider range of coverage from these different insurers.

What matters most is the competence of the agent or broker, who can range from inexperienced part-time salespeople to highly knowledgeable professionals. Business insurance brokers can be particularly helpful when you are deciding which kinds of coverage are most appropriate for your business because their expertise is concentrated in this area.

When selecting an insurance agent or broker, ask associates in your field for recommendations. Take the time to shop around. Ask questions to find out how they can help you. Ask for and check out references. It's important to find out how quickly payment is made for losses after claims are made.

Do your homework by finding out as much as you can about what kind of coverage you need before talking with an agent or broker. While agents and brokers can be very helpful, it's not wise to depend entirely on them for guidance. Other sources, like your trade association, may be able to give you guidelines relating to the customary coverages for your type of business.

Besides looking at the qualifications of the agent or broker, you'll also want to look closely at the insurance company providing the coverage. Besides the cost of the coverage, which types of coverage are offered is also important. The more kinds of insurance you can get from one source, the less time you'll have to put into administering the risk management function.

These days, it's wise to check into the stability of the firm insuring your risks. The best insurance policy is worthless if the carrier doesn't have the financial resources to pay its claims. Your state insurance commission may provide information on the financial condition of insurers in your state, as does the *Best Insurance Company Ratings* available at your library.

How To Save Money On Insurance

Even though paying insurance premiums is a necessity, it doesn't make sense to pay more than you have to. Here are some tips for keeping your insurance costs at a minimum:

- Compare quotes from different carriers and agents

- Investigate lower rate group plans like those offered by many trade associations

- Insure for your actual exposure only, don't carry excess coverage

- Increase deductibles; increasing the deductible from $100 to $1000 can reduce premiums 15 - 30%

- Pay small claims yourself; if an accident costs $600 and your deductible is $500, it's better to pay the whole claim out of pocket than have the insurance company pay its $100 and then raise your rates later

- Keep employees with poor driving records off the company's automobile policy

- Ask about premium discounts for loss prevention programs, such as burglar alarms, fire sprinklers, and fire alarms.

By making risk management an essential part of your business planning, you'll be in a good position to control premium costs and keep future increases to a minimum.

Tips for Using the Following Form:

Note: You are encouraged to copy this form for your own use. Keep the unmarked original in a safe place and make copies of it to work from.

Insurance Worksheet – In order to better understand and communicate your insurance needs, complete this form before meeting with an insurance agent or broker. In the column headed Coverage Amount, to the right of each category, enter the amount of coverage you think is appropriate for your business to carry. Place the initials "n/a" in each space that represents a category that doesn't apply to your business. Then make enough copies of the form that you have one for each agent you're going to get quotes from. Discuss the coverages you've selected and enter the quotes in the spaces provided to the right of the Coverage Amount. Add up the annual premium costs and place the total in space provided. Use the last column to note coverage specifics, exclusions, and any comments you may have. Using one of these forms with each agent gives you a way of comparing the prices of different insurers to help you get the most insurance for you money.

INSURANCE WORKSHEET

Basic Coverages Available	Coverage Amount	Cost	Comments
Building related			
Building structure			
Fire	_____	_____	_____
Windstorm	_____	_____	_____
Lightning	_____	_____	_____
Vandalism	_____	_____	_____
Earthquake	_____	_____	_____
Trees, plants and shrubs	_____	_____	_____
Glass damage	_____	_____	_____
Exterior signs	_____	_____	_____
Total			_____
Property related			
Inventory			
Base level	_____	_____	_____
Peak season (plus 25-40%)	_____	_____	_____
Employee dishonesty	_____	_____	_____
Robbery and burglary	_____	_____	_____
Money and securities	_____	_____	_____
Accounts receivable	_____	_____	_____
Valuable papers	_____	_____	_____
Boiler and machinery	_____	_____	_____
Personal effects	_____	_____	_____
Automobile	_____	_____	_____
Total			_____
Business operations related			
General business liability			
Bodily injury to others	_____	_____	_____
Damage to property of others	_____	_____	_____
Personal injury to others	_____	_____	_____
Professional liability	_____	_____	_____
Key person	_____	_____	_____
Loss of income			
Direct	_____	_____	_____
Indirect	_____	_____	_____
Extra expenses following loss	_____	_____	_____
Loss of refrigeration	_____	_____	_____
Total			_____
Other			
Medical (owner/employees)	_____	_____	_____
Disability (owner/employees)	_____	_____	_____
Worker's Compensation	_____	_____	_____
Life (owner/employees)	_____	_____	_____
Total			_____

Complete the first two columns of this form prior to meeting with an insurance broker or agent in order to better understand and communicate your needs. At or following the meeting you will be able to complete the entire form and compare agents or companies.

LEGAL

Small Business Legal Considerations

Starting and operating a business involves a number of legal considerations. First there are the government rules and regulations which must be understood and obeyed, and then there is the ever-present threat of litigation initiated against your business by individuals or other businesses.

While the business owner who is willing to do a little homework can often handle many of the legal situations arising during the course of business, there are times when hiring an attorney is a better option. This section is intended to give you an overview of the most common legal considerations in small business and to help you decide how you want to handle them.

When and How to Hire an Attorney

Many traditional small business experts, such as those in an SBA booklet on starting a small business, often give the following advice: "Even the smallest and newest business needs help from at least two kinds of specialists: an attorney and an accountant."

While this can be good advice in some cases, it may be overkill in others. It's not legally necessary to hire a lawyer to start a business. Corporations and partnerships usually do hire an attorney, however, because of the relatively complex paperwork involved. But many sole proprietors have operated for years without needing an attorney's services.

When you stand to lose substantial amounts of money or time, you should definitely consult an attorney; having a lawyer on your side can make it more likely you won't take a loss. A typical case might be when you're called upon to sign a contract written in "legalese" by an attorney for the other party. If you've ever tried to read one of these documents, you already know how hard legal language can be to understand. A good lawyer can translate the legal jargon into ordinary language – which is the way good business agreements should be written in the first place.

Another time to hire a lawyer is when you're sued by someone. Failure to respond appropriately to legal papers can result in having a default judgement made against you – meaning that you automatically lose.

Because lawyers are expensive and can sometimes complicate simple matters, it is important to find a lawyer with whom you can establish a good rapport, and who honors your desire for simplicity and brevity, without sacrificing substance.

A good place to start looking for an attorney is by asking friends and business associates for recommendations. Call prospective attorneys on the phone and ask them about their business experience and fees before seeing them in person. If you like what you hear, ask to set up an initial consultation. Most lawyers in smaller firms offer a brief initial consultation at no charge.

Legal fees are generally handled in one of two ways. If you want legal help on a specific matter (e.g. filing a lawsuit or patent application), the attorney will generally request a retainer, or deposit, to begin work on the matter. If, however, you are only seeking to develop a relationship for help on infrequent legal matters, you will probably be billed as the work is done.

Recently legal service plans have been introduced that offer telephone and in-person consultation, document review, letter writing, debt collection, letters and calls, and other legal services for a fixed yearly fee, paid in advance. These services are adequate for most routine matters and the fee is relatively modest (approximately $800 per year) considering that a lawyer might charge over $200 for writing a single letter.

These plans don't, however, protect a business owner from the potentially enormous expense of major legal action. If your type of business is vulnerable to major liability lawsuits, you may want to get a special insurance policy that will pay the legal costs of your defense.

It's a good idea to have an attorney review contracts before you sign them.

■ Keep notes of telephone calls. In case of any disputes, this documentation can prove invaluable.

■ Send important documents by certified mail with return receipt requested.

■ One of the most important things you can do to avoid legal problems is to get all your business agreements in writing.

Avoiding Legal Problems

Since legal problems are costly, time-consuming, and distracting, avoiding them is a good idea for any business owner. Here are some of the chief ways you can avoid legal problems:

■ Be aware of and conform to all federal, state, and local laws and regulations related to business in general and your type of business in particular.

■ Have clear policies and make sure your employees and customers are aware of them.

■ Follow your own policies and keep your end of bargains by always doing what you say you'll do.

■ Develop forms for as many functions as you can so you'll have a systematic way of collecting information, and therefore be less likely to forget something that could lead to legal trouble later.

■ Always save dated copies of any correspondence you send out.

Business Agreements

In your business, customers may give you money in advance for products or services to be delivered in the future. Or you may provide the products and services first and then bill for them later. The same is true of relationships with your suppliers. Sometimes you pay first and wait for delivery and sometimes you receive the goods and services first and pay later.

All these situations imply agreements – that buyers are going to get what they ordered and that sellers are going to be paid for what they shipped. Putting these agreements in writing helps prevent costly and time-consuming misunderstandings and mistakes.

There is no substitute for written agreements. As the Chinese proverb goes, "The faintest ink is more lasting than the keenest memory." Any time either you or your business is in a situation that could cost you money or time, it's wise to get the details down on paper.

From a legal standpoint, many of the papers generated by a business are considered contracts. Purchase orders, for instance, are contracts. In some cases even letters are considered contracts whose wording can be legally binding on a company.

While these legalities are important to understand, it's also important to understand the process of entering into contractual agreements. Whether you're buying or selling something, arranging distribution, or hiring a key employee, you're making agreements.

A contract is a formal business agreement between two or more people or companies, called parties. Contracts either specify something that has to be done, such as selling certain goods at a specific price by a particular date, or prohibit something from being done, such as not entering into competition for a certain time. In either case, each party to the agreement has to give up something of value, termed consideration. This could be money, goods, services, or rights.

For a contract to be legally binding, the particulars of the agreement have to be both legal and possible. The language should make it is obvious that neither party is being taken advantage of.

Even when these requirements are satisfied, there is still much that can go wrong. After an agreement has been reached, the parties may find that they have each interpreted the same words differently. That's why it is so important during the negotiation stage to clear up any possible misunderstandings. If differences aren't resolved at this stage, they can lead to problems, hard feelings, and legal action.

Here are some of the most common situations calling for contracts:

Financial transactions

■ Loans (bank or individual)

■ Sale or purchase of equity

■ Investment agreements

■ Insurance policies

■ Sale or purchase of a business

Purchasing

■ Any long-term buying arrangement

■ Any purchase on non-standard terms

Sales

■ Any long-term selling arrangement

■ Any sales on non-standard terms

General

■ Consulting services

■ Benefit plans

■ Cooperative arrangements with other companies

■ Partnerships

Once you have determined that a contract is necessary in a situation, you have four basic options to consider to obtain an agreement:

■ **Draw up your own.** If you are comfortable developing your own contracts, use the "Key Contract Terms " on the following page to remind you of the types of conditions that might be needed in your contract.

■ **Use a standard contract, such as those sold in stationery stores.** Many common legal situations, such as routine leases, sales agreements, and the like can be conveniently handled through these "fill in the blanks" contracts. While these contracts aren't tailored to the specifics of your situation, they can be useful for simple matters.

- **Hire an attorney.** Whenever the situation is extremely complex, or you have a lot to lose, hiring an attorney, even though expensive, can save you lots of money in the long run. You may want to hire an attorney to review any contracts you draw up or any standard contracts you use.

- **Allow the other party to prepare the first draft.** While this option may reduce the time and expense you have to put into it at first, it also gives the other party somewhat more initial control.

The Old Pro says: *"Contact an attorney when you think you are headed for trouble, don't wait until it happens."*

Key Contract Terms

Vendor or Customer Contracts
Indemnification
Passage of title, risk of loss, & security interests
Nondisclosure of confidential information
Conflict of interests
Non-compete clause
Payment terms, including late & pre-payment
Termination clauses, including penalties
Default, trigger & remedies
Governing law
Assignability
Modification procedure
Warranties
Ordering time & procedure
Right to balance inventory
Vendor support
Change in vendor status (ownership)

Agent, Dealer, Distributor Contracts
Commission schedule and rates
Draws, if any
Reimbursable expenses
Right to terminate
Manner of representation
Services to be provided, including reports
Limitations of liability
Indemnification by agent for negligent acts
Governing law
Advertising support and uses
Ability to audit
Responsibilities of both parties
Length of contract
Assignability
Independent contractor status

Partnership Agreement
Name and purpose of partnership
Duration of agreement
Type of partnership (general or limited)
Contributions by partners (dollars and time)
Business expense handling
Extent of each individual's authority
Separate debt handling
Books, records and accounting
Profit and loss division
Salaries and/or draws
Dissolution of partnership (death, termination)
Continuation of partnership (death, departure)
Employee management
Release of debts
Sale of partnership interest
Arbitration, settlement of disputes
Modification of agreement
Absence or disability

Consultant Contracts
Scope of the work
Product or service to be delivered
Schedule, including delivery date
Price to be paid, including payment schedule
Non-assignability
Product ownership with client
Indemnification
Conflict of interest
Nondisclosure of confidential information
Governing law
Insurance
Itemization of out-of-pocket expenses
Independent contractor status

Negotiating and Signing Agreements

Whenever you are called upon to sign an agreement, always read everything in the agreement, particularly the fine print. Remember that every agreement is negotiable, so feel free to propose whatever changes you feel are necessary to make the agreement more satisfactory. If there are parts of the agreement you don't like, cross them out. The other party will have a similar opportunity to amend the agreement to their liking, so the final agreement will often be a compromise, with each party giving up something of value in order to gain what they each want.

In dealing with large companies (whether as a customer or a supplier), there may be little opportunity to alter the terms. Often their legal departments have developed standard contracts that are required if you want to do business with them. And changes to these contracts are often subject to the review of the legal department.

If you ever find yourself in the position of feeling that you have to sign an agreement you feel uneasy about, delay signing in order to "sleep on it." The extra "cooling off" time may allow you to see the agreement in a new perspective. It also allows you to ask others for their opinions. Be especially cautious if the other party insists on an immediate signing; don't let anyone rush you into signing any agreement.

Negotiating is an important skill that every business owner should develop. So at least read a good book on negotiating, and try to attend a negotiating seminar where you have an opportunity to practice negotiation techniques. Before doing any negotiating reread the section on negotiating in the *Purchasing* section.

> *"A verbal contract isn't worth the paper it's written on"*
>
> Samuel Goldwyn

Copyrights, Trademarks, and Patents

One of the most misunderstood legal aspects in business involves copyrights, trademarks, and patents. Many business owners are confused about the differences between these three forms of protection due to the many misconceptions existing about them.

Entire books have been written about each of these subjects, so what follows covers only the most important points about each. While this information should answer your broad questions, specific questions should be referred to an attorney specializing in this field. With that in mind, here is a general overview:

■ **Copyrights.** Enacted to protect the rights of creators of intellectual property, copyrights cover: literary, musical, dramatic, choreographic, and visual works. Some of the specific types of work included in these categories are articles, stories, books, plays, songs, dances, photographs, paintings, sculptures, films, videos, records, and tapes. Contrary to popular belief, neither ideas nor titles are eligible for copyright protection. A copyright gives the holder the sole right to copy or reproduce the work. A standard copyright notice looks like this:

Copyright © 1991 by Wally Javitz

It costs $20 to register a copyright and you can get full details by requesting Circular 1, "Copyright Basics," from the Copyright Office (see *Directory of Small Business Resources* in **Resources**).

■ **Trademarks.** Trademarks are words, names, symbols, devices, or combinations of these adopted by manufacturers and merchants to identify their goods and distinguish them from those manufactured or sold by others. The purpose of a trademark is to prevent one company from exploiting the good reputation of another. A trademark must first be used in interstate commerce before it can registered, and a thorough trademark search should be made before using or applying for a trademark. The general format of the trademark is the symbol ® after every use of the trademark. The fee is $200 and registration can take several months or longer. For more complete information, request "Basic Facts About Trademarks" ($1.50) from the Superintendent of Documents (see *Directory of Small Business Resources* in **Resources**).

■ **Patents.** A patent gives an inventor the exclusive right to make, use, or sell any new and useful process (invention) for 17 years. This sounds good in theory, but in actual practice, it doesn't often work that way. According to many experts, a patent isn't a good way to protect an invention. Patents take years to get, and after being granted, they can be invalidated for being too similar to existing patents. A patent application can also attract lawsuits from other companies claiming that it infringes on their patents. Filing a patent is very complicated and shouldn't be undertaken without the assistance of a patent attorney, whose services will typically cost thousands of dollars. Once you have a patent it isn't easy to protect it. According to government figures "in over 70% of the infringement cases brought by patent holders to protect their patents, the patent itself was held invalid." More effective protection for your invention can often be obtained through other means, to find out how, talk to an attorney who specializes in trade secrets. For more information about patents, request "General Information Concerning Patents" from the Superintendent of Documents or "Can You Make Money with Your Idea or Invention?" ($.50) from the SBA (see *Directory of Small Business Resources* in **Resources**).

One of the most common misconceptions about copyrights, trademarks, and patents is that obtaining any of these forms of protection prevents someone from stealing your idea. It doesn't.

Nothing can prevent someone from infringing on your copyright, trademark, or patent. What these three forms of protection actually do is to acknowledge you as the rightful owner of the property you've registered.

In the event that someone infringes on your copyright, trademark, or patent, the government doesn't step in and punish them. You, as the holder of copyright, trademark, or patent, are responsible for bringing violators to justice through the courts. So in effect, your "protection" is the right to sue the infringer, an often costly and time-consuming proposition. And even if you prevail in court and are awarded damages, you may never be able to collect them. Even so, getting the proper protection for your intellectual property affirms your ownership and may discourage "copycats."

> *"If you get a patent, people don't just send you money. A patent is only a license to sue to protect your rights. The government doesn't come to your rescue."*
>
> Charlie Hall, Inventor of the waterbed.

Notes:

PERSONNEL

Your Most Valuable Asset

Everything in business is planned, produced, sold, and serviced by people. When customers or suppliers contact a business, they deal with the firm's employees. And the impressions they get of those employees are going to influence how they feel about the business itself. So it's easy to see how employees can be a company's greatest asset, whether that business has thousands of employees or only one – the owner.

This is particularly true in service and retail businesses, where how well employees serve customers and how well they get along with them, can determine whether a business succeeds or fails. But in any business, it is the employees who do the work, who make the business function, and who enable the business to grow.

Do You Need an Employee?

Hiring, training, and compensating workers, can be a considerable expense. In addition to wages, employers pay worker's compensation insurance and contribute to unemployment insurance and Social Security. To this can be added the costs of optional employee benefits: health and life insurance, vacation and holiday pay, and any other benefits the employer offers. Then there are the costs of preparing payrolls and other record-keeping chores.

With all these costs, a business owner has to be certain the profit potential of hiring an employee outweighs the expense. Overhiring is a common way that business owners get into financial trouble; anticipating a certain level of business, they staff up beforehand. If the anticipated business doesn't materialize, they don't have the money to pay for the additional employees, and all the other related expenses.

In addition to the expense, managing employees can be a challenging and sometimes frustrating task, especially for a business owner doing it for first time. Before hiring anyone, determine if you actually need an employee. There may be a more efficient and economical way to get the job done. If the job is a short-term need, a temporary worker can be hired from an agency. For some tasks, like bookkeeping, it may be better to use an outside bookkeeper on an as-needed basis.

But, if there is more work than you can handle, and hiring an employee is likely to enable your business to grow in some way, then it makes good sense to start looking for the right employee.

Finding the Right Employees

Most businesses need employees to help them grow to their full potential, in spite of the extra cost and paperwork involved. Assisted by the right employees, business owners can leverage their time and talents to accomplish more of what they do best, delegating the routine jobs in order to concentrate on making their businesses successful.

The key to finding the right employees is knowing what you're looking for. Even if you're just starting your business, it's a good idea to plan ahead to ensure that you have capable employees in every essential function (see the "Staffing Planner" at the end of this section). For each position, you'll need a job description explaining what it involves and how it fits into the overall business operation. You'll also need to be clear about the qualifications required for the position, including such things as experience, special skills, and education. For a convenient way to develop this information, use the "Effective Hiring Guide" at the end of this section.

The impression you and your employees make will determine how customers think about your business.

You'll be able to use the job description to better understand what kind of person you're looking for, to let the employee know your expectations, and for writing a classified ad for the job. Be flexible about the job requirements; it may not be easy to find a candidate who is a "perfect" match for your requirements. Look for compensating qualities such as initiative and enthusiasm. Naturally an employee's skills should be relevant to the job, but it may also be beneficial to hire an employee whose skills are complementary, rather than identical, to yours, especially if your operation is small.

Attracting the right employees depends on what you have to offer. Employees who are looking for a friendly and informal atmosphere where they can develop personal relationships will be most happy in a small business environment. Good candidates want competitive wages and benefits, pleasant working conditions, and a chance to grow on the job.

Where to Find Employees

Once you're clear about what you need done, the kind of employee you want to do it, and what you're willing to offer, then you're ready to start the hiring process. There are numerous sources of prospective employees. Here are some of them:

- **Recommendations.** Friends, business associates, or other employees can sometimes refer qualified applicants. Use your networking skills to get the word out about the kind of person you're looking for.

- **Placement bureaus.** High school, business school, and college placement bureaus are all good sources of students looking for full or part-time work.

- **Employment agencies.** Look for an employment agency that specializes in the type of position you have open. Be sure to investigate the reputation of the agency and be certain you understand the amount and payment method of their placement fees, which may be paid either by the applicant or the employer. Be wary of candidates who are paying an agency to find them a job; they probably don't have the qualities needed in a small business environment.

- **State employment offices.** Operated under the auspices of the federal government, there are nearly 2000 state employment offices across the nation. Their services are free to both job applicants and employers.

- **Trade and industrial associations.** Many trade groups maintain files on qualified employees seeking employment in that industry. This is a particularly good way to find highly skilled tradespeople.

- **Sign in the window.** For retail stores and restaurants, a "Help Wanted" sign in the window is a low cost way to attract local applicants.

- **Help-wanted ads.** Classified ads in local newspapers are generally used for lower paying jobs, while display ads in newspapers and trade publications are used for higher salaried positions. In either type of ad, running the job title as a headline is an effective way to call qualified readers' attention to the ad. Since this method can generate so much response, you're going to have to decide how you want the replies to be made – by phone, in person, or by mail. Many firms use a "blind ad" with a post office box number instead of the company name, either because they don't want their employees to know they are recruiting or because they don't want to be overwhelmed with phone calls or visits. Stating a specific salary range, reduces the responses from over-qualified or under-qualified candidates. This sample ad shows the major elements of an effective help-wanted ad:

be that the information they have provided is incomplete, messy, or indicates something that may be undesirable, such as frequent job changes.

The resumes or applications of the most promising candidates will be compared with each other to determine which of the applicants should be interviewed personally. While you don't want to eliminate potentially good employees, it's a good idea to keep the number of candidates called in for a personal interview manageable. Qualifying the applicants before interviewing them will save you, or whomever you delegate to do the interviewing, time and trouble.

For jobs that require technical skills, testing is often a good way to determine proficiency. Testing won't necessarily tell you which applicant will make the best employee, but it may be useful for weeding out those who are clearly unqualified.

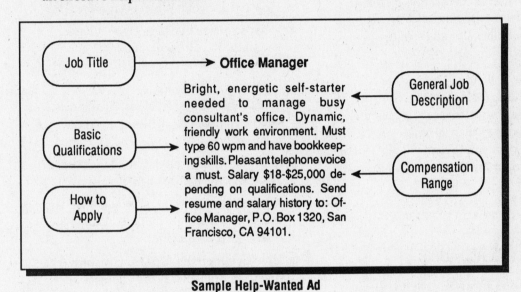

Sample Help-Wanted Ad

Qualifying the Applicants

Using any of the above sources of employees will generate applicants with varying degrees of suitability. You can expect resumes, often with a cover letter, from applicants for salaried positions, while hourly workers generally fill out employment applications in person at the place of business. At the end of this section, you'll find an "Employment Application" that you can make copies of for use in your business.

Your next step is to screen the letters, resumes, or applications to qualify the applicants for the position. Some of them will be eliminated on the basis of what you see on paper. It may be immediately obvious that they aren't qualified, or it may

The Interview

The application forms or resumes of the most qualified candidates serve as a basis for the interview, which is conducted to discover facts and additional details that can help you make an informed hiring decision. Conduct each interview in private. Put the applicant at ease by describing your business in general and the job in particular. Be honest about the pay range, hours, duties, and potential of the job. Don't try to "sell" the job to the applicants, but be sure they understand why your business would be a good place for them to work.

After you've described the job, encourage the applicant to talk by asking open-ended questions that allow them to answer freely, rather than questions with "yes" or "no" answers. Questions about former jobs, favorite subjects, and outside activities, can give you insight into the applicant's interests, expectations, and whether they will like the job. Asking why they left their last job is a good way to gain additional insight into the applicant's preferences and personality, whether they enjoy working, their strengths, and how they see themselves.

Even for applicants that seem otherwise qualified, there are certain intangibles that need to be discovered, such as their reliability and whether they get along well with others. During the interview listen closely for negative attitudes or other shortcomings that could affect their job performance. Interviews with candidates clearly lacking the qualifications or ability should be ended quickly, but politely.

Another factor for evaluating prospective employees is how compatible they are with you and your management style. Since most businesses in this country have fewer than 20 employees, it's likely that you and your employees will see a lot of each other, so it's important that you can get along well.

Questions Not to Ask Applicants

Almost all employers are aware that it is illegal to discriminate on the basis of race, color, religion, sex, or physical handicaps, but far fewer are aware that there are a number of additional questions an employer may not legally ask potential employees. Asking any of these questions opens up an employer to charges of discrimination. Here is a partial list of questions to avoid during a job interview:

■ What is your race? Your religion? Your national origin? What are your parents' nationalities?

■ Are married or single? Do you have children? Do you plan to have children? Who will take care of them while you're working? What is your spouse's occupation?

■ Do you have any friends or relatives working for this company?

If you have more work than you can handle alone, an employee can help your business grow.

■ How old are you? When is your birthday?

■ What's your native language? What language do you speak at home? (Questions about language skill are permitted if job-related)

■ What's the highest level of education you've completed? (Unless education level is job-related.)

■ How many times have you been arrested? What was the nature of these arrests?

■ What's your draft status? When were you discharged from the military? What type of discharge did you get?

■ How's your credit? Do you have any financial problems? Have you ever declared bankruptcy? Do you own a home or rent? Do you own a car? (Unless related to business necessity.)

■ Can you work on weekends and holidays? (Unless the job requires it and the question is not meant to exclude those of different religions.)

■ How tall are you? How much do you weigh? What physical disabilities do you have? (Unless these disabilities would interfere with job performance.)

■ What clubs and organizations do you belong to? (Unless referring specifically to union professional or trade association membership.)

In general, all interview questions should relate only to matter having a direct bearing on the applicant's ability to perform the job.

Hiring

Once you've selected the finalists after the interviews, be sure to check out the information given on their employment applications. Even though "resume padding" is a well documented phenomenon, a surprisingly large number of employers don't verify the information on employment applications.

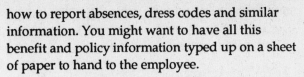

Make telephone calls to former employers and ask if they consider the applicant eligible for rehire, as well as asking about their work habits and skills. While some employers may give you detailed responses, others may not, out of concern about being sued by their former employee. Recently, employer references have tended to be purposely noncommittal to avoid legal problems with disgruntled employees.

When you've made a decision on which of the candidates you'd like to hire, make that applicant an offer covering all the important terms of the job, including salary, vacation, benefits, etc. Some candidates will try to negotiate your offer to get better terms for themselves, perhaps higher pay or more vacation. Unless you've made your best offer, be prepared to make some concessions if you really want that particular candidate.

Upon hiring, have the employee fill out an "Employee Information Form" (see sample at the end of this section). Also have them complete the other required government forms mentioned later in this section. File the completed form in a folder with the employee's name on it. Keep a separate personnel folder for each employee and use it to retain all documents relating to their employment.

Immediately after hiring an employee, introduce them to the company, first by describing the compensation and benefits in detail, the normal work hours, holidays, vacation, and sick leave, insurance coverage, and any other benefits you offer, along with when and how the employee qualifies for them. Also explain any company policies or procedures that the new employee should be familiar with, such as when paydays are,

how to report absences, dress codes and similar information. You might want to have all this benefit and policy information typed up on a sheet of paper to hand to the employee.

The next step is to introduce the employee to their co-workers to get them feeling like part of the business. Since beginning on a new job can be somewhat confusing, encourage questions and answer them promptly and patiently. Provide whatever assistance you can by giving the employee price lists, written instructions for operating equipment, and any other helpful information. In addition to telling them what to do, it's also helpful to explain why things are done a certain way.

The Basics of Becoming a Boss

In the nearly 70% of new businesses that are sole proprietorships, the owner often starts out as the only employee, perhaps with the assistance of family members. Later, when the business requires non-family employees, it becomes subject to additional government regulations and taxes, including:

■ Maintaining payroll records for each employee that show all the details of every pay check. Each employee should fill out an "Employee Timecard" every week. You'll find a sample of one in the back of this section. This information is then recorded on the "Employee Payroll Register" also found in the back of this section.

■ Federal income tax withholding from employees' pay checks. (See discussion of W-4 below)

■ Social Security tax withholding from employees' pay (over 7.5% of earnings currently) and employers are required match this amount themselves as the employer's contribution.

■ State income tax withholding (if applicable). Your accountant or state income tax office can advise you if this applies to your business.

■ State disability taxes (if applicable). Your accountant or insurance agent can advise you if this applies to your business.

■ Workers' compensation insurance (if applicable). Your accountant or insurance agent can advise you if this applies to your business.

■ Preparing quarterly and year-end reports on the above. You may have your accountant prepare these reports or advise you (or someone you delegate) on how to prepare them.

■ Federal and State workplace notices. After your business becomes an employer, you will receive notices in the mail from the state and federal governments containing notices that you are required to post where employees can see them easily.

The three main regulations every employer has to deal with are:

■ **Employer Identification Number (EIN).** Every employer needs an EIN for use on all government forms that ask for a "taxpayer identification number." See *Taxes* in **Finance** for a copy of #SS-4, "Application for Employer Identification Number." The Internal Revenue Service (IRS) can provide you with Publication #15, "Circular E – Employer's Tax Guide." This, as well as other IRS publications, can be ordered using the "IRS Publication & Form Request" also found in the *Taxes* section.

■ **W-4 Employee Withholding Form.** Every new employee must fill out a W-4 form which you provide upon hiring. This form records the employee's Social Security Number, marital status, and number of exemptions claimed. A "W-4 Employee Withholding Form" that you can copy and use is included at the end of this section.

■ **Employment Eligibility Verification , Form I-9.** The Immigration Reform and Control Act of 1986 imposes hiring requirements on all employers. The primary intention of the law is to prevent the employment of undocumented aliens. All employees hired after November 6, 1986 must complete a

form, and sign it under penalty of perjury, affirming their citizenship or lawful alien status. As the employer, you are responsible for verifying the proof provided. A copy of the "Employment Eligibility Verification, Form I-9" form is included at the end of this section. The information an employer needs to use the I-9 is found on the reverse side of the form. Keep the completed forms in each employee's personnel folder.

Though not required by law, keeping accurate attendance records allow you to document the attendance history of employees. This can be very handy in the event of a dispute over absence or tardiness. There's an "Employee Attendance History" at the end of this section that you can copy and use for this purpose.

> *"People are never problems.*
> *They are solutions."*
>
> Ted Nicholas, President
> Entrepreneurs of America

How to Keep Good Employees

A new employee's value to you increases through training, so be sure to allow sufficient time for training and don't expect too much of the trainee right away. Let the employee learn by performing under actual working conditions with close supervision. Follow up by checking the employee's performance on the job. If necessary re-explain key points and short cuts. Always encourage questions.

Once you've found good employees, pay them fairly, give them attractive employee benefits, provide good working conditions, give them an opportunity for personal growth, and above all, treat them with respect and consideration. You may also want to consider some type of profit-sharing with your employees to keep them focused on helping to make the business a success.

When you've done all this, you will have developed a team of employees dedicated to helping you build your business into the kind of success you envisioned when you started.

Providing a Quality Workplace

A quality workplace means more than providing a clean, safe working environment for employees. Creating an atmosphere of teamwork and common purpose is necessary for employee satisfaction and high productivity. There are many things you can do to improve the quality of your employees' work life that won't cost you any money.

Encouraging employees to participate in planning and implementing new operating procedures gives them a feeling of control over their work. Being open to feedback lets employees know their opinion is valuable and helps prevent frustration and resentment. Another factor contributing to a quality workplace is objective performance standards that let employees know what is expected of them.

While it may be difficult for some business owners to have enough faith in their employees to actually provide these kinds of working conditions, unless they do, they will have trouble keeping highly qualified employees.

Employee Compensation and Benefits

The amount and type of compensation an employee receives depends on the type of job, the prevailing wages in the area, their experience, and how much they're going to be able to contribute to the financial success of the business. The wages in many jobs are based on an hourly rate. In other jobs, like office work, the pay is usually a set monthly salary. Some employees receive tips, while others work on commission, either with or without a salary.

The method of compensation you choose should be designed to motivate your employees to work enthusiastically for you, be comparable to similar positions in your area, and when possible, tied to performance. You can use combinations of base pay, bonuses, and commissions to motivate, as well as compensate, your employees. To get an idea of prevailing salaries in you area, check with a local placement agency and request a free copy of their annual survey of compensation by job title.

Employee benefits are a big concern to many employees today. The benefits package you offer can be very influential in attracting and retaining top-notch employees. Since different benefits appeal to different people, the type you offer should be designed to appeal to the type of employee you want to retain. The "Employee Compensation & Benefit Planner" found at the end of this section, gives you a convenient way to list and compute the costs for various benefits you may consider offering.

In addition to the traditional benefits of vacation, holiday pay, and those mandated by federal or state law, there are a number of other benefit options your might want to consider, including:

- **Health or Medical Insurance.** The high cost of health care has made health care benefits very desirable to employees. This coverage is beyond the reach of many workers and they look to their employers to provide it. Employers get special group rates depending on the number of employees covered. Trade and professional associations may provide smaller employers a way to offer this kind of coverage. It is becoming increasingly common for employees to share in the cost of insuring their dependents. Medical coverage is most often offered, but some employers also offer dental and vision insurance as well.

- **Other Insurance.** Some employers offer life, accident, and additional disability insurance. As with health care benefits, group plans reduce the cost of coverage

- **Equity.** Giving employees a share of the company's success in the form of equity, or ownership, is an excellent way to get employees committed. As part owners of the business, they'll be more dedicated to its success. Consider this only for key employees whose skills are crucial to making the business successful. The best employees will often work for less salary if they have a stake in the business.

- **Profit Sharing/Retirement.** In these plans an employer agrees to make either a discretionary contribution based on profits or a set contribution based on the employee's compensation. These contributions will go to the employee at retirement, or be available after the employee has remained with the company for a set time, say three years at minimum. Properly set up, profit sharing plans are tax deductible to the employer. One common approach is called a 401(k) plan, named for the section of the tax code that authorizes its use. Your accountant can explain how it works. Profit sharing and retirement plans improve an employee's dedication to the company and help reduce turnover.

■ **Bonuses.** Employees will work harder and smarter when they personally benefit from the results of their efforts. Bonuses should be related to the goals of the company and be based on an employee's contribution to the achievement of the goal.

■ **Discounts.** Particularly effective for retail stores, employee discounts are very popular with employees and they require very little effort to administer.

■ **Education.** As your employees develop in knowledge and skills, they become more valuable to your business. That's why some employers offer full or partial tuition reimbursement for completed course work.

■ **Recreational Programs.** Employers can often get group discounts for activities, events, and entertainment that employees would enjoy, which can then be offered to the employees free or at a discount. Having employees do things together outside of work builds morale by fostering a sense of team.

■ **Financial Assistance.** Some companies offer loans to their employees, and others provide personal financial planning. Loans should generally be made in emergencies only.

■ **Personal Services.** Among the more recent benefits offered to employees, primarily by larger businesses, are child care and legal assistance services.

■ **Prestige.** For a business just starting out, where there may not be a lot of money for benefits, such things as flexibility in job titles

offers a way to provide something the employee wants at no cost to you. Other low cost perks include expense accounts, parking privileges, and professional or trade association memberships. More costly status benefits such as a company car and company paid travel should be provided only if the job warrants them.

Profit sharing builds morale and helps reduce turnover.

Your First Personnel Policy Manual

Having a written personnel policy manual can help an employer avoid misunderstandings, disagreements, and employee lawsuits. Even a very small business can benefit from having company policies and regulations in written form.

Employees appreciate knowing what is expected of them and what they can expect from the company. Putting these things in writing ensures fairness and consistent application.

Your first "manual" can be a few pages kept in a folder or loose-leaf binder. Upon hiring, each employee should be given the opportunity to go over it as part of their orientation. It's a good idea to give a copy of the manual (even if it is just one or two typed pages) to each employee.

The basic components of your first personnel policy manual might include:

■ **Employment.** Include the conditions of employment (performance expectations) and grounds for dismissal. Explain any probationary period and/or performance reviews.

- **Operations.** Discuss the work hours, starting and quitting times, work schedules, etc. Explain how lateness and absences are handled (whom to call and when). Include any policy you have on sick days and leaves of absence. Mention safety policies and explain how to report an accident in the workplace.

- **Wages.** Indicate when and how wages are paid. Mention how overtime is handled. And explain how and when salary reviews are conducted.

- **Benefits.** Include which kinds of insurance coverage are applicable. Mention paid holidays and vacation policy.

- **Workplace.** Explain any dress code and smoking policy. Include a discussion of breaks, personal phone calls, and keeping the workplace neat and clean.

How to Terminate an Employee

No matter how carefully you've selected an employee, there is always the chance they may not work out. If this happens, you can't just fire the employee without making your business vulnerable to legal action. While terminating an employee is often a difficult task, you can minimize both the unpleasantness and the risk of potentially damaging lawsuits by taking the following steps before terminating any employee:

- Discuss the problem with the employee. Try to find out what's behind the apparent problem. Look for alternatives to firing. Develop a specific, mutually agreeable plan for improvement.

- Issue written warnings if the agreed upon improvements do not occur. Ask the employee to sign the warnings, then file them in the employee's personnel file. If the employee won't sign them, note that on the document.

- Upon termination, conduct an exit interview with the employee, ask their opinion of the company and its working conditions in

order to see how you might prevent a similar occurrence in the future.

- Be courteous and tactful in dealing with the employee.

- Many employers give a dismissed employee two weeks notice, but in some cases it's better to give the employee two weeks pay and get them away from the worksite before they can cause additional problems or negatively affect morale.

- Pay all money due for wages and vacations when the employee leaves.

- Send out their wage and earnings statements (W-2) along with all others at the end of the year.

- Make sure the employee's personnel file contains copies of the prior warnings and the dismissal notice.

- Answer unemployment insurance inquiries promptly.

Independent Contractors

As mentioned earlier, an employer must pay and withhold taxes (income tax, social security tax, unemployment tax, etc.) for its employees. And in most cases the employer also provides employee benefits as well.

On the other hand, employers who use self-employed "independent contractors" can avoid the tax, benefit, and administrative costs associated with having employees.

In the past few years, however, the IRS has stepped up its efforts to reclassify thousands of workers who had formerly worked as independent contractors as employees.

Currently employers are losing 96% of all contested cases. Once workers are reclassified as employees, the employer may be subject to payment of back taxes and penalties.

To avoid these costly repercussions, employers should be aware of the 20 factors the IRS uses to reclassify workers. Many of these factors are subjective, and therefore create considerable uncertainty as to just which workers are employees and which are independent contractors. In some cases a single factor can be used to determine the worker's status, but generally it is a combination of the presence or absence of two or more of the following factors:

Employee versus Independent Contractor

Factor	Employee	Independent Contractor
Control	Is instructed how and when to do the job	Decides how and when to do a job
Employment	Works virtually full time for one company	Works for others on a regular basis
Employees	May not hire and supervise their own employees	Permitted to hire and supervise their own employees
Profit & Loss	Cannot realize either a profit or a loss	Can either make or lose money on a job
Tools	Furnished by company	Owns or rents their own tools
Remuneration	Paid on the basis of time worked	Paid by the job
Termination	Works "at will" and can be dismissed arbitrarily	By contract, cannot be dismissed without cause
Training	Training provided before performing job	Performs job without prior company training
Advertising	Does not offer their services to the general public	Offers to work for others and/or advertises
Reporting	Required to submit oral or written progress reports	Not required to submit frequent progress reports
Location	All work performed on company location	Work may be performed away from company location
Resignation	May terminate the relationship without penalty	Has a contractual responsibility which limits termination
Investment	Has little or no investment in his or her own business	Has a significant investment in his or her own business
Integration	Their work is substantially a part of the company's operation	Their work is independent of the company's operation
Labor	Personally performs the work	Has the work done by their employees
Relationship	Has a continuing relationship with the company	Has an intermittent relationship with the company
Hours	Determined by company	Determined by contractor
Control	Does not control events arising out of starting the job	Controls events arising out of starting the job
Billing	Does not render invoices	Bills for work performed, and charges appropriate sales tax
Reimbursement	Is reimbursed for all costs associated with the work	Is not reimbursed for costs not covered in the contract

Tips on Using the Following Forms:

Note: You are encouraged to copy these forms for your own use. Keep the unmarked originals in a safe place and make copies of them to work from.

Employee Compensation & Benefit Planner – Use this form to determine the types of benefits you plan to offer your employees, and to compute their approximate costs. Look down the left hand column and put a checkmark in the second column to the right of each of the items that applies to your business. Then in the third column enter a typical monthly cost range for each item checked. Some items have suggested ranges instead of blank spaces, which are normal for small business. In the last column convert all the other figures to monthly costs. Then total them at the bottom of the column to get the total monthly cost per employee. Dividing this figure by the typical monthly base wage (found by adding all the items under Compensation at the top of the form) provides your benefit cost factor, indicating how much more your employees are costing you than you would think from looking at the compensation alone. This cost factor will be useful in preparing your "Projected Expense Budget & Capital Expenditures."

Staffing Planner – Knowing the number and type of employees you need before you start your business will allow you to anticipate your labor costs. For each position you need to fill, place the title of that position in the first column. Use the second column to list the major duties and responsibilities of the position. In the third column write the date you want the position filled by. Enter the number of hours per week this person will be needed in the fourth column, then enter the estimated salary or wage in the fifth column. In the last column, compute the monthly cost per position. Then add up all the monthly costs in the space provided at the bottom of the form. This information can be used in your business plan (see *Business Plan*).

Effective Hiring Guide – Use this form to help prepare job descriptions. Enter each of the job titles from the "Staffing Planner" in the places indicated. Under each title, list the duties, experience needed, and the other pertinent considerations for each job in the spaces provided. The information on this form will help you clarify your personnel needs, give you a foundation for writing a help-wanted ad, and enable you to make a more informed hiring decision.

Employee Information Form – After hiring an employee, have them complete this form and place it in their personnel file. Keep this information current by updating it when changes occur during the course of employment. You could have employees supply you with the information at the top of the form as it changes.

Employment Application – This form was designed for use in any kind of business. It provides the basic information you need to judge whether the applicant is qualified enough for an interview, and to provide you with references to check. Upon hiring, keep this application in the employee's personnel file along the other employee-related documents mentioned in the text above. Store the applications of non-hired candidates in a separate folder.

Employment Eligibility Verification, Form I-9 – Each employee must complete one of these forms upon hiring. Keep them filed in the employees' personnel folders so you have ready access to them if they are requested by the government. Complete instructions are printed right on the form.

W-4 Employee Withholding Form – As required by law, one of these forms must be completed upon hiring and a new one filled out whenever an employee's status changes. Have the employee follow the instructions printed on the form. File the lower part of this form in the employee's personnel file, and give the upper part to the employee.

Employee Timecard – Every hourly employee should fill out one of these forms and turn it in each week. To ensure accuracy, the information should be recorded daily. After being used for preparing the payroll, these forms should be filed in a payroll folder by date. There are two identical forms on this page; cut it in half after photocopying.

Employee Payroll Register – This form will enable you to conveniently record the payroll information necessary for the legally required payroll reports. Each week enter the hours from the "Employee Time-card" in the appropriate spaces and do the necessary computations.

Employee Attendance History – This form gives you a record of the attendance of each employee. It should filed in the employee's personnel file. It is a convenient way to document the employee's attendance so that you have an objective way, rather than relying on your memory, to determine the extent of missed work. It could also prove useful as documentation in case you find it necessary to terminate an employee for excessive absence or lateness. This form is best used for "exception reporting," which means that nothing has to be indicated on the form unless it is an exception to what would be normally expected on a given day. Indicate each absence or lateness by using the appropriate code from the box at the right side. At the end of each month total the counts for each code and place these numbers in the boxes under the corresponding letters. At the end of the year, add each column to determine the and types of absences for that employee.

Compensation and Benefit Elements	Use in your Business ?	Typical monthly cost range	Monthly cost per employee
Compensation			
Base wage			
Hourly	_____	_____	_____
Monthly	_____	_____	_____
Commission	_____	_____	_____
Profit sharing	_____	_____	_____
Bonuses	_____	_____	_____
Mandatory Benefits			
Social Security (FICA)	✔	6.2% of wages (up to $53,400)	_____
Medicare	✔	1.45% of wages (up to $125,000)	_____
Federal Unemployment (FUTA)	✔	.8%-6.2% of wages (up to $7,000)	_____
State Unemployment (some states)	_____	2-4% of wages (up to $7,000)	_____
Worker's Compensation (some states)	_____	.5-1.5% of wages	_____
Optional Benefits			
Health insurance	_____	$150-300	_____
Life insurance	_____	$.09-.13 per $1000	_____
Disability insurance	_____	$35-75 per $1000 mo. benefit	_____
Maternity benefits	_____	often in medical plan	_____
Retirement benefits			
Pension plan	_____	1-10% of wages	_____
IRA contributions	_____	$500-2000	_____
Profit sharing	_____	Large range	_____
_____	_____		_____
_____	_____		_____
Non-Cash Benefits			
Vacations	_____	1-2 weeks per year	_____
Paid holidays	_____	4-8 days per year	_____
Sick leave	_____	3-5 days per year	_____
Unpaid leaves of absence	_____	varies	_____
Employee discounts	_____	10-20% off retail	_____
_____	_____		_____
_____	_____		_____
Total			_____

Benefit Cost Factor : (Total Monthly Cost per Employee
                 Divided by Typical Monthly Base Wage) _____

Note: Generally full benefits are reserved for full-time employees, part-time employees are typically provided a reduced package.

STAFFING PLANNER

BP

Position Title	Main Job Responsibilities	When First Needed	Hours Needed per Week	Estimated Salary or Wage	Monthly Cost
Total					

Monthly Cost is the monthly salary or wage multiplied by the Benefit Cost Factor calculated on the Employee Compensation & Benefit Planner

EFFECTIVE HIRING GUIDE

	JOB #1	JOB #2	JOB #3	JOB #4
Job Title				
Job Description (Major Duties)				
Experience Needed				
Necessary Skills				
Desired Personality Traits				
Sources of Prospects (Where you'll look for employees)				
Comments				

EMPLOYEE INFORMATION FORM

Name: _____

Address: _____

City: _____

State: _____ ZIP: _____

Phone #: _____

Soc. Sec. #: _____

Date of Birth: _____ Marital Status: _____

Emergency Contact

Name & Relationship: _____

Phone: _____

Starting Title: _____ Hire Date: _____

Employment History			
Date	Position	Rate of Pay	Pay Frequency

EMPLOYMENT APPLICATION

Position applied for _____

Name _____

        Last   First   Middle Initial

Address _____

        Street   City   State   ZIP Code

Phone ( ) _____ Social Security Number _____

Type of employment desired: Full-time ☐ Part-time ☐ Temporary ☐ Other ☐

Date available to start working: _____

If under 18, can you supply a work permit?..............................Yes ☐   No ☐

Are you legally eligible for employment in this country?.......Yes ☐   No ☐
(Proof of eligilibity will be required upon employment)

EMPLOYMENT HISTORY: List your 4 most recent employers or volunteer activities, starting with the most recent.

Company _____	Position/Title _____
Address _____	City & State _____
Phone number _____	Supervisor _____
Dates employed: From _____	To _____
Reason for leaving _____	Salary _____

Company _____	Position/Title _____
Address _____	City & State _____
Phone number _____	Supervisor _____
Dates employed: From _____	To _____
Reason for leaving _____	Salary _____

Company _____	Position/Title _____
Address _____	City & State _____
Phone number _____	Supervisor _____
Dates employed: From _____	To _____
Reason for leaving _____	Salary _____

Company _____	Position/Title _____
Address _____	City & State _____
Phone number _____	Supervisor _____
Dates employed: From _____	To _____
Reason for leaving _____	Salary _____

EDUCATIONAL BACKGROUND

School	City & State	Dates Attended	Degree	Course of Study

QUALIFICATIONS AND SPECIAL SKILLS: Please list any special training or skills you have

_____

_____

_____

REFERENCES

Name	Relationship	Phone Number

I understand and agree that any misrepresentation of facts on this application will be cause to either discontinue the consideration of this application or for termination of employment, if hired.

I also understand and agree that just as I am free to leave the company at any time, the company may terminate my employment at any time, with or without cause and with or without notice. I also understand that no other employee of the company has the authority to make representions to the contrary.

The company is given the right to contact all references and solicit information about me and my previous job performance.

Signed _____   Date _____

AN EQUAL OPPORTUNITY EMPLOYER

EMPLOYMENT ELIGIBILITY VERIFICATION

EMPLOYEE INFORMATION AND VERIFICATION: (To be completed and signed by employee.)

Name: (Print or Type) Last	First	Middle	Maiden

Address: Street Name and Number	City	State	ZIP Code

Date of Birth (Month Day Year)	Social Security Number

attest, under penalty of perjury, that I am (check a box):

☐ A citizen or national of the United States.

☐ An alien lawfully admitted for permanent residence (Alien Number A _____).

☐ An alien authorized by the Immigration and Naturalization Service to work in the United States (Alien Number A _____), or Admission Number _____ , expiration of employment authorization, if any _____).

attest under penalty of perjury, the documents that I have presented as evidence of identity and employment eligibility are genuine and relate to me. I am are that federal law provides for imprisionment and/or fine for any false statements or use of false documents in connection with this certificate.

nature	Date (Month Day Year)

PREPARER/TRANSLATOR CERTIFICATION (If prepared by other than the individual). I attest, under penalty of perjury, that the above was prepared by me at the request of the named individual and is based on all information of which I have knowledge.

Signature	Name (Print or Type)

Address (Street Name and Number)	City	State	ZIP Code

EMPLOYER REVIEW AND VERIFICATION: (To be completed and signed by employer.)

amine one document from those in List A and check the correct box, _or_ examine one document from List B _and_ one from List C and check the correct boxes. ovide the *Document Identification Number* and *Expiration Date*, for the document checked in that column.

List A Identity and Employment Eligibility	List B Identity	and	List C Employment Eligibility
United States Passport	☐ A State issued driver's license or I.D. card with a photograph, or information, including name, sex, date of birth, height, weight, and color of eyes. (Specify State) _____		☐ Original Social Security Number Card (other than a card stating it is not valid for employment
Certificate of United States Citizenship			
Certificate of Naturalization	☐ U.S. Military Card		☐ A birth certificate issued by State, county or municipal authority bearing a seal or other certification
Unexpired foreign passport with attached Employment Authorization	☐ Other (Specify document and issuing authority		☐ Unexpired INS Employment Authorization Specify form # _____
Alien Registration Card with photograph			
ocument Identification	*Document Identification* # _____		*Document Identification* # _____
xpiration Date (if any)	*Expiration Date (if any)*		*Expiration Date (if any)*

ERTIFICATION: I attest, under penalty of perjury, that I have examined the documents presented by the above individual, that they appear to be genuine, relate the individual named, and that the individual, to the best of my knowledge, is authorized to work in the United States.

Signature	Name (Print or Type)	Title

Employer Name	Address	Date

orm I-9 (03/20/87)

U.S. Department Of Justice
Immigration and Naturalization Service

Employment Eligibility Verification

> **NOTICE:** Authority for collecting the information on this form is in Title 8, United States Code, Section 1324A. It will be used to verify the individual's eligibility for employment in the United States. Failure to present this form for inspection to officers of the Immigration and Naturalization Service or Department of Labor within the time period specified by regulation, or improper completion or retention of this form may be a violation of 8 USC §1324A and may result in a civil money penalty.

Section 1. Employee's / Preparer's instructions for completing this form.

Instructions for the employee.

All employees, upon being hired, must complete Section 1 of this form. Any person hired after November 6, 1986 must complete this form. (For the purpose of completion of this form "hired" applies to those employed, recruited or referred for a fee.)

All employees must print or type their complete name, address, date of birth, and Social Security Number. The block which correctly indicates the employee's immigration status must be checked. If the second block is checked, the employee's Alien Registration Number must be provided. If the third box is checked, the employee's Alien Registration Number *or* Admission Number must be provided, as well as the date of expiration of that status, if it expires.

All employees must sign and date the form.

Instructions for the preparer of the form, if not the employee.

If the employee is assisted with completing this form, the person assisting must certify the form by signing it, and printing or typing his or her name and address.

Section 2. Employer's instructions for completing this form

(For the purpose of completion of this form, the term "employer" applies to employers and those who recruit or refer for a fee.)

Employers must complete this section by examining evidence of identity and employment authorization, and;
- checking the appropriate box in List A or boxes in both Lists B and C;
- recording the document identification number and expiration date (if any);
- recording the type of form if not specifically identified in the list;
- signing the certification section.

NOTE: *Employers are responsible for reverifying employment eligibility of aliens upon expiration of any employment authorization documents, should they desire to continue the alien's employment.*

Copies of documentation presented by an individual for the purpose of establishing identity and employment eligibility may be copied and retained for the purpose of complying with the requirements of this form and no other purpose. Any copies of documentation made for this purpose should be maintained with this form.

Employers may photocopy or reprint this form, as neccessary, for their own use.

RETENTION OF RECORDS.

After completion of this form, it must be retained by the employer during the period beginning on the date of hiring and ending:
- three years after date of such hiring, or;
- one year after the date the individual's employment is terminated, whichever is later.

U.S. Department of Justice
Immigration and Naturalization Service

1993 Form W-4

Department of the Treasury
Internal Revenue Service

Purpose. Complete Form W-4 so that your employer can withhold the correct amount of federal income tax from your pay.

Exemption From Withholding. Read line 7 of the certificate below to see if you can claim exempt status. If exempt, complete line 7; but do not complete lines 5 and 6. No Federal income tax will be withheld from your pay. Your exemption is good for one year only. It expires February 15, 1994.

Basic Instructions. Employees who are not exempt should complete the Personal Allowances Worksheet. Additional worksheets are provided on page 2 for employees to adjust their withholding allowances based on itemized deductions, adjustments to income, or two-earner/two-job situations. Complete all worksheets that apply to your situation. The worksheets will help you figure the number of withholding allowances you are entitled to claim. However, you may claim fewer allowances than this.

Head of Household. Generally, you may claim head of household filing status on your tax return only if you are unmarried and pay more than 50% of the costs of keeping up a home for yourself and your dependent(s) or other qualifying individuals.

Nonwage Income. If you have a large amount of nonwage income, such as interest or dividends, you should consider making estimated tax payments using Form 1040-ES. Otherwise, you may find that you owe additional tax at the end of the year.

Two-Earner/Two-Jobs. If you have a working spouse or more than one job, figure the total number of allowances you are entitled to claim on all jobs using worksheets from only one Form W-4. This total should be divided among all jobs. Your withholding will usually be most accurate when all allowances are claimed on the W-4 filed for the highest paying job and zero allowances are claimed for the others.

Advance Earned Income Credit. If you are eligible for this credit, you can receive it added to your paycheck throughout the year. For details, get Form W-5 from your employer.

Check Your Withholding. After your W-4 takes effect, you can use **Pub. 919,** Is My Withholding Correct for 1993?, to see how the dollar amount you are having withheld compares to your estimated total annual tax. Call 1-800-829-3676 to order this publication. Check your local telephone directory for the IRS assistance number if you need further help.

Personal Allowances Worksheet

For 1993, the value of your personal exemption(s) is reduced if your income is over $108,450 ($162,700 if married filing jointly, $135,600 if head of household, or $81,350 if married filing separately). Get Pub. 919 for details.

Enter "1" for **yourself** if no one else can claim you as a dependent . . . . **A** _____

Enter "1" if:
- You are single and have only one job; or
- You are married, have only one job, and your spouse does not work; or   } . . **B** _____
- Your wages from a second job or your spouse's wages (or the total of both) are $1,000 or less.

Enter "1" for your **spouse.** But, you may choose to enter -0- if you are married and have either a working spouse or more than one job (this may help you avoid having too little tax withheld) . . . . **C** _____

Enter number of **dependents** (other than your spouse or yourself) whom you will claim on your tax return . . . . **D** _____

Enter "1" if you will file as **head of household** on your tax return (see conditions under **Head of Household,** above) . **E** _____

Enter "1" if you have at least $1,500 of **child or dependent care expenses** for which you plan to claim a credit . . **F** _____

Add lines A through F and enter total here. Note: *This amount may be different from the number of exemptions you claim on your return* ▶ **G** _____

For accuracy, do all worksheets that apply.
- If you plan to **itemize or claim adjustments to income** and want to reduce your withholding, see the Deductions and Adjustments Worksheet on page 2.
- If you are **single** and have **more than one job** and your combined earnings from all jobs exceed $30,000 OR if you are **married** and have a **working spouse or more than one job,** and the combined earnings from all jobs exceed $50,000, see the Two-Earner/Two-Job Worksheet on page 2 if you want to avoid having too little tax withheld.
- If **neither** of the above situations applies, **stop here** and enter the number from line G on line 5 of Form W-4 below.

- - - Cut here and give the certificate to your employer. Keep the top portion for your records. - - -
---

Form W-4   Employee's Withholding Allowance Certificate

Department of the Treasury
Internal Revenue Service

▶ **For Privacy Act and Paperwork Reduction Act Notice, see reverse.**

OMB No. 1545-0010

1993

1 Type or print your first name and middle initial	Last name	2 Your social security number

Home address (number and street or rural route)	3 ☐ Single ☐ Married ☐ Married, but withhold at higher Single rate.
	Note: *If married, but legally separated, or spouse is a nonresident alien, check the Single box.*
City or town, state, and ZIP code	4 If your last name differs from that on your social security card, check here and call 1-800-772-1213 for more information . . . . ▶ ☐

5	Total number of allowances you are claiming (from line G above or from the worksheets on page 2 if they apply) .	**5**
6	Additional amount, if any, you want withheld from each paycheck	**6** $

7 I claim exemption from withholding for 1993 and I certify that I meet **ALL** of the following conditions for exemption:
- Last year I had a right to a refund of **ALL** Federal income tax withheld because I had **NO** tax liability; **AND**
- This year I expect a refund of **ALL** Federal income tax withheld because I expect to have **NO** tax liability; **AND**
- This year if my income exceeds $600 and includes nonwage income, another person cannot claim me as a dependent.

If you meet all of the above conditions, enter "EXEMPT" here . . . . ▶ **7**

Under penalties of perjury, I certify that I am entitled to the number of withholding allowances claimed on this certificate or entitled to claim exempt status.

Employee's signature ▶   Date ▶   , 19

8 Employer's name and address (Employer: Complete 8 and 10 only if sending to the IRS)	9 Office code (optional)	10 Employer identification number

Cat. No. 10220Q

Deductions and Adjustments Worksheet

Note: *Use this worksheet only if you plan to itemize deductions or claim adjustments to income on your 1993 tax return.*

1 Enter an estimate of your 1993 itemized deductions. These include: qualifying home mortgage interest, charitable contributions, state and local taxes (but not sales taxes), medical expenses in excess of 7.5% of your income, and miscellaneous deductions. (For 1993, you may have to reduce your itemized deductions if your income is over $108,450 ($54,225 if married filing separately). Get Pub. 919 for details.) **1** $ _____

2 Enter:
- $6,200 if married filing jointly or qualifying widow(er)
- $5,450 if head of household
- $3,700 if single
- $3,100 if married filing separately

2 $ _____

3 **Subtract** line 2 from line 1. If line 2 is greater than line 1, enter -0- **3** $ _____

4 Enter an estimate of your 1993 adjustments to income. These include alimony paid and deductible IRA contributions **4** $ _____

5 **Add** lines 3 and 4 and enter the total **5** $ _____

6 Enter an estimate of your 1993 nonwage income (such as dividends or interest income) **6** $ _____

7 **Subtract** line 6 from line 5. Enter the result, but not less than -0- **7** $ _____

8 **Divide** the amount on line 7 by $2,500 and enter the result here. Drop any fraction **8** _____

9 Enter the number from Personal Allowances Worksheet, line G, on page 1 **9** _____

10 **Add** lines 8 and 9 and enter the total here. If you plan to use the Two-Earner/Two-Job Worksheet, also enter the total on line 1, below. Otherwise, **stop here** and enter this total on Form W-4, line 5, on page 1. **10** _____

Two-Earner/Two-Job Worksheet

Note: *Use this worksheet only if the instructions for line G on page 1 direct you here.*

1 Enter the number from line G on page 1 (or from line 10 above if you used the Deductions and Adjustments Worksheet) **1** _____

2 Find the number in **Table 1** below that applies to the **LOWEST** paying job and enter it here **2** _____

3 If line 1 is **GREATER THAN OR EQUAL TO** line 2, subtract line 2 from line 1. Enter the result here (if zero, enter -0-) and on Form W-4, line 5, on page 1. **DO NOT** use the rest of this worksheet **3** _____

Note: *If line 1 is LESS THAN line 2, enter -0- on Form W-4, line 5, on page 1. Complete lines 4–9 to calculate the additional withholding amount necessary to avoid a year-end tax bill.*

4 Enter the number from line 2 of this worksheet **4** _____

5 Enter the number from line 1 of this worksheet **5** _____

6 **Subtract** line 5 from line 4 **6** _____

7 Find the amount in **Table 2** below that applies to the **HIGHEST** paying job and enter it here **7** $ _____

8 **Multiply** line 7 by line 6 and enter the result here. This is the additional annual withholding amount needed **8** $ _____

9 Divide line 8 by the number of pay periods remaining in 1993. (For example, divide by 26 if you are paid every other week and you complete this form in December 1992.) Enter the result here and on Form W-4, line 6, page 1. This is the additional amount to be withheld from each paycheck **9** $ _____

Table 1: Two-Earner/Two-Job Worksheet

Married Filing Jointly		All Others	
If wages from **LOWEST** paying job are—	Enter on line 2 above	If wages from **LOWEST** paying job are—	Enter on line 2 above
0 - $3,000	0	0 - $6,000	0
3,001 - 8,000	1	6,001 - 11,000	1
8,001 - 13,000	2	11,001 - 15,000	2
13,001 - 18,000	3	15,001 - 19,000	3
18,001 - 22,000	4	19,001 - 24,000	4
22,001 - 27,000	5	24,001 - 50,000	5
27,001 - 31,000	6	50,001 and over	6
31,001 - 35,000	7		
35,001 - 40,000	8		
40,001 - 60,000	9		
60,001 - 85,000	10		
85,001 and over	11		

Table 2: Two-Earner/Two-Job Worksheet

Married Filing Jointly		All Others	
If wages from **HIGHEST** paying job are—	Enter on line 7 above	If wages from **HIGHEST** paying job are—	Enter on line 7 above
0 - $ 50,000	$350	0 - $30,000	$350
50,001 - 100,000	660	30,001 - 60,000	660
100,001 and over	730	60,001 and over	730

EMPLOYEE TIMECARD

This form to be filled out and signed by employee (Please print)

Name _____

Department _____   Normal Hours _____

Week ending : _____-_____-_____		A.M.		P.M.		Overtime		Total	
		In	Out	In	Out	In	Out	Regular	Overtime
Monday	_____-_____-_____								
Tuesday	_____-_____-_____								
Wednesday	_____-_____-_____								
Thursday	_____-_____-_____								
Friday	_____-_____-_____								
Saturday	_____-_____-_____								
Sunday	_____-_____-_____								
						Weekly Total			

Signatures:

Employee: _____

Manager: _____

- -

EMPLOYEE TIMECARD

This form to be filled out and signed by employee (Please print)

Name _____

Department _____   Normal Hours _____

Week ending : _____-_____-_____		A.M.		P.M.		Overtime		Total	
		In	Out	In	Out	In	Out	Regular	Overtime
Monday	_____-_____-_____								
Tuesday	_____-_____-_____								
Wednesday	_____-_____-_____								
Thursday	_____-_____-_____								
Friday	_____-_____-_____								
Saturday	_____-_____-_____								
Sunday	_____-_____-_____								
						Weekly Total			

Signatures:

Employee: _____

Manager: _____

EMPLOYEE PAYROLL REGISTER

Name :

Address :

Social Security # :

Number of Exemptions :

Single / Married

Week ended	Hours Worked							Total Hours		Hourly Wage	Gross Wages				Deductions						Net Pay	Check #
	Mon	Tue	Wed	Thu	Fri	Sat	Sun	Reg	O/T		Reg	O/T	Total	FICA %	Fed w/h	State w/h	Other %	Other %			
1																					
2																					
3																					
4																					
5																					
6																					
7																					
8																					
9																					
10																					
11																					
12																					
13																					
Quarter Total																					

1																					
2																					
3																					
4																					
5																					
6																					
7																					
8																					
9																					
10																					
11																					
12																					
13																					
Quarter Total																					

PERSONNEL
FORMS

ADMINISTRATION

EMPLOYEE ATTENDANCE HISTORY

Name: _____

Department: _____

Vacation Days Alloted: _____

Hire Date: _____

Phone Number: _____

Attendance Codes:

V: Vacation   J: Jury Duty
H: Holiday   A: Leave of Absence
I: Illness   U: Unexcused Absence
L: Late   F: Illness in family
E: Excused   D: Death in family

YEAR : _____

	1	2	3	4	5	6	7	8	9	10	11	12	13	14	15	16	17	18	19	20	21	22	23	24	25	26	27	28	29	30	31
Jan																															
Feb																															
Mar																															
Apr																															
May																															
Jun																															
Jul																															
Aug																															
Sep																															
Oct																															
Nov																															
Dec																															

Total

Summary by Code *

V	H	I	L	E						

* Note all "Critical Events" (such as major illnesses, disciplinary discussions, or approved leaves) on the reverse side of this form.

Critical Events Log: Record all relevant facts, sign and date

FILING & RECORDKEEPING

Business Means Paperwork

If you're like most people, you're not wild about paperwork. But like it or not, dealing with paperwork is a necessity in any business. Laws and regulations require that you keep certain documents for taxes and other purposes. But beyond that, so many business papers – invoices, sales receipts, employment applications, income tax returns, lease agreements, inventory records, and the like – are vital for other reasons, that it's difficult to imagine a business functioning effectively without them.

Business Recordkeeping Basics

The key to effective recordkeeping is not to save any unnecessary papers; to save only what is necessary and toss the rest. It's been estimated that over 75% of all files are never opened after filing, so be selective about what goes into your files. But be sure to retain the documents required for legal reasons, even if you never use them for anything else. Before filing any document, ask yourself these questions:

■ **Am I legally required to retain this document?** Refer to the document retention chart later in this section. It lists the major business documents and how long they should be kept. Papers related to your income taxes should be kept readily accessible in case of a tax audit.

■ **When will I need this information?** If you can't answer this question, and it isn't legally

necessary to keep the document, then you should probably discard it. If you're in the process of buying or upgrading a product, you'll probably want to keep whatever promotional literature you receive on that subject. But if you don't have an immediate need, then just throw it away rather than cluttering your files with material you won't ever use.

■ **Is this information stored somewhere else?** If the information is in off-site storage, or on backed-up computer files, you may not need to keep a copy.

■ **Has the information already served its purpose?** If you've learned what you need to learn from it, or it's out of date, toss it. When you receive a new price list, for instance, discard the old one. If someone else needs to know the information, just pass it along to them.

Records You Should Keep

Having the right piece of paper when you need it can save you time, money, and trouble. Good records can help clear up mistakes and misunderstandings before they become serious problems, and can even help you prevail in the event a problem escalates into a lawsuit. Even though there are plenty of good reasons for keeping records, many business owners still think of recordkeeping as something they have to do primarily for tax reasons. The IRS, however, doesn't specify which records a business must keep. As their guidelines put it:

> "The law does not require any special kind of records. You may choose any system that is suited to your business and that will clearly show your income.
>
> Your permanent books (including inventory records) must show not only your gross income, but also your deductions and credits. In addition, you must keep any other records and data necessary to support the entries in your books and on your tax and information returns. Paid bills, cancelled checks, etc., that support entries in your books should be filed in an orderly fashion and kept in a safe place. For most small businesses, the business checkbook is the main source for entries in the business records."

Record Retention Guidelines

Retaining the documents shown below (as well as any that are unique to your business), for the time indicated, will allow you to support the entries made in your records:

Type of Document	Retention	Type of Document	Retention
Accident reports	7 years	Inventory records	7 years
Accounts payable ledgers	7 years	Invoices to customers	7 years
Accounts receivable ledgers	7 years	Invoices from vendors	7 years
Accountant's audits	Permanent	Journals	Permanent
Bank account reconciliations	2 years	Leases	Permanent
Bank statements	3 years	Mortgages/deeds	Permanent
Bills of sale	Permanent	Notes receivable	7 years
Cash books	Permanent	Patents	Permanent
Chart of accounts	Permanent	Payroll records	7 years
Checks (cancelled)	7 years	Personnel records (after termination)	7 years
Checks (important purchases)	Permanent	Petty cash vouchers	3 years
Check register	Permanent	Physical inventory tags	3 years
Contracts (active)	Permanent	Plant cost ledgers	7 years
Contracts (expired)	7 years	Property appraisals	Permanent
Corporate minutes, bylaws etc.	Permanent	Property records	Permanent
Correspondence (routine)	1 year	Purchase orders	7 years
Correspondence (critical)	Permanent	Receiving sheets	1 years
Deeds	Permanent	Sales records	7 years
Depreciation schedules	Permanent	Stock & bond records	Permanent
Deposit slips (copy)	2 years	Stock certificates (cancelled)	7 year
Employment applications	3 years	Tax returns and worksheets	Permanent
Financial statements	Permanent	Timecards/books	7 years
Garnishments	7 years	Trademark registrations	Permanent
General ledgers	Permanent	Training manuals	Permanent
Insurance policies (active)	Permanent	Vouchers for payments	7 years
Insurance policies (expired)	3 years	Union agreements	3 years
Internal reports	3 years	Withholding tax statements	7 years

Filing Systems

Small business filing systems can be arranged either by:

■ **Name.** Filing names in alphabetical order from A to Z, like the white pages of your telephone book, is probably the easiest and most commonly used method for filing records. This method is used extensively for storing information on customers, employees, and suppliers. If you use this method, be sure to leave extra space in the file drawers for new files.

■ **Subject.** For files that are more dependent on what the information is about than who it pertains to, filing by subject is useful. In this method filing is done by topic, grouping all related information together like the yellow pages of your phone book. This is how the small business filing and record-keeping system explained on the next page is organized.

■ **Geographic location.** This method doesn't have much application to small businesses. It is used primarily by companies that have branch offices in different cities or are most interested in the geographic location of their customers. These files can be set up by country, region, state, county, or city.

■ **Consecutive number.** In this method each file is stored in numerical order (1, 2, 3, etc.). This system requires a register book to identify which subject each number represents, and an alphabetical index to determine which numbers are assigned to various topics. The consecutive number method makes filing simple and provides a way to

A good filing system minimizes the time you have to spend filing and retrieving information

discover quickly if any files are missing, but keeping up the index and register book are a lot of work.

■ **Chronological.** In the chronological method the files are set up sequentially by year, month, and day, with the most recent files in front. Also called "tickler" files, this method is best used as a reminder of actions that need to be taken at a later date. Salespeople and those who make collections commonly use this system for follow up. If a prospect says to call back in two weeks, then a note to that effect goes into the folder for that date, say June 1. The folder for that date moves closer to the front of the file each day, and then on June 1, that folder is the first one in the file.

Filing and Recordkeeping Basics

Once you've accepted the necessity of retaining business papers, the next step is deciding how you're going to organize them. Merely having papers stored somewhere isn't enough, they also have to be easily found. The best way to organize business papers for most business purposes is a standard filing system, which uses file folders to store groups of similar papers, with the contents indicated on the folder's tab. Often several file folders are stored in a hanging file, which is then housed in a storage container.

For a new business a file drawer or file box is usually adequate. As your business grows, increasing the number of files, you'll want to transfer them to a either a two- or four-drawer filing cabinet. A filing system minimizes the time spent filing and retrieving papers, and results in greater business efficiency.

How to Set Up a Small Business Filing System That Will Grow With Your Business

The small business filing system explained here is designed to enable you to file important papers quickly, and then find them again just as quickly. It's set up to make routine recordkeeping chores as simple and easy as possible.

Filing Tips

Here are some tips to help make your filing easier:

- Throw away anything you don't have an immediate use for.

- Date stamp all letters and correspondence when they arrive so that you have a record of when they were received.

- Don't file extra photocopies. File the original and then make photocopies of it as needed.

- As a rule, don't save drafts of contracts or agreements. Keep only the final signed agreement. Earlier versions could cause confusion. If drafts are needed to show intent, or for some other reason, clearly mark them as such.

- Staple related papers together. Don't use paper clips; they catch on other papers.

- Copy or mount smaller documents onto regular-sized paper.

- Fold larger documents to fit the folder or reduce them on a copy machine.

- Avoid filing similar information in separate places.

Color coding speeds up finding and replacing files. It can reduce filing time by nearly 50%. That's why we recommend using color coded hanging files to identify major headings, similar to the tabs used in this guide: Business Development (Blue), Marketing (Red), Operations (Orange), Administration (Yellow), and Finance (Green). Each of these major headings is subdivided into five topics, each of which gets its own file folder of the same color as the major tabbed heading. For instance, the red hanging file for the major tabbed heading, Marketing, would contain red file folders for Marketing Plan, Market Research, Sales & Distribution, Promotion, and Product Development.

These file folders are used to store the business papers related to those topics. For example, all of your documents related to promotion would be put into the file folder labeled "Promotion." The contents of this file folder might include such things as:

- articles, reports, or notes on the subjects of advertising, publicity, or marketing communications

- lists of potential publications to advertise in or send news releases to

- media kits and rate cards from various media

- samples of your competitors' ads and brochures

- drafts and sketches for your own ads

- copies of insertion orders, as records of ads you've placed

- copies of correspondence related to advertising and publicity

- tracking sheets to tabulate response to your ads and publicity

- names and addresses of copywriters, designers, and ad agencies

- tear sheets (printed copies) of ads and publicity that has already appeared

- worksheets showing costs and estimated returns of various ads

- and just about anything else that concerns promotion.

Of course this is just a preliminary list and once your business is under way, you'll find many more things to file under the heading of "Promotion." Once this folder becomes too crowded, you might find it convenient to set up separate file folders labeled "Advertising," "Publicity," and "Marketing Communications" to hold the various papers related to those topics. This would be Stage 2 as shown below.

What you've done is expanded the advertising section from a file folder to a hanging file labeled "Advertising" to hold all the new file folders you've made, "Advertising General Info," "Competitors' Ads," "Media Kits," etc.

Eventually, many, if not all of the file folders could become hanging files. And each major tabbed heading that started out as a hanging file (Business Development, Marketing, etc.) will expand to become an entire drawer in a file cabinet. For example, let's say you keep copies of invoices you send to your customers or clients in the "Accounting" file folder under the major tabbed heading "Finance." As you get more and more invoices you may want to start a separate file folder called "Invoices," and perhaps later, if you get a lot of repeat business, a separate file folder for each customer.

With this system it doesn't matter how large your business gets, you stay organized because the basic structure stays the same. When too many different kinds of information get into a single file folder, it's time to upgrade that heading to a hanging file and divide all the materials that were in the folder into separate file folders with their own headings. By maintaining the color coding as you expand your record keeping system, you always know where everything goes. You'll save time by readily being able to identify a folder or file's general contents just by looking at its color.

Expansion of the recommended small business filing system

At Stage 3, you have so many materials in one of these Stage 2 files that the topic heading is too broad. At this point you can convert that heading into a hanging file and divide the information into more specific categories. Let's take Advertising for example. One of the folders you put into this hanging file could be called "Advertising General Info" to contain articles and reports on advertising. Maybe you'll want another file folder called "Competitors' Ads," so you can keep up with how similar businesses are presenting and positioning themselves. The same is true for each of the other topics related to advertising.

The power and beauty of this system is that it grows right along with your business. Let's say you've started the file folders mentioned above.

FINANCE

ACCOUNTING

BANKING

TAXES

CASH MANAGEMENT

BUDGETING

ACCOUNTING

Why You Need to Understand Accounting

You may find accounting confusing, even a bit "scary." If so, you've got a lot of company, and not entirely without reason. Some accounting terms are used in different ways, and sometimes different words are used to describe the same thing. Because of this confusion, too many business owners are convinced they'll never understand accounting and consequently decide that once they hire someone to take care of it for them, they won't have to think about it anymore. This is a serious mistake because an understanding of accounting basics is a necessity for every business owner. And these basics aren't that difficult to grasp once you realize that accounting is merely a way to collect key information about your business.

Running any business requires a series of informed decisions. The better the information going into those decisions, the better the decisions will be. That's why you need to understand the meaning of the information you use when making business decisions. It's smart to rely on accountants for advice, but it's even smarter to realize that since it's your money at stake, you're going to have to make the final decisions yourself. Otherwise you will be placing the future of your business in someone else's hands.

Even though most business owners are aware of the necessity of accounting records for tax purposes, not all realize their true value. Understanding the many uses of accounting information will give you an idea of just how important it is. Accounting records and reports give you vital information about your business: what your sales are, how much you're spending, and whether you're making any money.

Accounting records also provide a wealth of facts about your customers, such as who your best customers are and who owes you money. The financial information from your accounting records can also tell you which of your products or services are selling the best, and when your peak sales periods are. Of course, any time you want to get a loan you'll be required to submit financial statements. And if you ever decide to sell your business, the prospective buyer will certainly want to see all the pertinent financial information.

Accounting Basics

While accounting is a complex, and seemingly mysterious subject, the accounting concepts and issues discussed in this section will provide you with a framework for understanding the all-important financial aspects of your business, and give you enough basic knowledge to communicate intelligently with your accountant, bookkeeper, or banker.

The first decision to make about accounting is which of the two major methods to choose: cash basis, where you report income the same year it is received and deduct expenses the same year they are paid; or accrual basis, where you report income the same year it is earned, even if it hasn't been received, and deduct expenses in the year they were incurred, regardless of when they are paid.

In most cases, the method you choose for accounting will also be used for tax purposes. Due to its simplicity, cash basis accounting is generally used by sole proprietorships and partnerships unless inventory is involved, in which case the IRS mandates the use of the accrual method. Most corporations use the accrual method. Your accountant can advise you on which one is preferable, or required, for your business.

Another early decision will be the choice of an accounting period for tax purposes. You can choose to have your accounting period be a calendar year (ending on December 31) or a fiscal year (ending on the last day of any other month). Some businesses choose a fiscal year to avoid having to prepare financial statements during their busiest times, or when their inventory is at minimum levels. On the other hand, all personal service businesses, including consultants (even if incorporated), must operate on a calender year. Ask your accountant about which is best for you.

Regardless of what type of business you have, there are certain common accounting terms and functions that you should be aware of:

Cash Receipts. Cash receipts are the currency and checks you receive at the time of a sale. Many businesses, retail stores in particular, are "cash" businesses. If you only have a few cash sales each day, you can record them in a cash receipt book (available at stationery stores). If, on the other hand, you have a large volume of cash sales every day, a cash register may be the best way to keep track of them. You'll also want to record your sales in an income ledger either daily, weekly, or monthly, depending on your sales volume (see "Daily Sales Journal" at the end of this section).

Check Register. Every business should have a checking account into which all business receipts are deposited, and out of which all business expenses are paid. This account should be separate from the owner's personal account to avoid recordkeeping and tax problems. Enter each check in the check register, which becomes a record of your business expenses. Later these expenses will be categorized by type for accounting and tax purposes. To make this easier for you, your accountant can give you a chart of accounts that gives each type of expense a

unique account number, or you can use the "Chart of Accounts" at the end of this section. Some check writing systems, called "One-Write," record the important account information as you write the checks, making it easier to group expenses, and eliminating the need to enter each expense twice.

For many small businesses the checkbook is the primary record of income and expenses.

Cash Expenditures. For incidental, out-of-pocket expenses not paid by check, set up a petty cash fund. One hundred dollars or less is probably the maximum you'll want to keep on hand for petty cash. Here's how it works: say you spend $12.75 of your personal money to purchase some small item for your business. Take $12.75 from petty cash and attach the receipt to a petty cash ledger and record the transaction. All you have to do is write the date, nature of the expense, and amount (see "Petty Cash Record" at the end of this section). At least once a quarter, or earlier if the fund runs out of cash, add up the expenditures, reconcile them to the remaining balance, and cash a check written to "Petty Cash" to replace the depleted funds.

Accounts Receivable. When you sell on credit, the money owed to you for products and services already delivered is called accounts receivable. When you make a credit sale, record it on a uniquely numbered invoice (see "Invoice" at the end of this section) and separately onto a ledger card, if you expect frequent sales to the same customers. Besides the copy of the invoice you send to your customer, you'll need at least two other copies; one for the customer file and another for a numerical control file. You can prepare an invoice from scratch (using the sample invoice mentioned above as a guide) and then make the copies you need, or you can purchase multi-part invoices from a stationery store. The simplest ledger cards will show the date of sale, the customer's name, invoice number, amount of sale, have a space for the date paid, and a running balance of the total amount owed. They, too, are available at stationery stores. If you don't ordinarily make frequent sales to the same customers, it may be more convenient to keep track of who owes you money by entering the information from each invoice you bill onto an "Accounts Receivable Journal With Aging" (you'll find a blank one at the end of this section).

Accounts Payable. Accounts payable are the amounts your business owes for goods and services purchased from outside suppliers. When bills come in, keep them all in a payables folder. Once a week, go through the folder and pay each bill that's due. Enter each payment in your check register and in an expense ledger if you're using one (books that contain both income and expense ledgers are available at stationery stores). Use a chart of accounts, either from your accountant or from the back of this section, to assign an account number to each expenditure. This allows you to group your expenses into categories for tax purposes. After you've paid each bill, you can store your copy of the bill in a file or large envelope marked with the month and year. Paid bills you might need to refer to again, such as those from a major supplier, should be kept in a separate file so you have a purchase history from that supplier.

Payroll. Payroll consists of two major functions: paying employees for their work, and withholding and remitting a variety of federal and state taxes. At the end of each quarter (more frequently for large payrolls and less frequently for smaller ones) employers are required to report and remit all the taxes withheld from their employees, as well as the employers' portion of the FICA

due, on a Form 941 (see *Taxes*). There are a number of computerized services that can handle most of the payroll paperwork relatively inexpensively. You can find them in the business yellow pages under "Payroll Preparation Services," or by asking your accountant for a recommendation. A separate payroll ledger is needed for each employee you have (see "Employee Payroll Register" in the *Personnel* section).

Profit & Loss. Every business owner must have an understanding of the importance of the concept of profit and loss because to be successful, a business has to be profitable. But there is some confusion among business owners because the word "profit" is used in at least four different ways:

■ **Gross profit** is what's left when the cost of goods sold, but not operating expenses, are subtracted from sales. It is the difference between what you bought your product for and what you sold it for, and can indicate whether you are pricing your product or service correctly. This figure is more accurately referred to as gross margin.

■ **Operating profit** is what's left when the cost of goods sold and operating expenses are subtracted from sales. It derives from the primary operations of a business and doesn't include non-operating income and expense (such as interest paid or received), or income taxes.

■ **Pre-tax profit** is the operating profit plus non-operating income less non-operating expenses, before income taxes are deducted. It is most often found on the income statements of corporations.

■ **Net profit** is the pre-tax profit minus income taxes paid by the business. Often called "the bottom line," net profit is also referred to as income, net income, and earnings. In a sole proprietorship or partnership, net income will be the same as pre-tax profit since taxes are paid by the individual owner(s). Corporations, however, do have a separate tax liability. While net profit is important, it doesn't represent spendable money, and shouldn't be confused with cash flow which is discussed in *Cash Management*.

Financial Statements: Keeping Score in Business

There is only one way to keep score in business: dollars and cents. Complete, accurate financial records help you monitor your business so that you know what's going on currently, and they help you plan intelligently for the future. Because the ongoing success of your business depends on its financial health, you should be familiar with financial statements and what they can contribute to your business:

■ An accurate statement of sales, fixed and variable costs, profits, receivables, and inventory levels to let you know exactly where your business stands financially, and what factors are influencing its profitability

■ A comparison of current financial information with prior years' results and with this year's projections to gauge your growth and performance, and to indicate areas where improvement is needed

■ Financial information suitable for use by management, investors, lenders, and creditors in many kinds of decision making

■ Information necessary for tax filings and other reports to regulatory agencies

■ A way of discovering losses, shortages, theft, and error.

The various financial statements outlined below will, when used together, provide you with an overview of the financial condition of your business at any given time:

Income Statement. Also called a Profit & Loss Statement, the income statement shows the income of a business for any given time period (typically a month, quarter, or year), the expenses incurred in obtaining the income, and the resulting profit or loss. It is a historical account of what happened financially during that period. The annual income statement represents the operations of the business for the fiscal year. It is the financial report used most often in business to prepare budgets and forecasts, and it is also used to determine some of the key ratios discussed later. Refer to the accompanying "Income Statement" as you review the major items found on an income statement:

Advantage Office Supplies
Income Statement
Period ended June 30,1990

Sales	Quarter	% Sales	Year-to-date	% Sales
Product Sales	187,000	100.0%	370,000	100.0%
Returns and allowances	(1,300)	(0.7%)	(2,000)	(0.5%)
Discounts allowed	(200)	(0.1%)	(500)	(0.1%)
Total Sales	185,500	99.2%	367,500	99.3%
Beginning inventory	113,000	n/a	117,000	n/a
Purchases	84,892	n/a	163,000	n/a
Ending inventory	106,000	n/a	113,000	n/a
Cost of Goods Sold	91,892	49.1%	167,000	45.1%
Gross Margin	93,608	50.1%	200,500	54.2%
Operating Expenses				
Salaries	39,467	21.1%	81,000	21.9%
Payroll expenses	5,792	3.1%	11,020	3.0%
Advertising	5,896	3.2%	8,034	2.2%
Promotion	538	0.3%	948	0.3%
Selling expenses	1,896	1.0%	4,278	1.2%
Computer operations	268	0.1%	567	0.2%
Travel and entertainment	427	0.2%	1,275	0.3%
Dues and subscriptions	48	0.0%	146	0.0%
Rent & Utilities	5,879	3.1%	10,845	2.9%
Professional services	1,398	0.7%	474	0.1%
Outside services	147	0.1%	93	0.0%
Office supplies	245	0.1%	1,039	0.3%
Equipment rental	297	0.2%	594	0.2%
Repairs and maintenance	67	0.0%	175	0.0%
Shipping	104	0.1%	257	0.1%
Telecommunications	721	0.4%	1,838	0.5%
Depreciation	327	0.2%	654	0.2%
Insurance - general	468	0.3%	978	0.3%
Licenses, permits & taxes	60	0.0%	197	0.1%
Interest & bank charges	698	0.4%	1,465	0.4%
Other expenses	2,530	1.4%	6,723	1.8%
Bad debts	276	0.1%	723	0.2%
Total Operating Expenses	67,549	36.1%	133,323	36.0%
Operating Income	26,059	13.9%	67,177	18.2%

Revenue is the amount of sales a business makes in a particular period. Gross sales are the total sales, while net sales are the gross sales less returns and allowances.

Cost of Goods Sold is the cost, or expense, of all goods actually sold in a period. It is derived by adding the beginning inventory and the items purchased during the period, to determine the total goods available for sale; and then subtracting the ending inventory (what hasn't yet been sold). The difference between these figures represents your cost for the products sold in that period. Service-only businesses rarely have any cost of goods sold.

Operating Expenses are the other costs of running a business, such as salaries and wages, advertising, rent and utilities, etc.

Depreciation is a bookkeeping expense that represents the loss in value of an asset as it ages. Unlike the other expenses, it does not require a cash outlay at the time it is deducted from revenues.

Profit has been already covered by the discussion above in the subsection on Profit & Loss.

Balance Sheet. The balance sheet is a snapshot of the financial position of a business on the particular day it is drawn up. It shows the assets, the liabilities, and the owner's equity. The balance sheet is based on the equation Assets = Liabilities + Equity, meaning that what the business owns (assets) is equal to what it owes to others (liabilities) plus the net worth, or owner's portion, of the business (equity). Like the Income Statement, which it usually accompanies, this report can be generated at the end of a month, quarter, or fiscal year. Refer to the accompanying "Balance Sheet" while reviewing the following key components of the balance sheet:

Assets are the things a business owns or is due. **Current assets** include cash, accounts receivable, and inventory, which can all be converted into cash within a year. **Fixed assets**, like buildings, equipment, and furniture, can't be converted to cash without interfering with business operations. **Intangible assets**, such as copy-

rights, trademarks, patents, licenses, and franchises, may or may not be shown on the balance sheet.

Liabilities are what the business owes to others. **Current liabilities** include accounts payable, accrued salaries, short-term loans, and unpaid taxes that are due within a year. **Long-term liabilities** include mortgages, long-term loans, and other obligations due over a period longer than a year.

Advantage Office Supplies
Balance Sheet
As of June 30,1990

	Current Quarter	Prior Quarter
Assets		
Current Assets:		
Cash	23,754	45,368
Investments, Short-term	20,000	0
Notes receivable	0	0
Acounts receivable	26,300	24,597
Inventory	106,000	113,000
Total Current Assets	176,054	182,965
Fixed Assets:		
Machinery and equipment	9,078	6,476
Furniture and fixtures	23,476	18,375
Automotive equipment	0	0
Less: Accum. depreciation	-1,377	-1,050
Total Fixed Assets	31,177	23,801
Other Assets:		
Deposits	1,600	1,600
Investments, Long-term	0	0
Total Other Assets	1,600	1,600
Total Assets	208,831	208,366
Liabilities		
Current Liabilities		
Notes payable, Short-term	0	0
Accounts payable	55,389	51,385
Wages payable	5,167	6,849
Taxes payable	2,978	4,867
Accrued expenses	678	754
Total Current Liabilities	64,212	63,855
Other Liabilities		
Mortages payable	0	0
Notes payable, Long-term	25,000	50,000
Contracts payable	0	0
Loans from owners	0	4,000
Total Other Liabilities	25,000	54,000
Total Liabilities	89,212	117,855
Owner's Equity		
Net Worth	119,619	90,511
Total Liabilities & Equity	208,831	208,366

Owner's Equity or **Net Worth** is the value of the owner's share of a business. It equals the total assets minus the total liabilities. Owner's equity represents the owner's investment plus any additional value the business has created. The actual value of a business isn't necessarily indicated by the net worth since its intangible assets and potential for future earning, which could be its most valuable assets, may not be reflected on the balance sheet.

Cash Flow Statement. The cash flow statement indicates the cash position of a business at the end of certain period. It shows what the cash balance was at the start of the period and then shows how much cash was received from various sources and the reasons cash was paid out. It provides a way to plan the short-range cash needs of a business. This statement is useful because many of the items that affect cash, such as capital purchases, do not show up on an income statement, so a company can show profit yet still run out of cash. Refer to the accompanying "Cash Flow Statement" as

you review the following key components of a cash flow statement:

Sources of Cash are those items which brought cash into the business.

Uses of Cash are those items which used cash in the business.

Increase in Assets shows the use of cash to obtain something.

Decrease in Assets shows the conversion of an asset into a source of cash.

Increase in Liabilities shows the use of a bank or supplier as a source of cash.

Decrease in Liabilities shows the use of cash to pay off an obligation.

Financial Ratios

Besides what the various figures taken from the income statement, balance sheet, and cash flow statement reveal on their own, the relationships between certain of these figures, called ratios, can indicate even more about the financial health of a business. These ratios are best used to pinpoint areas of possible concern by comparing changes in a business over time. Ratios vary widely between different industries, and even within the same industry depending on the size and location of the specific business. Trade associations often publish the average ratios of their members, giving you a chance to compare your business with others in the field. Here are a few of the most widely used ratios that you should know about, along with sample calculations from the financial statements in this section:

■ **Current Ratio.** The current ratio, sometimes called the **working capital ratio,** is used to measure liquidity, or the ability of a business to pay its current debts using only current assets. The higher this ratio, the more solvent the business is, though a value of 2 is popularly accepted as a reasonable target. Derived from the balance sheet, the current ratio is determined by dividing current assets by current liabilities.

Current Assets ÷ Current Liabilities = Current Ratio
$176,000 ÷ $64,212 = 2.74

Advantage Office Supplies
Cash Flow Statement
Period ended June 30,1990

	Quarter	Year-to-date
Sources of Cash:		
Net Product Sales	185,500	367,500
Other Receipts	3,000	5,000
Non-Cash Expenses	327	654
Total Sources	188,827	373,154
Uses of Cash		
Operating Expenses	67,549	133,323
Capital Purchases	0	0
Items Purchased for resale	84,892	163,000
Total Uses	152,441	296,323
Increase in Assets (use)	465	1,965
Decrease in Liabilities (use)	-28,643	-33,643
Net Cash Flow	7,278	41,223
Beginning Cash Position	36,476	2,531
Ending Cash Position	43,754	43,754

■ **Quick Ratio.** Closely related to the current ratio is the quick ratio, or **acid test**, which is considered to be one of the best ways to determine if a business could meet its obligations if it lost all revenue. The general target for the quick ratio is a value of 1. To calculate this ratio all cash, accounts receivable, and marketable securities are added together and divided by the current liabilities. The quick ratio differs from the current ratio in that it excludes inventory.

(Cash + Accounts Receivable + Marketable Securities) ÷ Current Liabilities = Quick Ratio

($23.754 + 26,300 + 20,000) ÷ $64,212 = 1.09

Financial ratios are good indicators of the financial health of your business.

■ **Leverage Ratio.** Also derived from the balance sheet, the leverage ratio, sometimes called the **debt to equity ratio**, compares the liabilities of a business to its net worth. The higher the ratio the more debt a business is carrying. A very high ratio indicates that the business may not be able to repay its debts, while too low a ratio may mean the business isn't being allowed to grow to its potential. The leverage ratio is computed by dividing liabilities by net worth.

Liabilities ÷ Net Worth = Leverage Ratio

$89,212 ÷ $119,619 = 75%

■ **Net Profit Ratio.** This measure of profitability shows how much profit is derived from each dollar of sales. While net profit will always be a fraction of sales, the higher it is, the more operating efficiency it indicates. The net profit ratio is determined by dividing net profit by net sales. Both these figures are taken from the income statement.

Net Profit ÷ Net Sales = Net Profit Ratio

$67,717 ÷ $367,500 = 18%

■ **Average Collection Period.** Also called the **accounts receivable turnover**, this ratio indicates how quickly receivables are being collected. The lower it is, the faster a business is collecting what it is owed. In general, this number should be less than 1.33 times

your normal credit term (e.g. if your credit term is 30 days, the average collection period should not exceed 40 days). It is computed by dividing the accounts receivable, taken from the balance sheet, by the average credit sales per day (obtained by dividing net credit sales by the number of days in the accounting period).

Accounts Receivable ÷ Average Daily Credit Sales = Average Collection Period

$26,300 ÷ $710 = 37 days

■ **Inventory Turnover.** This ratio shows how fast your merchandise is moving. Usually the higher the turnover the better, because it shows that the business has been able to operate with a relatively small investment in inventory. It is obtained by dividing the cost of goods sold by the average inventory (which is found by adding the inventory at the beginning of the period to the ending inventory, and then using half that figure as an average).

Annual Cost of Goods Sold ÷ Average Inventory = Inventory Turnover

$668,000 ÷ $109,000 = 6.1 times

What to Do and When to Do It

Keeping your financial records up-to-date won't be a problem if you do what is necessary on a regular basis. Though your particular accounting needs may vary somewhat, here is a guide that will help you understand the most common tasks required to maintain accurate accounting records:

The result of not staying current with your bookkeeping.

Daily:

■ **Total Cash on Hand.** Total the amount of cash in the cash drawer or register.

■ **Record Income.** Add up receipts and invoices, and print cash register tapes. Enter a summary of sales and cash receipts in an income ledger. Use the "Daily Sales Journal."

■ **Record Payments.** Deduct checks from the checking account balance; record cash payments in the petty cash account.

■ **Enter Deposits.** Add deposits to your business checkbook to keep the balance current.

■ **Record Inventory.** Add items received to inventory records, using an "Inventory Control Card."

Weekly:

■ **Review Accounts Receivable.** Enter billed invoices on "Accounts Receivable Journal With Aging" form. Scan to see who owes you money; be particularly alert for past due accounts and take action to collect from slow payers.

■ **Review Accounts Payable.** Pay bills when due, but time your payments to manage your cash flow, remembering to take advantage of discounts.

■ **Prepare Payroll.** Compute each employee's payroll on the "Employee Payroll Register."

■ **Deduct Items Sold from Inventory.** Adjust inventory records to reflect the week's sales on an "Inventory Control Card."

Monthly:

■ **Balance Checkbook.** Reconcile your checking account records to the statements sent by your bank to make sure that both sets of records are in agreement, using the "Bank Account Reconciliation" found in *Banking*.

■ **Total All Ledgers.** Compute monthly totals for sales, expenses, and payroll.

■ **Make Tax Deposits.** Report and remit withheld employee income taxes and FICA taxes. Also file and remit any federal or state income taxes due. Depending on the amounts involved, these tax deposits may be due quarterly, or irregularly instead of monthly. See *Taxes* for additional details.

■ **Age Accounts Receivable.** Update your unpaid accounts, listing them by length of time on the books, i.e., 30, 60, 90 days, etc. Use this list to discover which slow and bad accounts require extra collection attention.

■ **Review Inventory.** Review the "Inventory Control Cards" to check inventory levels to see which items aren't moving so you can replace them with new stock.

■ **Reconcile Petty Cash.** Use the "Petty Cash Record" to make sure the actual cash in the petty cash box plus the total of the paid-out receipts for expenses from petty cash is equal to the starting balance. Replenish if necessary.

Quarterly:

- **File Estimated Tax Returns.** File federal and state estimated income taxes. See "Federal Tax Calendar" in *Taxes* for actual due dates.

- **Remit Sales Taxes.** If required, fill out a state sales tax report and send it in along with a check for the amount of sales tax you've collected. You may be required to remit sales taxes monthly or annually instead of quarterly, depending on the amounts involved.

- **Prepare Income Statement.** This will reflect the sales, expenses, and profit for that quarter and for the year-to-date. Many larger businesses generate this report monthly as well as quarterly.

- **Prepare Balance Sheet.** This will indicate the financial position of the business at the end of the quarter. Many larger businesses generate this report monthly as well as quarterly.

- **Prepare Cash Flow Statement.** This will reflect the cash activity and ending position for the quarter. Many larger businesses generate this report monthly as well as quarterly.

Annual:

- **Total All Ledgers.** Using the forms mentioned earlier, compute yearly totals for sales, expenses, and payroll.

- **Prepare Income Statement.** This will reflect the sales, expenses, and profit for the year.

- **Prepare Balance Sheet.** This will indicate the financial position of the business at the end of the year.

- **Prepare Cash Flow Statement.** This will indicate the cash activity and ending position of the business at the end of the year.

- **Send Out 1099 Forms.** Complete and mail a 1099 form (Statement for Recipients of Miscellaneous Income) to each independent contractor who earned over $600 from you in the previous year.

- **Send Out W-2 Forms.** Complete and mail a W-2 form to each employee who worked for you in the previous year.

- **Assemble Tax Papers.** Pull together all the documentation you're going to need for filing your income taxes.

- **Meet With Your Accountant.** Turn over your tax documentation and set up a time to discuss your financial condition and tax strategy for the coming year.

- **Set Up New Books.** Prepare for the coming year by setting up your ledgers.

The Accounting Cycle:
How the Pieces Fit Together

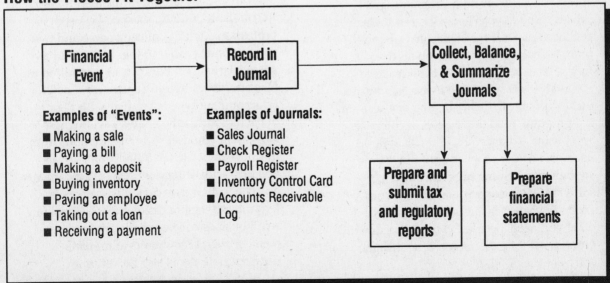

Financial Event → Record in Journal → Collect, Balance, & Summarize Journals

Examples of "Events":
- Making a sale
- Paying a bill
- Making a deposit
- Buying inventory
- Paying an employee
- Taking out a loan
- Receiving a payment

Examples of Journals:
- Sales Journal
- Check Register
- Payroll Register
- Inventory Control Card
- Accounts Receivable Log

Prepare and submit tax and regulatory reports

Prepare financial statements

How to Handle Your Accounting

By now you should agree that the question about accounting isn't whether you need to do it, but how you're going to do it. Fortunately there are a number of ways to ensure that your accounting gets done accurately:

- **Your own ledger books** are one way to handle the accounting needs of your business – if you're motivated and have the time it takes to keep your finances current. You can purchase ledger sheets at a stationery store and set up your own books. *Small Time Operator* by Bernard Kamoroff provides an excellent explanation of how to do it, as well as including sample ledger sheets that you can copy for use in your business.

- **An accounting system book**, like those published by Dome, Ideal, and Keith Clark, are available at stationery stores. These books contain the ledgers you need for recording sales, expenses, and payroll, and some of them come in weekly, monthly, or annual versions, and there are even special versions for certain businesses. Everything is set up for you; all you have to do is enter the numbers. Many small businesses, with fewer than five employees, find these books to be adequate for their accounting needs.

- **Accounting software** is becoming more and more popular with small business owners because of the way it can increase both the speed and accuracy of the accounting process. You have to be very careful when purchasing an off-the-shelf software program to make sure that it supplies the functions and reports your business needs, and that it is easy enough to learn and use to make it practical. Before buying any accounting program, read the reviews in computer and business magazines, and talk to both users and dealers. Some accounting firms specialize in helping select accounting software. The clearer you are about your needs the better chance you have of getting what you need. See the *Equipment* section in **Operations** for a discussion of accounting software.

- **Bookkeeping services** can provide a wide range of services to help you with your accounting needs. There are some services that specialize in taxes or payroll, and others that offer the full range of services. They can put your accounting data on their computers and print out standard or customized reports. Because your company's finances are too important to take a chance with, talk with clients who have used the firm's services for more than three years before turning your bookkeeping over to a them.

- **A part-time bookkeeper** may be all the bookkeeping help many small sole proprietors need, particularly those whose income and expenses are fairly straightforward. The main function of a bookkeeper is to maintain the company's journals and ledgers by recording all financial transactions. To find a part-time bookkeeper, ask business associates for recommendations or look in the yellow pages. Be sure to check references before retaining anyone to do your bookkeeping. Since their knowledge of accounting practices is often limited, don't seek accounting or tax advice on complex matters from bookkeepers.

- **An accountant** can set up an easy-to-follow bookkeeping system specifically designed for your business. Accountants can also give you advice on taxes, cash management, and other financial matters. A Certified Public Accountant, or CPA, is a state-licensed professional with a college degree and two years of on-the-job training. He or she has passed a qualifying exam and is required to take additional training each year. Look for an accountant who is familiar with your type of business and who shows a willingness to work with you. Get recommendations from business associates or other professionals you deal with. Interview several accountants and check their experience, references, and fee structure before making a decision. Many small businesses keep their own books and then use their accountants to prepare financial statements and tax returns.

Tips for Using the Following Forms:

Note: You are encouraged to copy these forms for your own use. Keep the unmarked originals in a safe place and make copies of them to work from.

Chart of Accounts – This chart of accounts is designed to be used in most small business accounting systems. It contains the various components that make up the balance sheet and income statement. To the right of the expenses are the Schedule C lines that show where each item is reported on the non-incorporated business owner's tax returns. Your accountant can advise you whether any additional items need to be included for your particular business.

Daily Sales Journal – The first column contains the days of the month. Enter your daily taxable sales in the second column across from the appropriate date. Enter the sales tax in the third column. In the fourth column enter the non-taxable sales, either out of state or wholesale. Enter any shipping charges in the fifth column. Add up the row for that day's entries from each of the columns and put the total in the next to last column. At the end of the month, total each of the columns.

Invoice – This sample invoice will acquaint you with the basic information that should appear on an invoice. Since the purpose of an invoice is to get you paid, it should give customers as much information as they need to pay it. With the addition of your business name and address in the upper left corner, this form is ready to be copied and used.

Petty Cash Record – Enter the beginning balance in the space indicated. For each expense make an entry under each column and subtract the amount from the balance. At the end of the period, total the amounts and place the ending balance in the bottom row of the last column. The total amount spent and the ending balance should equal the beginning balance. Use the part of the form in the lower right for reconciliation. In the Summary part of the form group together the expenses by account number from your Chart of Accounts.

Accounts Receivable Journal With Aging Each week add any accounts that owe you money. When the page is filled, start a new journal and list the oldest unpaid bills at the top of the form and check the corresponding box to indicate their age. Keep adding the new billings each week, and cross off those who have paid. Every two weeks check the Age column and put a check in the new category if appropriate.

1000 SERIES - ASSETS

1110	Cash
1120	Investments, short-term
1130	Notes receivable
1140	Acounts receivable
1150	Inventory
1160	Prepaid expenses
1170	Deferred charges
1210	Machinery and equipment
1220	Furniture and fixtures
1230	Automotive equipment
1240	Leasehold improvements
1250	Depreciation
1310	Deposits
1320	Investments, long-term
1330	Deferred charges

2000 SERIES - LIABILITIES

2110	Bank overdraft
2120	Notes payable, short-term
2130	Accounts payable
2140	Wages payable
2150	Taxes payable
2160	Accrued expenses
2170	Deferred credits
2210	Mortages payable
2220	Notes payable, long-term
2230	Contracts payable
2240	Less current portion
2310	Loans from shareholders

3000 SERIES - EQUITY ACCOUNTS

3100	Capital stock
3110	Common stock
3410	Retained earnings
3420	Treasury stock

4000 SERIES - REVENUE ACCOUNTS

4100	Sales
4200	Returns and allowances
4300	Discounts allowed

5000 SERIES - COST OF GOODS

5100	Purchases
5110	Freight-in
5120	Development costs
5410	Beginning inventory
5420	Ending inventory

6000 SERIES - EXPENSE ACCOUNTS

		Sch. C Line #
6100	Salaries	27
6110	Payroll expenses	14
6120	Advertising & promotion	8
6140	Selling expenses	11
6150	Computer operations	19
6160	Travel and entertainment	25
6170	Automobile	10
6180	Dues and subscriptions	28
6190	Office rent	21
6200	Professional services	18
6210	Outside services	28
6300	Utilities	26
6310	Office supplies	23
6320	Equipment rental	21
6330	Repairs and maintenance	22
6340	Shipping/Freight	15
6350	Telecommunications	19
6500	Depreciation	13
6600	Insurance - general	16
6610	Licenses and permits	28
6620	Taxes	24
6630	Contributions	28
6700	Interest	17
6710	Bank charges	28
6800	Bad debts	9

7000 SERIES - OTHER INCOME ACCOUNTS

7110	Other Income

8000 SERIES - OTHER EXPENSE ACCOUNTS

8110	Loss on asset sales
8120	Miscellaneous losses

9000 SERIES - INCOME TAX ACCOUNTS

9110	Federal taxes
9120	State taxes

Note: These accounts can be used in any manual or automated accounting system.

DAILY SALES JOURNAL

MONTH:

	Date	Taxable Product Sales	Sales Tax	Non-Taxable Sales	Shipping	Total Sales	Comments
1							
2							
3							
4							
5							
6							
7							
8							
9							
10							
11							
12							
13							
14							
15							
16							
17							
18							
19							
20							
21							
22							
23							
24							
25							
26							
27							
28							
29							
30							
31							
	Total						

INVOICE

Send payment to:

Sold to:

Ship to:

Account Number:	Invoice Number:
Order Number:	Invoice Date:
Salesperson:	Shipping Date:

Quantity Ordered	Item Number	Description	Unit Price	Amount
Total				

Please pay from this invoice.
No statement will be sent.

Sales Tax

Shipping

THANK YOU FOR YOUR ORDER !

Amount Due

PETTY CASH RECORD

Beginning Balance:

Date	Purpose	Amount	Spent by	Account	Balance
Total					

Summary

Account	Amount

Beginning Balance

Less: Total Amount Spent   - _____

Expected Cash on Hand   = _____

Actual Cash on Hand   - _____

Shortage/(Overage)   = _____

Balanced by: _____

Date: _____

Approved: _____

ACCOUNTS RECEIVABLE JOURNAL WITH AGING

Date Prepared: _____ By: _____

	Date Billed	Customer	Amount	Invoice #	Payment	Date Paid	Age (Days) Curr.	30	60	90	120+
1											
2											
3											
4											
5											
6											
7											
8											
9											
10											
11											
12											
13											
14											
15											
16											
17											
18											
19											
20											
21											
22											
23											
24											
25											
26											
27											
28											
29											
30											
31											
32											
33											
34											
35											
36											
37											
38											
Total											

BANKING

Choosing a Bank

Every business needs a separate checking account. Mixing personal and business funds not only leads to confusion, but it can cause problems at tax time. Using a business account gives you a convenient way to document your business deductions for tax purposes and also helps establish your credibility with suppliers. So one of the first things you need to do when starting a business is to open a business checking account.

You may already know a banker where you do your personal banking. An existing personal relationship with a bank officer can be the most important factor in choosing a bank. Convenience is also a factor, but the bank's range of services, fees, and employees can be much more important to your business. Before walking into the nearest bank and opening an account, call a number of banks in your area and ask to speak with the manager. Interview each manager to find out what particular benefits that bank can offer to a business like yours.

Try to cultivate a relationship with the manager by presenting yourself as a fellow professional, but don't try to make an impression by exaggerating the facts about your business. The relationship you build with the bank manager can benefit you in the future. You probably can't expect any big favors, but in the case of a loan application that could go either way, it doesn't hurt to have the manager on your side. Having already dealt with a number of small businesses, a banker can be a valuable source of financial advice, referrals, and suggestions about your business plan.

Bankers are generally adverse to risk, especially when it comes to new businesses. They prefer dealing with known quantities, which is why establishing an ongoing relationship is so important. So, in selecting a bank, think about it as choosing a banker too. Look for a banker with whom you have rapport and who understands your business.

What to Look for in a Bank

When comparing banks for your business banking needs, several factors need to be taken into account. Following are some of the criteria you'll want to use for comparison. Use the "Bank Comparison Worksheet" at the end of this section to record the information given by each bank. The figures quoted below for fees are typical ranges only, and may differ in your area.

- **Prior relationship.** As mentioned earlier, if you already have an ongoing relationship with a banker, you need only deepen the existing relationship, rather than having to build it from scratch.

- **Small business orientation.** Look for a bank that cultivates small business accounts. If a bank isn't knowledgeable about and sympathetic toward small business concerns, then it isn't a very good candidate for your new account.

- **Fees.** Some banks charge for each deposit and each check written. These fees may vary from 10¢ to 50¢ per transaction. A monthly service fee of around $5 to $10 may also be charged, particularly if your balance falls below a certain amount, say $1000 or $2500. Most, but not all, banks charge for bounced checks deposited into your account as well as any written on it. These fees generally range between $3 and $10 per check.

■ **Interest.** Try to find a bank that pays interest on your checking account balance; many do if you maintain a high enough balance. Typically the rates paid are between 5 and 7%. At some banks it is possible to get accounts that pay money market interest rates, though they usually require maintenance of a minimum balance, and allow only minimal transactions.

■ **Merchant status.** It's getting more difficult for small businesses to get authorization to accept credit cards, particularly those who take orders by mail or phone. So if you have any intention of accepting credit card orders, make sure the bank you choose will grant you merchant status. If it is especially difficult to get merchant status in your area, you may want to make granting it a condition for opening your account.

■ **Loans and credit lines.** Ask if your business will be eligible for either a line of credit or a loan. Small businesses have traditionally had a difficult time borrowing money, so any cash sources you can set up ahead of time can be of tremendous assistance if you ever have a need for ready cash. And though banks don't generally lend to new businesses, it doesn't hurt to ask. For information on how to get money for your business see the section called *Raising Money* in **Business Development**.

■ **Freebies.** The days of toaster give-aways for new accounts are long gone, but many banks still offer some free services. Preprinted checks, endorsement stamps, and safe deposit boxes are the most common freebies.

The size of the bank is another factor to consider. In a large bank with many branches, your account may not even be noticed. At a small independent bank, or a small chain, you may get better, more personalized service because your account could be more important to them. And lastly, make sure the bank you choose is solvent. Last year over two hundred banks failed, and when this happens banking operations can be disrupted.

Comparing a number of banks, based on those considerations you consider most important, should allow you to find a bank that is right for your business.

The Old Pro says:

"The best time to establish a relationship with a banker is when you don't need a loan, plan ahead!"

Opening a Bank Account

Business accounts are easy to open, but since requirements vary from bank to bank, check with the bank you've selected to find out what they require. For most businesses, a fictitious name statement is required before you can open an account under a business name. Corporations usually need to present a copy of their Certificate of Incorporation and other corporate papers as well. You may also be asked to show a driver's license, credit card, and to provide your social security number.

One last point about opening an account: conventional wisdom says the larger your opening deposit, the more respect you'll get, and the more clout you'll have with your banker.

Using Your Bank Account

Use your business checking account to pay all your business expenses, and be sure to deposit all your business income, both checks and cash, into it. Entering all your income and expenses into your check register gives you a well documented record of your business activities.

Avoid making checks out to "cash," and don't use your business account to pay for non-business expenses. When you want to withdraw money from your business account for yourself, make the check payable to yourself.

Each month when you receive your statement, use it to balance your account. This way you'll catch errors early and avoid embarrassing and costly mistakes, such as overdrafts, which bankers hate. To make it easy to balance your account, use the "Bank Account Reconciliation" form found at the end of this section.

Credit Card Sales

Using credit cards has become such a habit with many customers that many businesses depend on credit card sales for survival. If your competitors accept credit cards, then you probably should too. A business that accepts credit cards is said to have "merchant status." Other reasons to obtain merchant status are:

- Credit cards make it easier for your customers to buy from you

- Credit cards save you the trouble and expense of billing customers

- Customers who use credit cards are generally more affluent

- Credit card orders tend to be higher than purchases made in other ways.

For consumers, the most popular credit cards are VISA and MasterCard. Business customers often use the American Express card. Diner's Club and Discover are also popular cards. Your bank can give you information on being granted VISA and MasterCard merchant status, though as mentioned

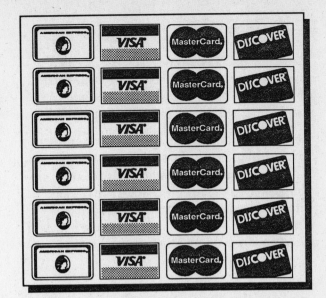

earlier, it may be difficult to obtain. If your local banks won't let you accept these cards, look for banks outside your area, even outside your state, that specialize in granting merchant status. For the other cards, contact the companies that offer them directly.

When a business accepts credit cards, billing and collection are handled by the issuer of the card. In return they receive a certain percentage, or discount, of each sale. The typical fees range from about 2.5 to 6.5%, with the lowest fees charged for high monthly volume with large average sale amounts, and the highest fees charged for low monthly volume with low average sale amounts.

Credit card fraud has made it necessary for businesses accepting credit cards to be cautious. Unless they follow certain procedures, the business that accepted the card may have to assume liability for any losses. Purchases made on expired cards are another way a business can take a loss. Stolen cards are a widespread source of credit fraud, so merchants are often required to check each card against a "hot" list sent monthly by the issuer.

There is usually a limit set by the bank on how large a purchase can be made on the card without authorization. Any sales over this amount require a phone call to a verification center for approval. Failure to get authorization can result in any loss coming out of the business owner's pocket. New automated verification and draft printing systems, which allow for rapid authorization, speed the card acceptance process for retailers.

Banking Tips

Once you open an business account at a bank, it's a good idea to keep it there. It's hard to establish a good credit reference if you move your account repeatedly.

Become acquainted with as many bank employees as possible, and treat them with respect. There are a number of situations that can occur in business which require the cooperation of bank employees, including clerks and tellers. In these situations, you'll be more likely to get the help you need if you've been courteous to them in the past.

Ask your bank to have your statement period end on the last day of the calendar month instead of sometime in the middle of the month. This makes keeping track of your account much easier.

If you find that your bank account regularly has balances that exceed your operating needs, it's a good idea to put the excess cash into a higher interest savings account to earn greater interest. Particularly large amounts can be put into certificates of deposit (CDs) or money market funds.

Tips for Using the Following Forms:

Note: You are encouraged to copy these forms for your own use. Keep the unmarked originals in a safe place and make copies of them to work from.

Bank Comparison Worksheet – Have this form at hand when you speak with various bank managers over the phone. First put a check mark beside the most important factors for your business. Then enter your expected monthly volume levels in the second column for each of the types of service you're interested in comparing. Bankers will need to have some idea of monthly volumes to quote fees to you. Cross off any services that don't apply to you. Write the names and phone numbers of three different banks in the spaces provided in the top row. Call each bank and record the fees quoted for each service. Use more forms to include additional banks in your comparison. When you've collected all the information you need, look at how the banks compared on the factors you checked as most important.

Bank Account Reconciliation – First go through your check register and make a mark beside every check number and deposit that appears on your statement. Be sure the amounts of each check and deposit are the same on the statement as they are in the check register.

Any valid charges (service fees, check printing charges, unrecorded checks) or credits (interest payments or unrecorded deposits) on the statement, but not appearing in your check register, should be entered in it. Any checks or deposits that don't appear on the statement should be entered in the appropriate columns in the Outstanding Transactions portion of the form. Next, in the spaces provided in the lower part of the form, write in the ending balance from your statement on line 1 and the ending balance from your check register on line 5. Enter the total amount of outstanding checks on line 2 and the total of outstanding deposits on line 3. When all these figures have been entered, do the necessary addition and subtraction. If line 6 is anything other than 0, recheck your arithmetic. Then recheck the addition and subtraction in your check register. If the amount of the difference is the same amount as any cleared or outstanding check, or any deposit, examine your check register to make sure that item has been recorded correctly. Report any errors in your statement to your bank immediately.

BANK COMPARISON WORKSHEET

Key Considerations	Need or expected monthly volume	Bank 1	Bank 2	Bank 3
Types of services offered				
Checking				
Savings				
Investments				
Federal tax deposits				
Small business counseling				
Loans/Lines of credit				
Pension administration				
Business credit cards				
Fees				
Checking account				
Monthly fee				
Minimum balance				
Per check charge				
Interest paid				
Other				
Savings account				
Interest rate				
Minimum balance				
Transaction fee				
Other				
Credit card processing				
Monthly fee				
Discount rate (fee)				
Other				
Other factors				
Convenient location				
Existing relationship				
Interest in small business				

BANK ACCOUNT RECONCILIATION

Date	Check Number	Description	Check Amount	Deposit Amount
		Outstanding Transactions		
Total				

1.) Balance from Bank Statement $ _____

2.) Less: Total outstanding checks   - $ _____

3.) Plus: Total outstanding deposits   + $ _____

4.) Adjusted Balance per Bank Statement $ _____

5.) Check Register Balance   - $ _____

6.) Difference (line 4-line 5) $ _____

If a difference exists check your calculations:
    a. if the amount of the difference is the same as a check,
      or deposit, then check to be sure it has been entered properly
    b. report any errors in your statement to the bank immediately.

If the statement is correct and you want to make a single adjustment,
if the difference is positive, add it to your check register; if negative, subtract it.

TAXES

Taxes: A Business Reality

For most small business people, few subjects are as unpleasant to contemplate as taxes. Just about every business owner complains that small business involves too much paperwork and red tape. And many of these complaints are directed squarely at the labyrinth of numerous and confusing federal, state, and local tax laws. Yet payment of these taxes is the lawful responsibility of every business owner. Failure to comply can lead to penalties, fines, or worse. And ignorance isn't an excuse.

In addition to paying taxes, business owners are required to collect or withhold certain federal and state taxes from customers and employees. There are also a number of forms that have to be completed on either a quarterly or annual basis. Since some businesses have been shut down for failure to make tax deposits in a timely fashion, it's imperative that you know what your tax obligations are and how to meet them.

Types of Taxes

Individuals accustomed to working as employees and filing only annual federal and state tax returns can become bewildered by the new tax obligations they take on when they become business owners (see "Key Tax and Regulatory Requirements" and "Federal Tax Calendar" at the end of this section). Because they're self-employed, sole proprietors and partners are required to make quarterly estimated income tax deposits. Corporations are also required to make quarterly pay-

ments. Just as when you were an employee, the IRS doesn't wait until the end of the year to collect the taxes due it. Here are some of the more common types of taxes your business may be responsible for:

■ **Federal income tax (including estimated income tax deposits).** Filing for sole proprietors is fairly simple. Use Form 1040 (Schedule C) for annual filing and Form 1040-ES for quarterly estimates. Partnerships are not taxed, but partnership income is taxed as personal income to each of the partners according to their share of ownership. The federal government also requires that a partnership return be filed for informational purposes on Form 1065. Since a corporation has an identity apart from its owners, it must file a tax return and pay taxes. The return is filed on Form 1120 and it utilizes a different rate structure than an individual. The corporation's estimated taxes are filed on Form 1120-W.

■ **Federal withholding taxes on employee wages.** After obtaining an employer's identification number (see *Personnel* in **Administration**), have employees fill out W-4 forms. The IRS document, "Employer's Tax Guide," gives the amounts to withhold from each paycheck. The amount will depend on wage level, payroll period, number of exemptions, and marital status. Employers are required to file a Form 941 return according to a schedule determined by the amounts owed. This schedule appears on the back of the "Federal Tax Calendar."

- **FICA (Social Security).** Employers are required to match employee contributions. Currently, the employee and employer each contribute 6.2% of the employees gross pay (up to $53,400). Sole proprietors and members of a partnership pay self-employment tax instead of Social Security for themselves. The filing and payment of the tax is the same as for Federal Withholding.

- **Medicare.** Medicare premiums were separated from FICA in 1991. The amount is collected along with FICA and is currently 1.45% of gross pay (up to $125,000) for both employees and employers.

- **FUTA.** Most employers are also subject to Federal Unemployment Tax (FUTA). While the Form 940 return is filed annually, the employer may have to make quarterly deposits. The amount paid depends on the claims history of the business.

- **State income tax.** Most states require payment of a state income tax for individuals engaged in sole proprietorships and partnerships, and a franchise tax for corporations. The requirements vary from state to state but tend to be similar to federal requirements, check with your state's Franchise Tax Board for details (it may be called by a different name in your state).

- **State withholding taxes on employee wages.** In addition to withholding state taxes from employee paychecks, most states also require the payment of state unemployment taxes, and in some cases, disability insurance as well. On a periodic basis, employers are required to file returns and remit the funds withheld. Contact your state employment department for details.

- **State sales tax.** Almost all states have sales taxes that businesses are required to collect and remit to the state. Permits are required for businesses that purchase items intended for resale from other vendors. These allow the holder to make purchases without paying sales tax on them. The sales tax collected from customers must be remitted to the state on a regular basis. You will receive the information you need upon application for a resale permit.

- **Local property or inventory tax.** Many locales have annual taxes on such things as inventory, equipment, office supplies, and other tangible personal property. Property and buildings are also taxed in many areas. Once you have a business license, the local authorities will contact you if your business is subject to these taxes.

- **Local sales tax.** In addition to state sales taxes, many municipalities and transit districts have sales taxes that must be collected in the same manner as state taxes.

- **Federal excise tax.** Most small business aren't required to pay federal excise tax, but certain manufacturers in several industries are. These include the manufacture of trucks and truck parts, hunting and fishing equipment, and fossil fuels; and the resellers of heavy trucks and certain fuels. A more complete list can be found on the back of the "Federal Tax Calendar."

Tax evasion is a crime but tax avoidance is a sound business practice.

Use the "Federal Tax Calendar" to determine when various tax obligations are due for your business. You'll also find explanations of how to compute withholding of federal income tax, FICA, and FUTA on the back of the "Federal Tax Calendar." Contact your local IRS office for free federal tax information, and your state and local tax offices for further information about their requirements.

You are permitted to prepare the tax returns for your business, but it's a good idea to have an accountant or professional tax preparer do them for you. Refer to the section on *Accounting* for tips on finding an accountant for your business.

Tax Elections

Although most tax matters are mandated by Congress or the IRS, you do have some choices concerning how your business is taxed. You may select:

- **Calendar or fiscal tax year.** You can choose to have your tax year end on December 31, called a calendar year, or to have it end on the last day of any other month, called a fiscal year. See the *Accounting* section for additional information about choosing a tax year.

- **Cash or accrual basis.** You can choose to have your business taxed on a cash basis, where you report income the same year it is received and deduct expenses the same year they are paid; or on an accrual basis, where you report income the same year it is earned, even if it hasn't been received, and deduct expenses in the year they were incurred, regardless of when they are paid. See the *Accounting* section for more information about these two methods.

- **Inventory valuation.** If your business has inventory, you can also choose how it is valued for tax purposes, either as FIFO (first in, first out) or LIFO (last in, first out). FIFO assumes that your inventory sells in the same order it was acquired or produced, while LIFO assumes that the most recently acquired inventory sells first. For more details on this topic, see *Inventory* in **Operations.**

Business Deductions

Only expenses related to your business activities are deductible. The general rule is that a deductible expense be both necessary and ordinary to your type of business. Documentation is necessary when claiming tax deductions. As suggested in the section on *Banking*, paying all business expenses out of your business checking account provides a portion of the necessary documentation. Certain types of deductions which require additional documentation are:

- **Travel, meals, and entertainment.** Two types of documents are required:

  1. **Evidence of payment.** A receipt, cancelled check, or charge slip showing the amount and proof of payment is needed, except for expenses under $25.

  2. **Log or diary.** Also required is a log or diary showing the:

     - ☐ Business purpose or benefit of the expense.

     - ☐ Names and business relationships of all the individuals entertained or met on the trip.

     - ☐ Cost of the travel or entertainment.

     - ☐ Dates of the travel or entertainment. If meal precedes or follows an actual business discussion, the date and length of the business deduction.

     - ☐ Place the expenses were incurred. The name of the city and location of the entertainment.

- **Automobile.** Documentation is required to show the business mileage, destination, and the business purpose of the trip. Keeping a log in your car is the best way to assure the validity of this information. If your business use of a car is consistent from month to month, and you have a way of showing this, you may use records for a portion of the year to report usage for the entire year. If you use your own car for business over 50% of the time, you are allowed to prorate your automobile expenses and depreciation for tax purposes. If your business usage is under 50%, you're only allowed to claim the mileage charges.

A "Business Expense Report" is provided at the end of this section to help keep track of daily expenses. It provides a convenient way to document your travel and entertainment expenses for tax purposes. The section on *Filing & Recordkeeping* in **Administration** explains what other documents are necessary to keep and how long they should be retained.

Ordinary Business Tax Deductions

While business deductions are frequent targets of changes in the tax code, there are still a large number of business deductions available. Many of these deductions are overlooked by new business owners. The following list of deductions, though extensive, doesn't include every possible deduction for every business. Your accountant can advise you of any additional deductions applicable to your business and keep you informed about changes in the tax code that affect deductions.

Accounting and bookkeeping services
Advertising expenses
Automobile expenses (business related)
Bad debts
Bank service charges
Books (business related)
Bonuses to employees
Briefcases
Business development expenses (except for start-up)
Business gifts (within prescribed limits)
Christmas cards (business related)
Cleaning services (office, uniforms, etc.)
Coffee service
Collection expenses
Commissions (sales reps, agents, etc.)
Company picnic or event
Consulting fees
Convention & trade show expenses
Delivery charges
Depreciation of office furniture, fixtures and equipment
Donations (charitable)
Dues (professional or trade associations)
Educational expenses (seminars, books, etc.)
Employee awards
Entertainment (some restrictions)
Equipment lease costs
Equipment purchases (if not depreciated)
Flowers and other temporary decorations
Freight and shipping charges
Home office expenses (with some restrictions)
Insurance premiums: liability, life, health, etc.

Interest (business debt)
IRA and Keogh deposits (some restrictions)
Labor costs (independent contractors)
Legal fees and professional fees
Licenses and permits
Mailing list expenses
Maintenance contracts (equipment)
Membership fee (business related)
Moving expenses
Obsolete inventory
Office furnishings (depreciated)
Office rental
Office supplies
Postage
Product displays
Professional services (artists, writers, etc.)
Refunds
Repairs to equipment
Repairs to office (some restrictions)
Research and development expenses
Safe deposit box
Social security taxes (employer's share)
Stationery and printing
Subscriptions (business periodicals)
Supplies and materials
Tax preparation fee
Taxes (some types)
Telephone and answering service
Tools (necessary for your business)
Travel expenses (some restrictions)
Uniforms (necessary for business)
Utilities
Wages (employees, family members, etc.)

Homebased Business Deductions

If you decide to operate your business from your residence, you can deduct the expenses for the portion of your home or apartment used exclusively for the business. This deduction cannot, however, exceed the business's gross income less all other business expenses. If the expenses involved with your home office or shop, do exceed your net income, the difference may be deducted in future years.

You can also deduct the use your home phone, but be prepared to thoroughly document the business usage for tax purposes. You may also be able to deduct a percentage of your home expenses for gas, electric, and heat as well. Your accountant or tax preparer can advise you on how to compute these deductions for your homebased business.

Expenses You Can't Deduct

Certain expenses cannot be deducted on your tax returns because they are specifically disallowed by law. Non-deductible expenses include:

- **A nonexclusive home office.** Intermittent use of your home as an office, or use on a part-time basis is not deductible. Even if your home office is used regularly, it isn't deductible unless it is used exclusively for business purposes.

- **Loan repayments.** Since a loan isn't considered income when received, it isn't considered a deductible expense when paid. Interest paid on a business loan is deductible however.

- **Payments to yourself.** The exception to this is if your business is incorporated and you are paid a salary by the corporation.

- **Federal taxes.** State income taxes are, however, deductible on your federal returns.

- **Commuting expenses.** Getting to your place of business from home isn't deductible, but other business travel generally is.

- **Fines for legal violations.** Parking tickets, even received during the course of business, cannot be deducted.

- **Other non-deductible expenses.** Clothing (suitable for wearing outside of work), meals at work (unless entertaining clients or prospects), and expenses unrelated or unnecessary to your business.

It comes as surprise to new business owners that many of the expenses they incur when starting up their business are not immediately deductible. Instead of being deducted, start-up expenses are amortized, or spread out, over the first sixty months of business. Ask your accountant for more specific guidance about which expenses are considered as part of your start-up costs.

"The difference between death and taxes is that death doesn't get worse every time Congress meets."

How to Cut Your Tax Bill

Although tax evasion is illegal and is severely punished, reducing your tax bill is not only legal, it is the mark of an astute business person. Tax laws are designed to stimulate or discourage certain activities, so when a deduction or opportunity exists, you are entitled to take it. If you don't, it might not be available the next year.

Tax laws are constantly changing, with Congress making a new "overhaul" of the tax laws every couple of years. Things change so fast that a recent survey indicated that over 40% of the information given out by IRS employees to assist taxpayers was wrong. So while the information in this section is the best currently available, it is bound to change.

Even after the last "tax reform" there are still some ways to cut your taxes legally. But bear in mind that these too are subject to change at some later session of Congress. Here are some of the tax-saving strategies that could be of benefit to you:

■ **Accelerated cost recovery.** Business property is given a depreciation class based on its "useful life," which the government sets for different kinds of property. The accelerated cost recovery program (called MACRS) allows you to deduct the cost of the equipment faster than would be allowable under a depreciation method that deducts the same amount each year.

■ **Expensing equipment.** Current law allows a business to expense (deduct) the cost of most types of equipment up to $10,000 per year instead of depreciating it over the life of the equipment. This amount begins to decrease, however, as equipment purchases exceed $200,000. This is referred to as a Section 179 election.

■ **Plan year-end equipment purchases.** For the best depreciation allowances, major equipment purchases should be made before the end of the third quarter. If at least 60% of your depreciable equipment is bought in the first nine months of your tax year, you can deduct the equivalent of six months depreciation; if not, you will lose a month or two of the depreciation deductions.

■ **Pay or accrue next year's expenses this year.** If you know you are going to be making large expenditures right after the beginning of the new year, either purchase and pay for them (if you are operating on a cash basis), or enter into contracts to purchase and accrue (if you are operating on an accrual basis) as many of them as you can before the end of the year. This allows you to take the deductions in the current year.

Accelerated Cost Recovery Example

Let's assume you purchased a computer system in May and that you are a calendar year taxpayer. The system had a total purchase price of $4,756.

Under the MACRS depreciation method the cost of this asset will be recovered (depreciated) over 60 months (covered by 6 tax years) according to the following schedule*:

Year	Percent	Amount
Year 1	20.00%	$ 951.20
Year 2	32.00%	$ 1,521.92
Year 3	19.20%	$ 913.15
Year 4	11.52%	$ 547.89
Year 5	11.52%	$ 547.89
Year 6	5.76%	$ 273.95
Total	100.00%	$ 4,756.00

By using the MACRS depreciation method you are able to deduct the entire cost of the asset (less any potential value at the end of 60 months) from your tax return. Assuming an average federal tax rate of 30% these deductions will reduce your tax bill by $1,427, and lower the actual cost of this computer system from $4,756 to $3,329.

*This assumes that you have not elected to take the Section 179 election explained above.

Tips for Using the Following Forms:

Note: You are encouraged to copy these forms for your own use. Keep the unmarked originals in a safe place and make copies of them to work from.

Key Tax and Regulatory Requirements – To give you a convenient way to see all the requirements in one place, this form lists the tax and key regulatory items required of a small business. The first part of the form has the requirements for every business; the second part has those requirements added when the first employee is hired. The other parts of the form show the additional requirements when specific numbers of employees are hired. Check off each requirement as you complete it. Cross off any items that don't apply to your situation. Using this form will help prevent you from getting entangled with the bureaucracy due to neglecting any of the necessary requirements.

Federal Tax Calendar – This handy guide shows you when federal taxes are due so you can avoid late payments and penalties. It shows the filing dates for all the different taxes along with the types of business they apply to. Keep it in a convenient place so you don't miss any filing deadlines. The other side of this form explains the point at which the taxes must be deposited, and which activities are subject to excise taxes.

Business Expense Report – Use this form to keep track of your automobile, travel, and entertainment expenses. The upper part of the Daily Expense Record portion of the form is for recording your daily business mileage. Below the mileage information are spaces for other daily expenses. Add each day's expenses and show the totals in the spaces provided. At the end of the week add the daily totals to get the weekly total and put it in the space shown. For any entertainment expenses, enter all the information asked for in the Entertainment Detail portion of the form. Keeping this form current will give you the documentation you need to back up your tax deductions for these items.

IRS Publication & Form Request - Use this form to order IRS publications regarding topics of interest to small businesses and the forms needed to help you meet your business tax obligations.

IRS Form SS-4 and Instructions - This is your Application for Federal Employer Identification Number. Use it before hiring your first employee. Complete instructions accompany the form.

Required of all businesses

General

- Federal Estimated Taxes
- Federal Income Tax Returns
- State and/or Local Income Taxes
- Application for Federal I.D. Number (Form SS-4) [Partnership & Corporation]
- Form 1099 Information Returns

- Local Business License
- State Sales and Use Tax Permit & Returns [if selling tangible property]
- Fictitious Business Name Statement [if using fictitious name]
- Registration as employer with state [most states]

Required when first employee is added (in addition to above)

General

- Application for Federal I.D. Number (Form SS-4) [Sole Proprietorship]
- Payroll Tax Returns (Federal)
- File and provide W-2s to employees
- Complete INS Form I-9 for each new hire
- State Fair Employment laws [many states]
- Federal and state child labor laws
- Federal wage and hour regulations and laws
- State wage and hour regulations and laws
- Workers' Compensation Insurance required

Federal Fair Employment laws

- Equal Pay Act [equal pay for women]
- No discrimination in federal contracts
- Posting of other non-discrimination notices by some federal contractors

OSHA - Job Safety Regulations

- Health and Safety Regulations
- Posting of Job Safety and Health Notices
- Posting of Employee Rights Notice [regarding OSHA]
- Reporting fatalities or multiple injuries to OSHA

ERISA - For employees' pension or profit-sharing plan

- Provide Summary Plan Description to employees
- File Summary Plan Description with Department of Labor
- File Form 5500-C or 5500-R Annual Report
- Provide Summary Annual Report to employees
- File and provide to employees Summary of Material Plan Modifications
- File Termination Report [if plan terminated]
- Bonding requirement for plan officials

ERISA - For unfunded or insured employee "welfare" plans

- Provide Summary Plan Description to employees

ERISA - For funded employee "welfare" plans

- Provide Summary Plan Description to employees
- File Summary Plan Description
- File Form 5500 Annual Report
- Provide Summary Annual Report to employees
- File and provide to employees Summary of Material Plan Modifications
- File Termination Report [if plan is terminated]

Required when eleventh employee is added (in addition to above)

Federal Fair Employment laws

- No discrimination on account of race, color, religion or sex, etc.
- Post notice regarding non-discrimination OSHA - Job Safety Regulations
- Log of industrial illnesses and injuries

Required when twentieth employee is added (in addition to above)

Federal Fair Employment laws

- Age discrimination laws
- Post notice regarding age non-discrimination

Required when hundredeth employee is added (in addition to above)

Federal Fair Employment laws

- File Form EEO-1

ERISA - For unfunded and insured employee "welfare" plans:

- File Summary Plan Description
- File Form 5500 Annual Report
- Provide Summary Annual Report to employees
- File and provide to employees Summary of Material Plan Modifications
- File Termination Report [if plan is terminated]

ERISA - For employees' pension or profit-sharing plan

- File Form 5500 Annual Report

FEDERAL TAX CALENDAR

Date	Tax Payment or Return Required	Form	Type of Organization			
			Sole Prop.	Partner-ship	C Corp.	S Corp.
Jan. 15 *	Federal Income - Estimate, 4th installment	1040ES	xx	xx		
Jan. 31	Distribute W-2s to employees	W-2	xx	xx	xx	xx
Jan. 31 **	Federal Withholding Return	941	xx	xx	xx	xx
Jan. 31 **	Federal Unemployment Tax (FUTA)	940	xx	xx	xx	xx
Jan. 31	Distribute Information Returns (1099)	1099	xx	xx	xx	xx
Feb. 28	Submit W-2's to IRS	W-3	xx	xx	xx	xx
Feb. 28	Submit Information Returns (1099) to IRS	1099	xx	xx	xx	xx
Mar. 15 *	Annual Tax Return	1120 or 1120-A			xx	
Mar. 15 *	Annual Tax Return	1120S				xx
Apr. 15 *	Federal Income - Estimate, 1st installment	1040ES	xx	xx		
Apr. 15 *	Federal Income - Estimate, 1st Installment	1120-W			xx	
Apr. 15	Annual Tax Return	Sch. C, Form 1040	xx			
Apr. 15 *	Annual Tax Return	Form 1065		xx		
Apr. 15	Self Employment Tax	Sch. SE, Form 1040	xx	xx		
Apr. 30 **	Federal Withholding Return	941	xx	xx	xx	xx
Jun. 15 *	Federal Income - Estimate, 2nd installment	1040ES	xx	xx		
Jun. 15 *	Federal Income - Estimate, 2nd Installment	1120-W			xx	
Jul. 31 **	Federal Withholding Return	941	xx	xx	xx	xx
Sep. 15 *	Federal Income - Estimate, 3rd installment	1040ES	xx	xx		
Sep. 15 *	Federal Income - Estimate, 3rd Installment	1120-W			xx	
Oct. 31 **	Federal Withholding Return	941	xx	xx	xx	xx
Dec. 15 *	Federal Income - Estimate, 4th Installment	1120-W			xx	
Various	Federal Excise Taxes	Various	See table on reverse			

Extensions available (tax must still be paid on original due date)						
Apr. 15	Annual Tax Return (extends 4 months)	4868	xx			
Apr. 15 *	Annual Tax Return (extends 3 months)	8736		xx		
Mar. 15 *	Annual Tax Return (extends 6 months)	7004			xx	
Mar. 15 *	Annual Tax Return (extends 6 months)	7004				xx

* Dates are for calender year taxpayers, if you have selected a different tax year, please adjust the dates according to their occurrence in your tax year. For example, a July 31 date is the last day of the 7th month of the tax year. So if your tax year begins in May that date would become November 30.

** See table on reverse for deposit requirements

Note: Any filing falling due on a Saturday, Sunday or holiday is due on the next date that is not a Saturday, Sunday or holiday.

Continued on other side

FICA, Medicare & Federal Income Tax Withholding

If total liability is:	Then:
less than $500 per quarter	No deposit required Remit payment with return (Form 941)
Monthly depositors	Deposit required by 15th of month following withholding from employees.
Semi-weekly depositors: Paydays: Wednesday, Thursday, Friday Paydays: Saturday, Sunday, Monday	 Deposit the following Wednesday Deposit the following Friday

Generally users of this book will be monthly depositors or fall into the under $500 exemption.
To be monthly depositor your withholding tax liability for the prior four quarters must be less than $50,000.
Once you are established as a depositor the IRS should notify you of your required payment frequency.

Federal Umemployment Tax (FUTA)

If total liability is:	Then:
over $100 for any quarter, or cumulative with any preceeding quarter(s)	deposit required (Form 8109), on last day of month following quarter end

Federal Excise taxes

If your business is engaged in the manufacturing, distribution or sale of any of the items listed below, it MAY be liable for excise taxes. If your product is on this list obtain IRS Publication 510 to determine what, if any, liability you may have.

Petroleum.crude oil and gasoline	Sport fishing equipment
Coal	Bows and arrows
Chemicals	Firearms, shells and cartridges
Toll or local telephone service	Tires
Teletypewriter exchange service	Highway use - trucking companies
Air transportation	Alcholic beverages

Information current as of government publications issued January 1993.

BUSINESS EXPENSE REPORT

Name: _____   Week of: _____

Daily Expense Record

	Day	Monday	Tuesday	Wednesday	Thursday	Friday	Saturday	Sunday
	Date	/ /	/ /	/ /	/ /	/ /	/ /	/ /
Beginning Mileage								
Ending Mileage								
Total Miles Driven								
Gas / Service								
Parking / Tolls								
Car rental / Cab / Bus								
Lodging								
Breakfast								
Lunch								
Dinner								
Laundry								
Phone								
Tips								
Other:								
Other:								
Entertainment (below)								
Daily Total								
Total for Week								

Entertainment Detail

Date	Item	Person Entertained & Business Relationship	Location & Place Name	Business Purpose	Amount

Purpose of travel: _____   Signature: _____

_____   Date: _____

_____

The bottom half of this page is a duplicate of the IRS's form for ordering tax forms, instructions and publications.

These publications can be used to supplement the information in the *Taxes* section of **The New American Business System**.

The forms listed to the right are the most useful for a new or small business.

Mail completed form to:

**Forms Distribution Center
Rancho Cordova, CA 95743-0001**

Commonly Used IRS Business Publications

Publication Number	Subject
15	Employer's Tax Guide (Circular E)
17	Your Federal Income Tax
334	Tax Guide for Small Business
463	Travel, Entertainment, and Gift Expenses
505	Tax Withholding and Estimated Tax
509	Tax Calendar
533	Self-Employment Tax
534	Depreciation
535	Business Expenses
538	Accounting Periods and Methods
541	Tax Information on Partnerships
542	Tax Information on Corporations
583	Taxpayers Starting a Business
587	Business Use of Your Home
589	Tax Information On S Corporations
910	Guide to Free Tax Services
917	Business Use of a Car
937	Business Reporting (Employment Taxes and Information Returns

Detach at this Line

Order Blank- We will send you 2 copies of each form and 1 copy of each set of instructions or publication you circle. Please cut the order blank on the line above and be sure to print or type your name and address accurately on the bottom portion. This will be the label used to return material to you. Enclose this order blank in your own envelope and address your envelope to the IRS address shown above. To help reduce waste, please order only the forms, instructions, and publications you think you will need to prepare your return. Use the blank spaces to order items not listed. If you need more space attach a separate sheet of paper listing the additional forms and publications you may need. Be sure to allow 2 weeks to receive your order.

1040	Schedules A & B (1040)	Schedule SE (1040)	Pub. 15	Pub. 533	Pub. 583	
Instructions for 1040 & Schedules	Schedule C (1040)		Pub. 17	Pub. 534	Pub. 587	
1040A			Pub. 334	Pub. 535	Pub. 589	
			Pub. 463	Pub. 538	Pub. 910	
			Pub. 505	Pub. 541	Pub. 917	
			Pub. 509	Pub. 542	Pub. 937	

Internal Revenue Service

Name

Number and Street

City or town, State, and ZIP Code

Please print legibly. This is your address label.

Application for Employer Identification Number

(For use by employers and others. Please read the attached instructions before completing this form.)

EIN

OMB No. 1545-0003
Expires 4-30-94

Please type or print clearly.

1 Name of applicant (True legal name) (See instructions.)

2 Trade name of business, if different from name in line 1

3 Executor, trustee, "care of" name

4a Mailing address (street address) (room, apt., or suite no.)

5a Address of business (See instructions.)

4b City, state, and ZIP code

5b City, state, and ZIP code

6 County and state where principal business is located

7 Name of principal officer, grantor, or general partner (See instructions.) ▶

8a Type of entity (Check only one box.) (See instructions.)

☐ Individual SSN _____
☐ REMIC   ☐ Personal service corp.
☐ State/local government   ☐ National guard
☐ Other nonprofit organization (specify) _____
☐ Other (specify) ▶ _____

☐ Estate
☐ Plan administrator SSN _____
☐ Other corporation (specify) _____
☐ Federal government/military ☐ Church or church controlled organization
If nonprofit organization enter GEN (if applicable) _____

☐ Trust
☐ Partnership
☐ Farmers' cooperative

8b If a corporation, give name of foreign country (if applicable) or state in the U.S. where incorporated ▶

Foreign country

State

9 Reason for applying (Check only one box.)

☐ Started new business
☐ Hired employees
☐ Created a pension plan (specify type) ▶
☐ Banking purpose (specify) ▶

☐ Changed type of organization (specify) ▶ _____
☐ Purchased going business
☐ Created a trust (specify) ▶ _____
☐ Other (specify) ▶

10 Date business started or acquired (Mo., day, year) (See instructions.)

11 Enter closing month of accounting year. (See instructions.)

12 First date wages or annuities were paid or will be paid (Mo., day, year). **Note:** If applicant is a withholding agent, enter date income will first be paid to nonresident alien. (Mo., day, year) · · · · · · · · · · · · · ▶

13 Enter highest number of employees expected in the next 12 months. **Note:** If the applicant does not expect to have any employees during the period, enter "0." · · · · · · · ▶

Nonagricultural	Agricultural	Household

14 Principal activity (See instructions.) ▶

15 Is the principal business activity manufacturing?
If "Yes," principal product and raw material used ▶

☐ Yes   ☐ No

16 To whom are most of the products or services sold? Please check the appropriate box.   ☐ Business (wholesale)
☐ Public (retail)   ☐ Other (specify) ▶   ☐ N/A

17a Has the applicant ever applied for an identification number for this or any other business? · · · · · · · · · ☐ Yes   ☐ No
Note: If "Yes," please complete lines 17b and 17c.

17b If you checked the "Yes" box in line 17a, give applicant's true name and trade name, if different than name shown on prior application.

True name ▶   Trade name ▶

17c Enter approximate date, city, and state where the application was filed and the previous employer identification number if known.

Approximate date when filed (Mo., day, year)	City and state where filed	Previous EIN

Under penalties of perjury, I declare that I have examined this application, and to the best of my knowledge and belief, it is true, correct, and complete

Telephone number (include area code)

Name and title (Please type or print clearly.) ▶

Signature ▶   Date ▶

Note: Do not write below this line.   For official use only.

Please leave blank ▶	Geo.	Ind.	Class	Size	Reason for applying

For Paperwork Reduction Act Notice, see attached instructions.   Cat. No. 16055N   Form **SS-4** (Rev. 4-91)

General Instructions

(Section references are to the Internal Revenue Code unless otherwise noted.)

Paperwork Reduction Act Notice.—We ask for the information on this form to carry out the Internal Revenue laws of the United States. You are required to give us this information. We need it to ensure that you are complying with these laws and to allow us to figure and collect the right amount of tax.

The time needed to complete and file this form will vary depending on individual circumstances. The estimated average time is:

Recordkeeping	7 min.
Learning about the law or the form	21 min.
Preparing the form	42 min.
Copying, assembling, and sending the form to IRS	20 min.

If you have comments concerning the accuracy of these time estimates or suggestions for making this form more simple, we would be happy to hear from you. You can write to both the **Internal Revenue Service,** Washington, DC 20224, Attention: IRS Reports Clearance Officer, T:FP; and the **Office of Management and Budget,** Paperwork Reduction Project (1545-0003), Washington, DC 20503. **DO NOT** send the tax form to either of these offices. Instead, see **Where To Apply.**

Purpose.—Use Form SS-4 to apply for an employer identification number (EIN). The information you provide on this form will establish your filing requirements.

Who Must File.—You must file this form if you have not obtained an EIN before and

• You pay wages to one or more employees.

• You are required to have an EIN to use on any return, statement, or other document, even if you are not an employer.

• You are required to withhold taxes on income, other than wages, paid to a nonresident alien (individual, corporation, partnership, etc.). For example, individuals who file **Form 1042,** Annual Withholding Tax Return for U.S. Source Income of Foreign Persons, to report alimony paid to nonresident aliens must have EINs.

Individuals who file **Schedule C,** Profit or Loss From Business, or **Schedule F,** Profit or Loss From Farming, of **Form 1040,** U.S. Individual Income Tax Return, must use EINs if they have a Keogh plan or are required to file excise, employment, or alcohol, tobacco, or firearms returns.

The following must use EINs even if they do not have any employees:

• Trusts, except an IRA trust, unless the IRA trust is required to file **Form 990-T,** Exempt Organization Business Income Tax Return, to report unrelated business taxable income or is filing Form 990-T to obtain a refund of the credit from a regulated investment company.

• Estates

• Partnerships

• REMICS (real estate mortgage investment conduits)

• Corporations

• Nonprofit organizations (churches, clubs, etc.)

• Farmers' cooperatives

• Plan administrators

New Business.—If you become the new owner of an existing business, **DO NOT** use the EIN of the former owner. If you already have an EIN, use that number. If you do not have an EIN, apply for one on this form. If you become the "owner" of a corporation by acquiring its stock, use the corporation's EIN.

If you already have an EIN, you may need to get a new one if either the organization or ownership of your business changes. If you incorporate a sole proprietorship or form a partnership, you must get a new EIN. However, **DO NOT** apply for a new EIN if you change only the name of your business.

File Only One Form SS-4.—File only one Form SS-4, regardless of the number of businesses operated or trade names under which a business operates. However, each corporation in an affiliated group must file a separate application.

If you do not have an EIN by the time a return is due, write "Applied for" and the date you applied in the space shown for the number. **DO NOT** show your social security number as an EIN on returns.

If you do not have an EIN by the time a tax deposit is due, send your payment to the Internal Revenue service center for your filing area. (See **Where To Apply** below.) Make your check or money order payable to Internal Revenue Service and show your name (as shown on Form SS-4), address, kind of tax, period covered, and date you applied for an EIN.

For more information about EINs, see **Pub. 583,** Taxpayers Starting a Business.

How To Apply.—You can apply for an EIN either by mail or by telephone. You can get an EIN immediately by calling the Tele-TIN phone number for the service center for your state, or you can send the completed Form SS-4 directly to the service center to receive your EIN in the mail.

Application by Tele-TIN.—The Tele-TIN program is designed to assign EINs by telephone. Under this program, you can receive your EIN over the telephone and use it immediately to file a return or make a payment.

To receive an EIN by phone, complete Form SS-4, then call the Tele-TIN phone number listed for your state under **Where To Apply.** The person making the call must be authorized to sign the form (see **Signature block** on page 3).

An IRS representative will use the information from the Form SS-4 to establish your account and assign you an EIN. Write the number you are given on the upper right-hand corner of the form, sign and date it, and promptly mail it to the Tele-TIN Unit at the service center address for your state.

Application by mail.—Complete Form SS-4 at least 4 to 5 weeks before you will need an EIN. Sign and date the application and mail it to the service center address for your state. You will receive your EIN in the mail in approximately 4 weeks.

Note: *The Tele-TIN phone numbers listed below will involve a long-distance charge to callers outside of the local calling area, and should only be used to apply for an EIN. Use 1-800-829-1040 to ask about an application by mail.*

Where To Apply.—

If your principal business, office or agency, or legal residence in the case of an individual, is located in: ▼	Call the Tele-TIN phone number shown or file with the Internal Revenue service center at: ▼
Florida, Georgia, South Carolina	Atlanta, GA 39901 (404) 455-2360
New Jersey, New York City and counties of Nassau, Rockland, Suffolk, and Westchester	Holtsville, NY 00501 (516) 447-4955
New York (all other counties), Connecticut, Maine, Massachusetts, New Hampshire, Rhode Island, Vermont	Andover, MA 05501 (508) 474-9717
Illinois, Iowa, Minnesota, Missouri, Wisconsin	Kansas City, MO 64999 (816) 926-5999
Delaware, District of Columbia, Maryland, Pennsylvania, Virginia	Philadelphia, PA 19255 (215) 961-3980
Indiana, Kentucky, Michigan, Ohio, West Virginia	Cincinnati, OH 45999 (606) 292-5467
Kansas, New Mexico, Oklahoma, Texas	Austin, TX 73301 (512) 462-7845
Alaska, Arizona, California (counties of Alpine, Amador, Butte, Calaveras, Colusa, Contra Costa, Del Norte, El Dorado, Glenn, Humboldt, Lake, Lassen, Marin, Mendocino, Modoc, Napa, Nevada, Placer, Plumas, Sacramento, San Joaquin, Shasta, Sierra, Siskiyou, Solano, Sonoma, Sutter, Tehama, Trinity, Yolo, and Yuba), Colorado, Idaho, Montana, Nebraska, Nevada, North Dakota, Oregon, South Dakota, Utah, Washington, Wyoming	Ogden, UT 84201 (801) 625-7645
California (all other counties), Hawaii	Fresno, CA 93888 (209) 456-5900
Alabama, Arkansas, Louisiana, Mississippi, North Carolina, Tennessee	Memphis, TN 37501 (901) 365-5970

If you have no legal residence, principal place of business, or principal office or agency in any Internal Revenue District, file your form with the Internal Revenue Service Center, Philadelphia, PA 19255 or call (215) 961-3980.

Specific Instructions

The instructions that follow are for those items that are not self-explanatory. Enter N/A (nonapplicable) on the lines that do not apply.

Line 1.—Enter the legal name of the entity applying for the EIN.

Individuals.—Enter the first name, middle initial, and last name.

Trusts.—Enter the name of the trust.

Estate of a decedent.—Enter the name of the estate.

Partnerships.—Enter the legal name of the partnership as it appears in the partnership agreement.

Corporations.—Enter the corporate name as set forth in the corporation charter or other legal document creating it.

Plan administrators.—Enter the name of the plan administrator. A plan administrator who already has an EIN should use that number.

Line 2.—Enter the trade name of the business if different from the legal name.

Note: *Use the full legal name entered on line 1 on all tax returns to be filed for the entity. However, if a trade name is entered on line 2, use only the name on line 1 **or** the name on line 2 consistently when filing tax returns.*

Line 3.—Trusts enter the name of the trustee. Estates enter the name of the executor, administrator, or other fiduciary. If the entity applying has a designated person to receive tax information, enter that person's name as the "care of" person. Print or type the first name, middle initial, and last name.

Lines 5a and 5b.—If the physical location of the business is different from the mailing address (lines 4a and 4b), enter the address of the physical location on lines 5a and 5b.

Line 7.—Enter the first name, middle initial, and last name of a principal officer if the business is a corporation; of a general partner if a partnership; and of a grantor if a trust.

Line 8a.—Check the box that best describes the type of entity that is applying for the EIN. If not specifically mentioned, check the "other" box and enter the type of entity. Do not enter N/A.

Individual.—Check this box if the individual files Schedule C or F (Form 1040) and has a Keogh plan or is required to file excise, employment, or alcohol, tobacco, or firearms returns. If this box is checked, enter the individual's SSN (social security number) in the space provided.

Plan administrator.—The term plan administrator means the person or group of persons specified as the administrator by the instrument under which the plan is operated. If the plan administrator is an individual, enter the plan administrator's SSN in the space provided.

New withholding agent.—If you are a new withholding agent required to file Form 1042, check the "other" box and enter in the space provided "new withholding agent."

REMICs.—Check this box if the entity is a real estate mortgage investment conduit (REMIC). A REMIC is any entity

1. To which an election to be treated as a REMIC applies for the tax year and all prior tax years,

2. In which all of the interests are regular interests or residual interests,

3. Which has one class of residual interests (and all distributions, if any, with respect to such interests are pro rata),

4. In which as of the close of the 3rd month beginning after the startup date and at all times thereafter, substantially all of its assets consist of qualified mortgages and permitted investments,

5. Which has a tax year that is a calendar year, and

6. With respect to which there are reasonable arrangements designed to ensure that: (a) residual interests are not held by disqualified organizations (as defined in section 860E(e)(5)), and (b) information necessary for the application of section 860E(e) will be made available.

For more information about REMICs see the Instructions for **Form 1066,** U. S. Real Estate Mortgage Investment Conduit Income Tax Return.

Personal service corporations.—Check this box if the entity is a personal service corporation. An entity is a personal service corporation for a tax year only if

1. The entity is a C corporation for the tax year.

2. The principal activity of the entity during the testing period (as defined in Temporary Regulations section 1.441-4T(f)) for the tax year is the performance of personal service.

3. During the testing period for the tax year, such services are substantially performed by employee-owners.

4. The employee-owners own 10 percent of the fair market value of the outstanding stock in the entity on the last day of the testing period for the tax year.

For more information about personal service corporations, see the instructions to **Form 1120,** U.S. Corporation Income Tax Return, and Temporary Regulations section 1.441-4T.

Other corporations.—This box is for any corporation other than a personal service corporation. If you check this box, enter the type of corporation (such as insurance company) in the space provided.

Other nonprofit organizations.—Check this box if the nonprofit organization is other than a church or church-controlled organization and specify the type of nonprofit organization (for example, an educational organization.)

Group exemption number (GEN).—If the applicant is a nonprofit organization that is a subordinate organization to be included in a group exemption letter under Revenue Procedure 80-27, 1980-1 C.B. 677, enter the GEN in the space provided. If you do not know the GEN, contact the parent organization for it. GEN is a four-digit number. Do not confuse it with the nine-digit EIN.

Line 9.—Check only one box. Do not enter N/A.

Started new business.—Check this box if you are starting a new business that requires an EIN. If you check this box, enter the type of business being started. **DO NOT** apply if you already have an EIN and are only adding another place of business.

Changed type of organization.—Check this box if the business is changing its type of organization, for example, if the business was a sole proprietorship and has been incorporated or has become a partnership. If you check this box, specify in the space provided the type of change made, for example, "from sole proprietorship to partnership."

Purchased going business.—Check this box if you acquired a business through purchase. Do not use the former owner's EIN. If you already have an EIN, use that number.

Hired employees.—Check this box if the existing business is requesting an EIN because it has hired or is hiring employees and is therefore required to file employment tax return for which an EIN is required. **DO NOT** apply if you already have an EIN and are only hiring employees.

Created a trust.—Check this box if you created a trust, and enter the type of trust created.

Created a pension plan.—Check this box if you have created a pension plan and need this number for reporting purposes. Also, enter the type of plan created.

Banking purpose.—Check this box if you are requesting an EIN for banking purpose only and enter the banking purpose (for example, checking, loan, etc.).

Other (specify).—Check this box if you are requesting an EIN for any reason other than those for which there are checkboxes and enter the reason.

Line 10.—If you are starting a new business, enter the starting date of the business. If the business you acquired is already operating, enter the date you acquired the business. Trusts should enter the date the trust was legally created. Estates should enter the date of death of the decedent whose name appears on line 1.

Line 11.—Enter the last month of your accounting year or tax year. An accounting year or tax year is usually 12 consecutive months. It may be a calendar year or a fiscal year (including a period of 52 or 53 weeks). A calendar year is 12 consecutive months ending on December 31. A fiscal year is either 12 consecutive months ending on the last day of any month other than December or a 52-53 week year. For more information

on accounting periods, see **Pub. 538,** Accounting Periods and Methods.

Individuals.—Your tax year generally will be a calendar year.

Partnerships.—Partnerships generally should conform to the tax year of either (1) its majority partners; (2) its principal partners; (3) the tax year that results in the least aggregate deferral of income (see Temporary Regulations section 1.706-1T); or (4) some other tax year, if (a) a business purpose is established for the fiscal year, or (b) the fiscal year is a "grandfather" year, or (c) an election is made under section 444 to have a fiscal year. (See the Instructions for **Form 1065,** U.S. Partnership Return of Income, for more information.)

REMICs.—Remics must have a calendar year as their tax year.

Personal service corporations.—A personal service corporation generally must adopt a calendar year unless:

1. It can establish to the satisfaction of the Commissioner that there is a business purpose for having a different tax year, or

2. It elects under section 444 to have a tax year other than a calendar year.

Line 12.—If the business has or will have employees, enter on this line the date on which the business began or will begin to pay wages to the employees. If the business does not have any plans to have employees, enter N/A on this line.

New withholding agent.—Enter the date you began or will begin to pay income to a nonresident alien. This also applies to individuals who are required to file Form 1042 to report alimony paid to a nonresident alien.

Line 14.—Generally, enter the exact type of business being operated (for example, advertising agency, farm, labor union, real estate agency, steam laundry, rental of coin-operated vending machine, investment club, etc.).

Governmental.—Enter the type of organization (state, county, school district, or municipality, etc.)

Nonprofit organization (other than governmental).—Enter whether organized for religious, educational, or humane purposes, and the principal activity (for example, religious organization—hospital, charitable).

Mining and quarrying.—Specify the process and the principal product (for example, mining bituminous coal, contract drilling for oil, quarrying dimension stone, etc.).

Contract construction.—Specify whether general contracting or special trade contracting. Also, show the type of work normally performed (for example, general contractor for residential buildings, electrical subcontractor, etc.).

Trade.—Specify the type of sales and the principal line of goods sold (for example, wholesale dairy products, manufacturer's representative for mining machinery, retail hardware, etc.).

Manufacturing.—Specify the type of establishment operated (for example, sawmill, vegetable cannery, etc.).

Signature block.—The application must be signed by: (1) the individual, if the person is an individual, (2) the president, vice president, or other principal officer, if the person is a corporation, (3) a responsible and duly authorized member or officer having knowledge of its affairs, if the person is a partnership or other unincorporated organization, or (4) the fiduciary, if the person is a trust or estate.

CASH MANAGEMENT

More Important Than Profit

Cash flow, the amount of cash moving through a business, is the vital element that keeps every business financially healthy. Cash is needed for operating expenses, payroll, and to pay for inventory and materials. At some point in its life, virtually every business will experience cash flow problems, particularly during its early stages. Running out of money indicates serious trouble; failure to manage cash properly is one of the leading causes of small business failure.

In practical terms, cash flow can be more important than profits, as evidenced by the fact that even "profitable" businesses have gone bankrupt because of cash shortages. The reason for this seemingly implausible happening is that profit is determined by accounting methods, and can include such non-cash items as accounts receivable and expenditures for inventory already paid for, but not yet expensed on an income statement or tax return. Cash flow, on the other hand, focuses on the actual amount of cash going into and out of a business.

With cash flow, timing is everything. Even when a company shows a profit on its income statement, it can still have a cash crunch if its bills are due immediately, but its income is in the form of uncollected invoices and inventory that won't generate cash until a later date.

Keys to Cash Management

Cash management is the key to avoiding cash flow problems. For a business to become or remain profitable and competitive, it is essential that its cash flow be managed properly. This means enhancing the flow of cash into the business, and slowing its flow out of the business. And it means planning ahead to anticipate cash needs before they become problems.

Receipts are the monies coming into a business from cash and credit sales. Obviously the more cash sales you have the better for your cash flow. Safeguarding cash on hand and depositing cash receipts daily are good policies for any business that has significant cash receipts. Credit card receipts are similar to cash, in that to receive fastest credit for them, they should be deposited daily or weekly as volume dictates.

Cash sales aren't the chief source of receipts in every business, so it's crucial for a business which receives significant receipts from credit sales to know how to maximize cash flow from accounts receivable. This is an area that causes many problems in small business. These problems arise from loose procedures in one or more of these functions:

Granting Credit. Extending credit often earns you loyal customers who tend to spend more than cash customers. And a customer list is a valuable asset you can use to solicit future sales, and that may be worth money if you ever decide to sell your business. Selling on credit can lead to problems, however, because you can lose money if customers don't pay, your working capital requirements are increased when the money you had to put out to make the sales is due before your customers pay you, and it costs you time and money to prepare invoices and make collections. One way to avoid cash flow problems from your credit sales is to have a credit policy. Ask new customers to fill out a credit application, and be sure to check it out thoroughly. This will help assure that those to whom you extend credit are actually creditworthy. If you sell to other businesses, use the "Trade Credit Application" found at the back of this section. When considering any customer for credit, judge them on the criteria professional lenders use, the four Cs:

- **Credit.** Does TRW show the individual or business owner as having good personal credit? Does Dun & Bradstreet indicate the business has an adequate credit history?

- **Capacity.** Does your customer have cash or other means of payment available? Does their bank report them as having a reasonable account balance?

- **Character.** Is your customer reputable? Does he or she operate a business known and trusted in the community?

- **Collateral.** Does the customer have a cushion to fall back on if cash gets short?

Billing Procedures. If possible, always render an invoice on the day the sale is made. The sooner you bill, the sooner you'll get paid. Business convention sets 30 days from purchase as the normal time invoices are due. In actual practice, however, some customers stretch out payments to 45, 60, 90, and even 120 days. If you specify due dates of 10, 15, or 20 days instead of the customary 30, it may speed up payments. When cash is very tight, consider offering discounts for prompt payment (e.g. 2% for payment in ten days, 5% for prepayment). Though these discounts speed payment, they also decrease profits. Follow customer billing instructions and try to find out the payment cycles of your largest customers to make sure your invoices are received before the deadline. Service businesses that work on a project basis often set up a payment plan, for example, 50% to initiate the contract, then 25% at some specified point, and the final 25% upon completion of the project.

Soon after an account becomes overdue call and request payment.

Collections. Overdue accounts get more difficult to collect as they "age," so take action quickly. While you have over a 98% chance of collecting an invoice when it is due, that percentage drops to less than 75% at ninety days, to around 58% at six months, and down to only about 26% after a year. To encourage prompt payments, it may a good idea to add a monthly late charge of 1.5%, if you can do it without hurting business.

The traditional way to begin the collections process is to send a "past due notice" three to five days after the invoice is due, and if this doesn't work, following up with a succession of more strongly worded letters. Since that approach is somewhat passive, you may find personal phone calls more effective. Three to five days after an invoice is due, call and say something like, "Our records show that we haven't yet received payment for our invoice #1234, dated June 1, for $128.74. Please check on it and tell me when the payment was sent." If they tell you the payment hasn't been sent yet, ask them when it will be. Write down the date they tell you and their name on a follow-up list. Later, if you don't receive the payment when promised, call that person back and find out why. Keep calling every week until you get the money. Use a friendly, but businesslike, tone. Be brief, but firm. Don't accuse or argue; it's better to be calm and insistent.

For some delinquent accounts, more extreme tactics are sometimes required, including collection agencies (whose fees can range from 25 to 50% of the collected amount), small-claims court (where winning still doesn't necessarily guarantee payment), and hiring a lawyer (for large amounts only). Each of these methods can be expensive, time-consuming, or both. Make sure what you can collect is worth the cost and effort. Don't go after someone just "to teach them a lesson." First, make sure that you have a reasonable chance of collecting the money owed you. If not, it could cost you more than it's worth. Use the "Accounts Receivable Journal With Aging" (see *Accounting*) to keep abreast of your receivables.

Cash Flow Problems

When a business runs out of cash, it's almost always due to one of the following problems:

- **Excessive investment in fixed assets.** Real estate, machinery, equipment, and furniture tie up a company's assets because they can't be quickly converted to cash without interfering with business operations. To reduce this problem, purchase only what you need and consider leasing as an option while cash is tight.

- **Receivables out of proportion with sales.** Receivables increasing faster than sales can mean either that collections are lagging, product demand is diminishing, salespeople are selling less, extended credit is being given to encourage orders, or that sales are being made to less creditworthy customers.

- **Poor billing procedures.** The longer it takes to send out invoices, the longer it's going to take to get paid. Incorrect and missent invoices also delay payment. Not including the customer's purchase order number or not following customers' invoicing requirements are other reasons payments aren't made promptly. Issuing prompt, accurate invoices will speed payments back to you.

- **Excessive inventories.** Although inventory is an asset, too much of it can be a real

liability to your business. In the first place, you usually can't deduct its cost from taxable income until you sell it. Idle inventory just doesn't sit there, it also costs money: 20-25% of its value each year has to be added to its cost for storage space, interest on the money borrowed to obtain it, and any losses or damages to it. See the *Inventory* section in **Operations** for ways to manage this important asset.

- **Excessive payables.** Over-spending is often the result of fast growth. A fast growing business has many demands on its cash, often occurring at the same time. Another reason for over-spending is extravagance, or the purchase of non-essentials that don't directly contribute to the growth of the business. New equipment, fancy office furniture and luxurious company cars are frequently purchased before the company's financial condition warrants them, often for status rather than business reasons.

The Old Pro says:

"Creditors have better memories than debtors."

Managing Your Payables

Another way to avoid cash flow problems is to carefully monitor the money your business pays out. For maximum control of cash flow, make sure only one person writes checks. Even in an equal partnership, only one person should have responsibility for paying all the bills.

Paying your bills when due is one of the best ways you have of getting and keeping a good credit rating, but try to time the payment so that the money going out of the business is matched by an money coming in. Plan your outgoing payments to be received on or just before the due date. There's no reason to pay early unless a discount is offered.

If you have sufficient operating cash, pay attention to which bills offer discounts for early payment, and take advantage of these chances to save by paying them in time to get the discounts. A common discount is "2% – 10, net 30." This means that you can deduct 2% of the bill if you pay in 10 days, with the full payment is due within 30 days if you choose not to take the discount. Another good discount to look for is the "prepayment discount" which allows you to deduct a certain percentage, sometimes as much as 5%, of the invoice by paying at the time of your order.

To avoid bad credit, if you do fall behind in your payments, don't hang your head in shame and avoid your creditors. As soon as you see you're going to have difficulty paying any bills, call and explain the situation. Either give them a date when they can expect full payment, or offer to make a partial payment "on account." Then keep your word.

Other Ways to Increase Cash Flow

While accounts payable is a critical part of managing the cash going out of your business, there are other ways to avoid cash shortages:

Leasing. When you need equipment or machinery, consider leasing it instead of buying. Leasing reduces your "up-front" costs, thereby conserving your cash. For tax purposes, the monthly lease payments are deductible as an expense, whereas most equipment purchases are depreciated over many years.

Trade Credit. Whenever possible try to get advantageous terms on your purchases from suppliers. The longer you have to pay for your purchases, the less likely you'll be caught in a pinch. The *Purchasing* section will give you suggestions for negotiating better terms with your suppliers.

Inventory. Don't tie up excessive amounts of your cash in inventories. Keep them as lean as possible. Get rid of slow moving items by cutting their price. If you've got items you can't sell at all, either write them off or donate them for the tax benefits.

Taxes. Don't overpay your estimated taxes. Defer tax payments as long as you can without incurring penalties. File for refunds as soon as you become aware that they're due to you.

Forecasting Cash Flow

Keep a running forecast, updated with your best estimates of your anticipated cash receipts and expenditures to assure you don't run out of cash. Use the "Cash Forecast" and other cash management tools explained in the next section, *Budgeting*.

Notes:

Tips for Using the Following Form:

Note: You are encouraged to copy this form for your own use. Keep the unmarked original in a
safe place and make copies of it to work from.

Trade Credit Application – Before selling
on credit to another business, have a
representative from that company
fill out one of these applications.
When the form is returned to you,
review it. If any of the requested
information is missing, call the
contact back to get the missing
information. Before granting credit,
call and/or write the references to
verify the applicant's good credit
history. Once the applicant becomes
a customer, store the application in
the customer's file.

TRADE CREDIT APPLICATION

General Information   (Please type or print responses to all sections)

Business name _____

Billing address _____   Shipping address _____

City/State/ZIP _____   City/State/ZIP _____

Telephone ( )_____   Telephone ( )_____

Contact person _____   Fed. Tax I.D. _____

Corporation ( )   Partnership ( )   Sole Proprietorship ( )

Years: in business ____   at present location ____

If unincorporated, name(s) of owner(s):

(1) _____   (3) _____

(2) _____   (4) _____

Principal corporate officer _____ Title _____

Trade References

Name	Address/City/State	Phone
(1)		
(2)		
(3)		

Bank Reference

Name	Address/City/State	Phone

Account Number(s)

(1) _____   (2) _____

I am applying for credit in order to facilitate purchases and agree to pay amounts owed when due.

Company: _____

By: _____

Title: _____

Date: _____

BUDGETING

Budgeting and Financial Forecasts are Important

Budgeting is a tool for dealing with the future. It helps you turn expectations into reality. In its simplest form, a budget is a detailed plan of future receipts and expenditures – a projected income (profit and loss) statement. As the budgeted period progresses, you can compare actual results with forecasted goals.

Of course without accurate information, forecasting becomes guessing rather than planning, so it is important to keep forecasts of sales and expenses realistic. There isn't any point in preparing a budget with over-optimistic projections. They won't fool anyone but you, and you should be the last person who wants to be fooled because you'll need accurate forecasts to prepare your business plan, apply for loans, and most importantly, to keep your business on target.

You need accurate forecasts to keep your business on track.

How To Prepare An Accurate Forecast (Budget)

An owner who has been in business a while can use the financial figures from previous years to make forecasts. A new business owner, however, doesn't have these figures, and so must look to other sources for information on which to base reasonable assumptions.

Approximate operating expenses can be determined with a little investigation. Check with commercial real estate agents to find out the typical rental rates for business space similar to what you'll need. Talk with other business owners in the vicinity to learn about the costs for utilities, local taxes, and trash removal. Your local telephone company can provide accurate estimates for telephone installation and monthly charges.

Most fields have trade or professional organizations that can provide industry averages for both income and expenses (see **Resources** for other organizations that provide this data). You can also check at your local library for statistics compiled by various government agencies. Tidbits of information about local competitors can also be found in articles about them appearing in local newspapers.

Preparing a budget may seem like a complicated and difficult process, but it doesn't have to be. If you view it as step-by-process, and work on just one part at a time, you won't be overwhelmed by the total task. Just follow these steps to prepare a budget for your business:

1. **Sales.** Start by forecasting your expected sales using the "Sales Forecast" included at the end of this section. Base this forecast on realistic figures for a start-up and be sure to check them against industry averages. If your estimate is significantly different, be sure to find out why.

2. **Staffing.** Use the "Staffing Planner" from *Personnel* to help you determine what staff will be needed to handle this level of sales. Include sales staff as well as production and support staff. And don't forget to include yourself.

3. **Expenses.** Determine the expenses associated with operating your business by using the "Projected Expense Budget & Capital Expenditures" found at the end of this section. Typical expenses will include:

   - Payroll and related expenses (from "Staffing Planner")

   - Advertising expenditures (from "Advertising Placement Planner" in *Promotion*)

   - Rent (from "Site Selection Worksheet" in *Facilities*)

   - Telephone & utilities

   - Insurance and banking from "Insurance Worksheet" (in *Insurance*) and "Bank Comparison Worksheet" (in *Banking*)

   - Legal, accounting, and consulting services

   - Travel and entertainment

   - Membership dues, subscriptions and supplies

   - Other items.

4. **Equipment.** Using the "Equipment & Supplies Needed Worksheet" (from *Equipment*), determine capital expenditures for any necessary equipment and record them

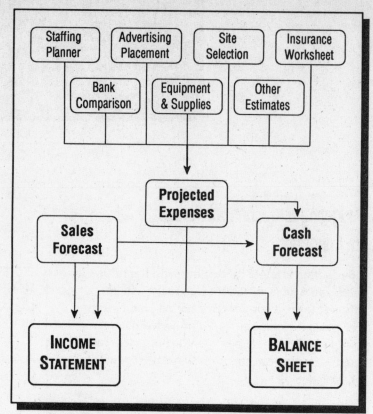

How the forms found in this manual provide information to each other that allows you to create an accurate forecast.

on the Capital Expenditures portion of the "Projected Expense Budget & Capital Expenditures." Be sure to include:

- Computers
- Software
- Office furniture
- Store fixtures
- And all other equipment and machinery mentioned on the "Equipment & Supplies Needed Worksheet."

5. **Cash Forecast.** Go to the "Cash Forecast" at the end of this section, and transfer to it the sales and expense figures from the "Sales Forecast" and the "Projected Expense Budget & Capital Expenditures." Include purchases of goods and materials for resale. Then:

   a. Enter opening cash on hand.

   b. Calculate cash position over planning period.

   c. Determine how much cash you need to obtain, if any, to finance your start-up.

6. **Income Statement.** Go to "Projected Income Statement" (also called a Projected Profit & Loss Statement) at the end of this section, and

   a. Transfer sales and expense information from the "Sales Forecast" and "Projected Expense Budget & Capital Expenditures."

   b. Compute depreciation by dividing total capital expenditures by 60 then enter the result under each month. This assumes five years (60 months) as the depreciable life of the equipment. While this is adequate for budgeting purposes, your accountant can determine the actual depreciation for tax purposes.

   c. Calculate operating income.

7. **Balance Sheet.** Go to "Projected Balance Sheet" at the end of this section, and

   a. Obtain cash balance from "Cash Forecast."

   b. Estimate accounts receivable based on expected credit sales.

   c. Estimate inventory based on the amounts needed to cover sales and necessary stock on hand.

   d. Obtain equipment, vehicle, and furniture and fixtures balances from the Capital Expenditures portion of the "Projected Expense Budget & Capital Expenditures."

   e. Enter depreciation (see 6b above).

   f. Estimate accounts payable based on expected credit purchases.

   g. Obtain short-term loan balance from "Cash Forecast."

   h. Estimate any long-term (over one year) obligations.

   i. Calculate owner's equity by subtracting total liabilities from total assets.

> The Old Pro says: *"If you don't understand the need for budgeting and forecasting, you don't have enough experience to be starting a business."*

> *"A budget is nothing more or less than a quantified list of assumptions or expectations."*
>
> Paul Resnick, Author
> *The Small Business Bible*

Budgeting Tips And Reminders

■ In preparing budgets it is better to err on the conservative side, and to be surprised by an excess of funds rather than have to deal with an empty bank account. As mentioned earlier, one of the best ways to ensure reasonable estimates is to check them against industry norms.

■ If possible, use a computer spreadsheet for budgeting. It will allow you to make changes more easily and see their impact immediately. You can test different assumptions to see what results they'd have on your business. See the *Equipment* section for suggestions on which programs are available.

■ A properly prepared budget gives you a tool for controlling your business. Once you've completed the budget, break it down into quarters. During the year, use the quarterly divisions to monitor expenses. Next quarter's budget can help you schedule stock purchases and staffing to handle anticipated peak periods; and to plan vacations, special promotions, and inventory taking during expected slow periods.

■ Quarterly income statements allow you to compare actual results with those forecasted, so you can pinpoint problem areas for that quarter and deal with them before they get out of control. That's why you should use this proven management technique in your business.

Tips for Using the Following Forms:

Note: You are encouraged to copy these forms for your own use. Keep the unmarked originals in a safe place and make copies of them to work from.

Sales Forecast – The top part of the form is designed for the first year's forecast. In the left hand column list each source of income from the sale of your products or services. Then in each of the monthly columns enter the amount of sales you estimate for that month from each source. Most businesses will have only one or two major sources of sales: a clothing store, for instance, may have only one source of sales – its merchandise; on the other hand, a beauty parlor will have two sources – its services and the sale of beauty products. Add up each column, deducting an allowance for any returns, to provide the Total Net Sales per month. Use the spaces in the lower part of the form to make quarterly estimates for the following two years.

Projected Expense Budget & Capital Expenditures – The upper part of this form contains the Projected Expense Budget. Estimate your monthly expenses in each of the categories shown. Use the other forms ("Staffing Planner," etc.) mentioned to obtain estimates. For the expenses that are not contained on a particular form, make estimates on your own. Your telephone company representative can give you a good idea of your monthly phone bill, and you can ask your accountant for an approximation of the year's accounting fees and when they'll be due. Adding down each monthly column gives the Total Operating Expenses for each month. Adding each item across gives the Total Annual Expenses for that item. At the bottom of the form are the

Capital Expenditures, which can be obtained from the "Equipment & Supplies Needed Worksheet" found in *Equipment*. For each piece of equipment, place its cost in the column under the month when you plan to acquire it. The back of the form provides space for quarterly estimates for the following two years.

Cash Forecast – At the top part of the form under Receipts, enter the figures from the "Sales Forecast." Then under Expenditures, place the figures from the "Projected Expense Budget & Capital Expenditures." Your accountant can help you estimate the amount of taxes and their due dates for your estimated sales (it varies depending on the legal structure of your business). Under Items Bought for Resale, enter the amount of money expected to be paid out each month for merchandise (finished goods) and materials (necessary for manufacture) intended for resale. Do the arithmetic indicated on lines 16 through 18. Use line 19 to enter any borrowed or invested capital that will put into the business during any given month. Put the amount of cash you're starting with on line 20. Add line 18 through 20 and put the Ending Cash Position on line 21. Then place that figure on line 20 of the next month as the Beginning Cash Balance for that month. Negative numbers on line 18 indicate that cash, either from your cash balance or from loans and investments, is needed to supplement your receipts. Simply put, it means your business is spending more money than it is making, which is common among new businesses. If line 21 is ever a negative number, it means the business is out of cash and some sort of financing is needed. This is how the "Cash Forecast" can prevent serious problems by alerting you to potential problems before they occur. The back of the form provides space for quarterly estimates for the following two years.

Projected Income Statement – Enter the Net Sales for each month from the "Sales Forecast." Under Cost of Goods Sold, add any inventory purchased that month to the value of the Beginning Inventory. Then subtract the value of the Ending Inventory, which will give you the Cost of Goods Sold. An alternative approach to determining Cost of Goods Sold is to multiply the number of units sold of a product by the cost per unit. This can be a simpler approach for a single product company. Subtracting Cost of Goods Sold from Total Revenue gives the Gross Margin. Next enter the expenses from the "Projected Expense Budget & Capital Expenditures." The computed depreciation (as explained in the discussion of the Income Statement in 6b above) is then entered for each month. Both these numbers are then added to obtain the Total Operating Expense. Subtracting this figure from the Gross Margin gives the Operating Income. The back of the form provides space for quarterly estimates for the following two years.

Projected Balance Sheet – Under Current Assets, enter the cash from the "Cash Forecast." Estimate the monthly accounts receivable from expected credit sales. Take the inventory figure from the "Start-Up Inventory Planner." Under Fixed Assets, transfer the figures for fixed assets from the Capital Expenditures portion of the "Projected Expense Budget & Capital Expenditures." Subtract the Accumulated Depreciation (which is the value previously computed in 6b above added to the prior period's Accumulated Depreciation) from the Total Fixed Assets to determine the Net Fixed Assets. Estimate your Accounts Payable based on projected credit purchases, your Taxes Payable based on estimates of payroll taxes, state sales taxes, and, if operating as a corporation, income taxes. Estimate your Short-term Loans based on any cash shortages as indicated on line 19 of your "Cash Forecast." Enter the outstanding balances of any Long-term Loans and Long-term Leases, then add all the Current Liabilities and the Long-term Liabilities to get Total Liabilities, which should be subtracted from Total Assets to arrive at Owner's Equity. The back of the form provides space for quarterly estimates for the following two years.

Following the blank forms in this section are examples of the budgeting forms. They are filled out for a retail camera shop just about to open and include line-specific instructions. Examples begin on page 25-17.

SALES FORECAST

YEAR:

Sales By Source	Jan	Feb	Mar	Apr	May	Jun	Jul	Aug	Sep	Oct	Nov	Dec	TOTAL
Less: Returns													
Total Net Sales													

Year:

Sales By Source	1st Q	2nd Q	3rd Q	4th Q	TOTAL
Less: Returns					
Total Net Sales					

Year:

Sales By Source	1st Q	2nd Q	3rd Q	4th Q	TOTAL
Less: Returns					
Total Net Sales					

PROJECTED EXPENSE BUDGET & CAPITAL EXPENDITURES

YEAR: _____

Operating Expenses	Jan	Feb	Mar	Apr	May	Jun	Jul	Aug	Sep	Oct	Nov	Dec	TOTAL
Owner's Salary													
Staff Salaries													
Payroll Taxes													
Benefits													
Advertising													
Promotions													
Office Rent													
Accounting Services													
Legal Services													
Telephone													
Utilities													
Consultants													
Repairs													
Mail/Shipping													
Insurance													
Bank Charges													
Office Supplies													
Travel & Entertainment													
Licenses & Permits													
Dues & Subscriptions													
Total													

Capital Expenditures	Jan	Feb	Mar	Apr	May	Jun	Jul	Aug	Sep	Oct	Nov	Dec	TOTAL
Computer Equipment													
Furniture													
Store Fixtures													
Software													
Other Equipment													
Total													

PROJECTED EXPENSE BUDGET & CAPITAL EXPENDITURES

YEAR: _____

Operating Expenses	1st Q	2nd Q	3rd Q	4th Q	TOTAL	1st Q	2nd Q	3rd Q	4th Q	TOTAL
Owner's Salary										
Staff Salaries										
Payroll Taxes										
Benefits										
Advertising										
Promotions										
Office Rent										
Accounting Services										
Legal Services										
Telephone										
Utilities										
Consultants										
Repairs										
Mail/Shipping										
Insurance										
Bank Charges										
Office Supplies										
Travel & Entertainment										
Licenses & Permits										
Dues & Subscriptions										
_____										
_____										
_____										
Total										

Capital Expenditures	1st Q	2nd Q	3rd Q	4th Q	TOTAL	1st Q	2nd Q	3rd Q	4th Q	TOTAL
Computer Equipment										
Furniture										
Store Fixtures										
Software										
Other Equipment										
Total										

CASH FORECAST

⒝⒫

YEAR:

Receipts	Jan	Feb	Mar	Apr	May	Jun	Jul	Aug	Sep	Oct	Nov	Dec	TOTAL
1 Product Sales													
2 Professional Fees													
3 Other													
4 Other													
5 Other													
6 **TOTAL SOURCES** (add 1 through 5)													
Expenditures													
7 Operating Expenses (from Projected Expenses)													
8 Capital Purchases (from Capital Expen.)													
9 Tax Payments													
10 Other													
11 **Sub-Total** (add 7 through 10)													
Items Bought for Resale													
12 Finished Goods													
13 Materials													
14													
15													
16 **Sub-Total** (add 12 through 15)													
17 **TOTAL USES** (add 11 + 16)													
18 Net Cash (Operations) (subtract 6-17)													
19 Cash Invested/borrowed													
20 Beginning Cash Balance													
21 **Ending Cash Position** (add 18 through 20)													

CASH FORECAST

YEAR: _____

	1st Q	2nd Q	3rd Q	4th Q	TOTAL	1st Q	2nd Q	3rd Q	4th Q	TOTAL
Receipts										
1 Product Sales										
2 Professional Fees										
3 Other										
4 Other										
5 Other										
6 **TOTAL SOURCES** (add 1 through 5)										
Expenditures										
7 Operating Expenses (from Projected Expenses)										
8 Capital Purchases (from Capital Expen.)										
9 Tax Payments										
10 Other										
11 **Sub-Total** (add 7 through 10)										
Items Bought for Resale										
12 Finished Goods										
13 Materials										
14										
15										
16 **Sub-Total** (add 12 through 15)										
17 **TOTAL USES** (add 11 + 16)										
18 Net Cash (Operations) (subtract 6-17)										
19 Cash invested/borrowed										
20 Beginning Cash Balance										
21 **Ending Cash Position** (add 18 through 20)										

PROJECTED INCOME STATEMENT

YEAR:

	Jan	Feb	Mar	Apr	May	Jun	Jul	Aug	Sep	Oct	Nov	Dec	TOTAL
Revenue:													
Net Sales													
Other Revenue													
Total Revenue													
Cost of Goods Sold:													
Beginning Inventory													
Plus: Purchases													
Less: Ending Inventory													
Cost of Goods Sold													
Gross Margin													
Operating Expenses:													
Expenses from Budget													
Depreciation													
Other Expenses													
Other:													
Total Operating Expenses													
Operating Income													

Projected Income Statement

YEAR:

	1st Q	2nd Q	3rd Q	4th Q	TOTAL	1st Q	2nd Q	3rd Q	4th Q	TOTAL
Revenue:										
Net Sales										
Other Revenue										
Total Revenue										
Cost of Goods Sold:										
Beginning Inventory										
Plus: Purchases										
Less: Ending Inventory										
Cost of Goods Sold										
Gross Margin										
Operating Expenses:										
Expenses from Budget										
Depreciation										
Other Expenses										
Other:										
Total Operating Expenses										
Operating Income										

PROJECTED BALANCE SHEET

YEAR: _____

Assets	Jan	Feb	Mar	Apr	May	Jun	Jul	Aug	Sep	Oct	Nov	Dec	TOTAL
Current Assets:													
Cash													
Accounts Receivable													
Inventory													
Other													
Total Current Assets													
Fixed Assets:													
Equipment													
Vehicles													
Furniture & Fixtures													
Total Fixed Assets													
Less: Depreciation													
Net Fixed Assets													
Other Assets													
Total Assets													
Liabilities													
Current Liabilities:													
Accounts Payable													
Taxes Payable													
Short-Term Loans													
Total Current Liabilities													
Long-Term Liabilities:													
Long-Term Loans													
Long-Term Leases													
Total Long-Term Liabilities													
Owner's Equity													
Total Liabilities And Equity													

FINANCE

25-15

PROJECTED BALANCE SHEET

YEAR: _____

Assets	1st Q	2nd Q	3rd Q	4th Q	TOTAL	1st Q	2nd Q	3rd Q	4th Q	TOTAL
Current Assets:										
Cash										
Accounts Receivable										
Inventory										
Other										
Total Current Assets										
Fixed Assets:										
Equipment										
Vehicles										
Furniture & Fixtures										
Total Fixed Assets										
Less: Depreciation										
Net Fixed Assets										
Other Assets										
Total Assets										
Liabilities										
Current Liabilities:										
Accounts Payable										
Taxes Payable										
Short-Term Loans										
Total Current Liabilities										
Long-Term Liabilities:										
Long-Term Loans										
Long-Term Leases										
Total Long-Term Liabilities										
Owner's Equity										
Total Liabilities And Equity										

Sales By Source	Jan	Feb	Mar	Apr	May	Jun	Jul	Aug	Sep	Oct	Nov	Dec	TOTAL
Cameras	300	600	1200	1800	2500	3000	3500	4000	5000	5500	16000	13000	50400
Other Equip	200	400	800	1200	1500	2000	2000	2500	2500	2500	5000	6000	26600
Film	1000	1200	1500	2000	2200	2500	2700	3000	3200	3400	5000	6000	33700
Processing	1500	2000	1800	2000	2000	2500	3000	3400	3600	4000	4000	4000	33800
Misc.	0	100	250	350	500	500	500	500	500	700	700	700	5300
Less: Returns			-125	-125	-150	-156	-200	-200	-200	-200	-250	-250	-1850
Total Net Sales	3000	4300	5425	7225	8550	10350	11500	13200	14600	15900	24450	29450	147950

Year: _____

Sales By Source	1st Q	2nd Q	3rd Q	4th Q	TOTAL
Less: Returns					
Total Net Sales					

Year: _____

1st Q	2nd Q	3rd Q	4th Q	TOTAL

The holidays are a busy time for retailers. This should be reflected in your forecast.

People also stock up on items for their own use during the holidays

These monthly and annual totals transfer to the "Projected Income Statement."

Separate your sales into categories that are meaningful to you. Often each category will have a different peak sales period. This format allows you to forecast each of them individually.

PROJECTED EXPENSE BUDGET & CAPITAL EXPENDITURES — EXAMPLE   YEAR: 1992

Operating Expenses	Jan	Feb	Mar	Apr	May	Jun	Jul	Aug	Sep	Oct	Nov	Dec	TOTAL
Owner's Salary	1500	1500	1500	1500	1500	1500	1500	2000	2000	2000	2500	2500	17000
Staff Salaries	1500	1500	1500	2000	2000	2000	2000	2500	2500	2500	2500	3000	25500
Payroll Taxes	150	150	150	350	350	350	350	450	450	450	500	550	4250
Benefits	105	105	105	245	245	245	245	315	315	315	350	350	2975
Advertising	500	500	500	700	700	700	700	900	900	900	900	1100	9000
Promotions	300	300	300	300	300	300	300	400	400	400	400	300	4000
Office Rent	1000	1000	1000	1000	1000	1000	1000	1000	1000	1000	1000	1000	12000
Accounting Services	250	300	100	100	100	100	100	100	100	100	100	125	1375
Legal Services	200	300	100	100	75	75	75	75	75	75	75	75	1325
Telephone	50	50	75	75	100	100	100	100	100	100	100	150	1100
Utilities	75	75	75	75	75	75	75	75	75	75	75	75	900
Consultants	0	0	0	0	0	0	0	0	0	0	0	0	0
Repairs	50	50	50	50	50	50	50	50	50	50	50	75	525
Mail/Shipping	50	50	60	60	60	60	70	70	70	70	80	80	770
Insurance	65	65	65	65	65	65	65	65	65	65	65	65	780
Bank Charges	20	20	20	20	20	20	20	20	20	20	20	20	240
Office Supplies	125	15	50	50	100	100	100	100	100	100	100	75	1025
Travel & Entertainment	0	50	15	15	50	50	50	50	50	50	100	125	725
Licenses & Permits	50	50	50	50	50	50	50	50	50	50	50	50	600
Dues & Subscriptions	35	35	35	35	35	35	35	35	35	35	35	35	420
Other	500	300	200	200	200	200	200	200	200	200	206	306	2900
Interest					76	76	76	76	76	76	76	0	531
Total	5075	4615	4510	7050	7151	7151	7161	8631	8631	8631	9216	10116	87941

Capital Expenditures	Jan	Feb	Mar	Apr	May	Jun	Jul	Aug	Sep	Oct	Nov	Dec	TOTAL
Computer Equipment	3000												3000
Furniture	1000												1000
Store Fixtures	2000					1000							3000
Software	1500												1500
Other Equipment	1000								1000				2000
Total	8500					1000			1000				10500

Annotations (callout boxes):

- *(Owner's Salary)* This must be consistent with what your business can afford.
- *(Staff Salaries)* This is based on the staff needed to run the business. (see "Staffing Planner")
- *(Benefits)* These can be estimated on the "Benefit and Compensation Planner"
- *(Office Rent)* Estimated on the "Facility Planner"
- *(Insurance)* Estimated on the "Insurance Worksheet"
- *(Bank Charges)* Estimated on the "Bank Comparison Worksheet"
- *(Interest)* Interest is calculated from the amount of outstanding debt in any month. It is: (Annual Interest Rate ÷ 12) x Amount of Outstanding Debt
- *(Operating Total)* These monthly and annual totals transfer to the "Projected Income Statement" and the "Cash Forecast" (line 7)
- *(Capital Expenditures)* These are the purchase prices (including sales tax) of items needed to open your business. They come from the "Equipment and Supplies Needed Worksheet"
- *(Capital Total)* These monthly and annual totals transfer to the "Cash Forecast" (line 8)

PROJECTED INCOME STATEMENT — EXAMPLE   PhotoCentral   YEAR: 1992

	Jan	Feb	Mar	Apr	May	Jun	Jul	Aug	Sep	Oct	Nov	Dec	TOTAL
Revenue:													
Net Sales	3000	4300	5925	7225	8550	10350	11500	13200	14600	15900	24450	29450	147950
Other Revenue													0
Total Revenue	3000	4300	5425	7225	8550	10350	11500	13200	14600	15900	24450	29450	147950
Cost of Goods Sold:													
Beginning Inventory	0	14000	16500	19000	20500				23000	25000	28500	28500	0
Plus: Purchases	15000	4000	4000	4000	4000				8000	9000	9000	3000	74000
Less: Ending Inventory	14000	16500	19000	20600	21500				25000	28500	28500	21000	21000
Cost of Goods Sold	1000	1500	1500	2500	3000	5500	7500	8200	6000	5500	9000	10500	53000
Gross Margin	2000	2800	3925	4725	5500	6850	7500	8200	8600	10400	15450	18950	94950
						66%	65%	62%					
Operating Expenses:													
Expenses from Budget	5075	4625	4510	7050	7151	7151	7161	8631	8631	8631	9216	10110	87941
Depreciation	142	142	142	142	142	142	158	158	175	175	175	175	1883
Other Expenses													
Other:													
Total Operating Expenses	5217	4767	4652	7192	7293	7309	7319	8189	8806	8806	9391	10285	89824
Operating Income	-3217	-1967	-727	-2467	-1743	-459	181	-589	-206	1594	6059	8665	5126

Callout annotations:

These numbers come directly from the "Sales Forecast"

These numbers go to the "Cash Forecast" (line 1)

These numbers go to the "Cash Forecast" (line 12 and/or 13)

These numbers go to the "Projected Balance Sheet"

These numbers come directly from the "Projected Expense Budget"

This monthly depreciation is the total cost of currently owned equipment divided by 60. (e.g. for September it is: $10,500 ÷ 60 = $175) The cumulative amount of depreciation is used on the "Projected Balance Sheet"

Operating Income is the Gross Margin minus Total Operating Expense.

Your first month's purchases will come from the "Start-up Inventory Planner"

For planning purposes it is often easier (and almost as accurate) to use an industry or projected gross margin percentage to calculate your Cost of Goods Sold (see June, July, August). Be aware that the Gross Margin will often vary between product lines, in this example Cameras have fairly low margins, while film processing has high margins. As your product mix changes so will your Gross Margin.

CASH FORECAST — EXAMPLE

Photo Central   **YEAR: 1992**

Receipts	Jan	Feb	Mar	Apr	May	Jun	Jul	Aug	Sep	Oct	Nov	Dec	TOTAL
1 Product Sales	3000	4300	5425	7225	8550	10350	11500	13200	14600	15900	24450	29450	147950
2 Professional Fees													
3 Other													
4 Other													
5 Other													
6 TOTAL SOURCES (add 1 through 5)	3000	4300	5425	7225	8550	10350	11500	13200	14600	15900	24450	29450	147950
Expenditures													
7 Operating Expenses (from Projected Expenses)	5075	4625	4510	7050	7151	7151	7161	8631	8631	8631	9216	10110	87946
8 Capital Purchases (from Capital Expen.)	8500												10506
9 Tax Payments						1000			1000				
10 Other													
11 Sub-Total (add 7 through 10)	13575	4625	4510	7050	7151	8151	7161	8631	9631	8631	9216	10110	98441
Items Bought for Resale													
12 Finished Goods	15000	4000	4000	4000	4000	4000	5000	5000	8000	9000	9000	3000	74000
13 Materials													
14													
15													
16 Sub-Total (add 12 through 15)	15000	4000	4000	4000	4000	4000	5000	5000	8000	9000	9000	3000	74000
17 TOTAL USES (add 11 + 16)	28575	8625	8510	11050	11151	12151	12161	13631	17631	17631	18216	13110	172441
18 Net Cash (Operations) (subtract 6-17)	-25575	-4325	-3085	-3825	-2601	-1801	-661	-431	-3031	-1731	6234	16340	-24491
19 Cash invested/borrowed	40000				7000							-7000	40000
20 Beginning Cash Balance	0	14425	10100	7015	3190	7589	5788	5128	4697	1666	-65	6169	0
21 Ending Cash Position (add 18 through 20)	14425	10100	7015	3190	7589	5788	5128	4697	1666	-65	6169	15509	15509

Callout notes:

- These numbers come directly from the "Projected Income Statement"
- These come directly from the "Projected Expense Budget"
- Once the business is profitable this will be estimated according to the schedule in the "Federal Tax Calender"
- For simplicity, this comes from the "Projected Income Statement"
- This number (all monthly values) transfers to Cash on the "Projected Balance Sheet", it is how much you have in the bank.
- This is your monthly cash flow, negative numbers mean you expect to spend more than is coming in (common for start-ups)
- One month's Ending Cash Balance is the next month's Beginning Cash Balance.
- This is a short-term loan. In this case it is being used to build up inventory.
- This is your initial cash investment in your business. It is best determined *after* you have completed the Cash Forecast through Line 18 for all months; you will then be able to see how much cash is required to get going.

Callout annotations:
- This number comes from Line 21 of the "Cash Forecast"
- This number comes from the Ending Inventory line of the "Projected Income Statement"
- These numbers come from the bottom portion of "Projected Expense Budget & Capital Expenditures"
- This is the cumulative amount of Depreciation expense shown on the "Projected Income Statement"
- This is the short-term loan shown on line 19 of the "Cash Forecast"
- Owners Equity is equal to Total Assets minus Total Liabilities (36,603 - 7,000 = 29,603)

Assets	Jan	Feb	Mar	Apr	May	Jun	Jul	Aug	Sep	Oct	Nov	Dec	TOTAL
Current Assets:													
Cash	14425	10100	7015	3196	7589	5788	5128	4697	1666	-65	6169	15509	15509
Accounts Receivable													
Inventory	14000	16500	19000	20500	21500	22000	23000	23000	25000	28500	28500	21000	21000
Other													
Total Current Assets	28425	26600	26015	23690	29089	27788	28128	27697	26666	28435	34669	36509	36509
Fixed Assets:													
Equipment	5500	5500	5500	5500	5500	5500	5500	5500	6500	6500	6500	6500	6500
Vehicles													
Furniture & Fixtures	3000	3000	3000	3000	3000	4000	4000	4000	4000	4000	4000	4000	4000
Total Fixed Assets	8500	8500	8500	8500	8500	9500	9500	9500	10500	10500	10500	10500	10500
Less: Depreciation	142	283	425	561	708	867	1025	1183	1358	1533	1708	1883	1883
Net Fixed Assets	8358	8217	8075	7933	7792	8633	8475	8317	9142	8967	8792	8617	8617
Other Assets													
Total Assets	36783	34817	34090	31623	36881	36422	36603	36013	35808	37402	43461	45126	45126
Liabilities													
Current Liabilities:													
Accounts Payable													
Taxes Payable													
Short-Term Loans	0	0	0	0	7000	7000	7000	7000	7000	7000	7000	0	0
Total Current Liabilities	0	0	0	0	7000	7000	7000	7000	7000	7000	7000	0	0
Long-Term Liabilities:													
Long-Term Loans													
Long-Term Leases													
Total Long-Term Liabilities													
Owner's Equity	36783	34817	34090	31623	29881	29422	29603	29013	28808	30402	36461	45126	45126
Total Liabilities And Equity	36783	34817	34090	31623	36881	36422	36603	36013	35808	37402	43461	45126	45126

RESOURCES

Directory of Small Business Resources

Contacts

Accounting Corporation of America
3945 Camono Del Rio South, Suite L
San Diego, CA 92108
(619) 563-0535
Publishes studies of the operating ratios for various industry groups.

American Association of Equipment Lessors
1300 North 17th Street, Suite 1010
Arlington, VA 22209
(703) 527-8655
Makes referrals to lessors who provide an alternative to purchasing equipment.

American Association of Professional Consultants
9140 Ward Parkway
Kansas City, MO 64014
(816) 444-3500
Refers businesses to qualified consultants. Distributes books and tapes on consulting, and conducts seminars.

American Entrepreneurs Association
2392 Morse Avenue
Irvine, CA 92714
(714) 261-2325
(800) 421-2300 (free catalog)
Offers publications on specific small businesses.

American Federation of Small Business
407 S. Dearborn Street
Chicago, IL 60605
(312) 427-0207
Provides information on pending legislation and offers educational programs to its 25,000 members.

American Home Business Association
397 Post Road
Darien, CT 06820
(800) 433-6361
(203) 655-4380
Provides business information and services to business owners working from their homes.

American Management Association
135 W. 50th Street
New York, NY 10020
(212) 586-8100,
Offers meetings, publications and videos to businesses.

American Marketing Association
250 S. Wacker Drive
Chicago, IL 60606
(312) 648-0536
Publishes marketing information.

American Small Business Association
Box 612663
Dallas, TX 75261
(800) 227-1037
Supports legislation and conducts business education programs for its 50,000 members.

American Society of Independent Business
777 Main Street, Suite 1600
Ft. Worth, TX 76102
(817) 870-1880
Helps its 9,200 members obtain insurance coverage for their employees.

American Woman's Economic Development Corporation (AWED)
60 East 42nd Street
New York, NY 10165
(212) 692-9100
Have trained over 96,000 women to start and operate their own businesse

Applegate Group
P.O. Box 637
SunValley, CA 93153-0637
(818) 768-7081
Small business communication and consulting firm founded by syndicated columnist and author Jane Applegate. Provides strategic planning, resource matching. Nationwide network.

Association of Small Business Development Centers
1050 17th Street, NW, Suite 810
Washington, DC 20036
(202) 887-5599
Organization of state centers providing advice for those planning to start a new business.

Best Employers Association
4201 Birch Street
Newport Beach, CA 92660
(714) 756-1000
Provides managerial, economic, financial, and sales information to its 25,000 members.

Business Assistance Service
Office of Business Liaison
U.S. Department of Commerce
14th & Constitution, Room 5898-C
Washington, DC 20230
(202) 377-3176
Helps small businesses navigate the federal bureaucracy.

Business Coalition for Fair Competition
American Council of Independent Laboratories
1629 K Street, NW, Suite 400
Washington, DC 20006
(202) 887-5872
National coalition of trade associations and small firms experiencing unfair competition from nonprofit organizations or government entities.

Business Radio Network
888 Garden of the Gods Road
Colorado Springs, CO 80907
(719) 528-7040 / (800) 321-2468
Offers a list of nationally syndicated radio business shows by geographic location.

The Business Strategy Seminar
120 East 34th Street #15L
New York, NY 10016
(212) 481-7075
Support group system for entrepreneurs based upon the Mastermind Principle.

Center for Entrepreneurial Management
180 Varick Street
New York, NY 10014
(212) 633-0060
Provides publications, books, and tapes on starting, financing, and operating a small business to 3000 members.

Center for Entrepreneurship
Wichita State University
Box 147
Wichita, KS 67208
(316) 689-3000
Offers courses, seminars and workshops in entrepreneurship, also offers a Bachelor of Business Administration in Entrepreneurship. Publishes an informational guide to entrepreneurship.

Consultant's National Resource Center / Professional Management Institute
Box 430
Clear Spring, MD 21722
(301) 791-9332
Provides information for consultants and refers business owners to experts.

Consumer Information Center
Dept. 517K
Pueblo, CO 81009
Distributes a number of free and low cost government publications.

Council of Better Business Bureaus, Inc.
4200 Wilson Blvd., Suite 800
Arlington, VA 22203
(703) 276-0100
Maintains complaint records of numerous businesses, and also provide free and low cost publications.

Creative Communications, Inc.
1402 E. Skyline Drive
Madison, WI 53705
(608) 231-3070
Publishes Continent-wide Directory of Seminars and Workshops.

Customs Service Public Information Division
1301 Constitution Avenue
Washington, DC 20229
(202) 566-8195
Provides information on customs requirements by phone, mail, or fax.

Direct Marketing Association
11 West 42nd Street
New York, NY 10036
(212) 768-7277
Provides publications and workshops on various marketing and direct mail topics.

Dun & Bradstreet, Inc.
Dun's Analytical Services
1 Diamond Hill Road
Murray Hill, NJ 07974
(201) 665-5769
Publishes key business ratios for over 100 types of businesses. Available free on request.

Federal Trade Commission
Division of Legal & Public Records
Pennsylvania Avenue & 6th Street, NW
Washington, DC 20580
(202) 326-2000
Agency that regulates interstate commerce.

H.A.L.T.
1319 F Street, NW, Suite 300
Washington, DC 20004
(202) 347-9600
Non-profit group that promotes low-cost and self-help law.

Hobby Industry Association of America
319 E. 54th Street
Elmwood Park, NJ 07407
(201) 794-1133
Organization devoted to helping companies in the craft or hobby industry attain business success.

Insurance Information Institute
110 William Street
New York, NY 10038
(212) 669-9200
(800) 942-4242 (Business and consumer hotline)
Offers free publications and telephone advice on getting more insurance coverage for less.

Internal Revenue Service
Taxpayer Information and Education Branch
1111 Constitution Avenue, NW
Washington, DC 20274
(800) 829-1040 (Taxpayer hotline)
(800) 829-3676 (To request forms only)
Provides free information by phone, as well as publications, and forms.

International Association for Business Organizations
Box 30149
Baltimore, MD 21270
(301) 356-2163
Encourages joint marketing services and international trade assistance.

International Council for Small Business
St. Louis University
3674 Lindell Blvd.
St. Louis, MO 63108
(314) 658-3896
Helps members exchange ideas on the development and improvement of small business management.

International Franchise Association
1350 New York Avenue, Suite 900
Washington, DC 20005
(202) 628-8000
Trade organization that offers publications and seminars for its members.

International Venture Capital Institute Inc.
Box 1333
Stamford, CT 06904
(203) 323-3143
Organization of venture capital clubs. Directory of 115 venture capital clubs $9.95. Also publishes directory of Business Incubators.

Invention Management Program
Arthur D. Little Enterprises
25 Acorn Park
Cambridge, MA 02140
(617) 864-5770
For a percentage of royalties, this group guides inventions through the patent and marketing processes.

Manufacturers Agents National Association
23016 Mill Creek Road, P.O. Box 3467
Laguna Hills, CA 92654
(714) 859-4040
Organization of manufacturers' sales agents and manufacturers.

Meridian Learning Systems
P.O. Box 21293
El Sobrante, CA 94820-1293
(510) 669-9000
(800) 462-2699
Promotes small business; publishes self-help business materials, including "The New American Business System," for entrepreneurs and small business owners.

Minority Business Development Agency (MBDA)
14th & Constitution Avenues NW, Room 6711
Washington, DC 20230
(202) 377-1936
Provides management, marketing, financial, and technical assistance to minority businesses.

National Association for the Cottage Industry
Box 14850
Chicago, IL 60614
(312) 472-8116
Publishes a newsletter and resource guide for those who work at home; offers workshops and telephone support.

National Association for the Self-Employed
2324 Gravel Road
Ft. Worth, TX 76118
(800) 232-6273
Provides insurance, counseling, and publications for the self-employed.

National Association of Credit Management
8815 Centre Park Drive
Columbia, MD 21045
(301) 381-7411
Offers information on all aspects of business credit.

National Association of Home Based Businesses
Box 30220
Baltimore, MD 21270
(301) 363-3698
Organization of 3000 home based businesses.

National Assocation of Private Enterprise
Box 470397
Ft. Worth, TX 76147
(817) 870-1971
Helps its 80,000 members obtain information on better ways to operate businesses and benefit from group buying and insurance programs.

National Association of Small Business Investment Companies (NASBIC)
1156 15th Street, NW, Suite 1101
Washington, DC 20005
(202) 833-8230
(202) 775-9158 (Fax)
200 SBICs across the country licensed by the SBA to invest in small businesses. They may also make below-market rate loans. Directory $10.

National Association of Women Business Owners
600 South Federal Street
Chicago, IL 60605
(312) 922-0465
Offers networking and seminars to its 2800 members in 48 chapters.

National Business Incubation Association
One President Street
Athens, OH 45701
(614) 593-4331
National organization of 580 business incubator managers across the country. Incubators provide new businesses with below market-rate rental space, office equipment, and business and technical consultation.

NCR Corporation
Product Marketing
1700 S. Patterson Blvd.
Dayton, OH 45479
(513) 445-5000
Publishes studies of the costs of operating over 50 kinds of retail businesses.

National Federation of Independent Business
600 Maryland Avenue, SW, Suite 700
Washington, DC 20024
(202) 554-9000
Organization of over 500,000 independent businesses. Provides information to members and lobbies Congress on small business issues.

National Small Business United
1155 15th Street NW, Suite 710
Washington, DC 20005
(202) 293-8830
Provides a newsletter and seminars to over 50,000 members; lobbies Congress.

National Venture Capital Association
1655 N. Fort Meyer Drive, Suite 700
Arlington, VA 22209
(703) 528-4370
Organization of venture capitalists. Send a self-addressed 9" x 12" envelope with $1.90 postage to receive a list of their members.

Network of Small Businesses
5420 Mayfield Road, Suite 205
Lyndhurst, OH 44124
(216) 442-5600
Provides financing for business expansion, start-ups, inventors and innovators

Office of Small and Disadvantaged Business Utilization
(202) 377-3387
Helps small, disadvantaged, and women-owned businesses sell to the Dept. of Commerce.

Office of the U.S. Trade Representative
600 17th Street, NW
Washington, DC 20506
(202) 395-3230
Provides details of trade agreements with other countries.

Patent and Trademark Office
U.S. Dept. of Commerce
Washington, DC 20231
(703) 557-3881
Provides information and forms for patent and trademark protection. To receive a copy of any patent send $1.50 and the patent number.

Price Waterhouse
Growing and Middle Markets
1251 Avenue of the Americas, 34th Fl.
New York, NY 10020
(212) 489-8900
Publishes five financial guides for small businesses.

Procurement Automated Source System (PASS)
Small Business Administration
Box 9000
Melbourne, FL 32902
(800) 368-5855
Federal program to locate small and minority businesses for government contracts. Write for a free form to have your business put on their list.

Register of Copyrights
Library of Congress
Washington, DC 20559
(202) 287-9100
Provides information and forms for copyright protection.

Robert Morris Associates
1650 Market St. Suite 2300
Philadelphia, PA 19103
(215) 851-9100
Publishes ratios for over 200 lines of business.

SBA Management Assistance Publications
Box 15434
Ft. Worth, TX 76119
Publishes a variety of free and low cost publications on small business topics.

SBA Office of Small Business Loans
1441 L Street, NW
Washington, DC 20416
(202) 653-6570
Businesses that have been turned down by banks for business loans may be eligible for a loan which is 90% guaranteed by the SBA.

SBA Small Business Development Centers
(800) 368-5855
Provide educational seminars, conferences, and other resources from over 600 locations across the country. Call to find the location nearest you and to receive a calendar of events.

Seed Capital Network, Inc.
8905 Kingston Pike, Suite 12
Knoxville, TN 37923
(615) 573-4655
Matches entrepreneurs with investors who are looking for small business opportunities.

Service Corps of Retired Executives (SCORE)
409 3rd Street, SW
Washington, DC 20416
(202) 205-6762
Provides free counseling from retired executives at over 760 locations.

Small Business Administration (SBA)
409 3rd Street, SW
Washington, DC 20416
(202) 205-6623
(800) 368-5855 (SBA Answer Desk)
The SBA is the federal government's main source of assistance to small businesses. It provides loans, loan guarantees, publications, and workshops. It also provides counseling through its sponsorship of SCORE. There are field offices across the country.

Small Business Assistance Center
554 Main Street
Worcester, MA 01601
(508) 756-3513
Offers planning and strategy programs to aid its 35,000 members in starting, improving, or expanding small businesses.

Small Business Foundation of America
20 Park Plaza, Suite 438
Boston, MA 02116
(617) 350-5096
Charitable organization that raises funds for organizations and research on small business.

Small Business Alliance
Bank of America
Small Business Product Managements
Dept. 3670
One South Van Ness Avenue
San Francisco, CA 94103
(800) 662-5837
Provides an array of services and discount buying opportunities to small businesses.

Small Business Service Bureau, Inc.
544 Main Street
Worcester, MA 01601
(617) 756-3515
Provides assistance on cash flow, taxes, and management problems.

Superintendent of Documents
U.S. Government Printing Office
Washington, DC 20402
(202) 783-3238
Provides a number of free and low cost pamphlets on a number of topics.

Support Services Alliance
Box 130
Scoharie, NY 12157
(518) 295-7966
Provides group contracts and services for its 10,000 members.

Telecommunications Research & Action Center
Box 12038
Washington, DC 20005
(202) 462-2520
Evaluates long distance telephone service. Guide to carriers available for $5.

U.S. Association for Small Business and Entrepreneurs (USASBE)
905 University Avenue, Room 203
Madison, WI 53715
(608) 262-9982
Organization of educators and entrepreneurs interested in the development of small business.

United States Trademark Association
6 E. 45th Street
New York, NY 10017
(212) 986-5880
Answers questions about trademarks and offers publications and seminars.

Venture Capital Network
201 Vasser Street, rm W59-219
Cambridge, MA 02139
(617) 253-7163
(6170 258-7264 (Fax)
A non-proft clearinghouse to connect start-up, early stage and high growth companies with potential investors or strategic partners.

Working from Home Hotline
Box 5172
Santa Monica, CA 90405
(213) 399-2028
(900) 456-9675 (hotline)
Toll call for new homebased business opportunities, reviews, and resources.

Publications & Software

Books

Businesspersons' Guide to Taxation in the 90's, Harry Gordon Oliver II, El Dorado Press, 70 Santa Rita Ave., San Francisco, CA 94116, (415) 564-8418

The Check Is Not In The Mail, Leonard Sklar, Baroque Publishing, 744 Jacaranda, Hillsborough, CA 94010

Conceptual Selling, Robert B. Miller & Stephen E. Heiman, Warner Books & Miller-Heiman, Inc., 1990 N. California Blvd, Ste. 940, Walnut Creek, CA 94596.

Deciding to Go Public, Ernst & Young, 2000 National City Center, Cleveland, OH 44114.

The E Myth: Why Most Businesses Don't Work and What to Do About It, Michael E. Gerber, Ballinger Publishing Co., 54 Church Street, Cambridge, MA 02138.

Empire Building by Writing and Speaking, Gordon Burgett, Communication Unlimited, Box 1001, Carpinteria, CA 93013.

FormAides for Direct Response Marketing, Ad-Lib Publications, Box 1102, Fairfield, IA 52556, (515) 472-6617.

Guerrilla Marketing, Jay Conrad Levinson, Guerrilla Marketing International, Box 1336, Mill Valley, CA 94942, (415) 381-8361.

The Guide to Venture Capital Sources, Capital Publishing Corp., 10 South LaSalle Street, Chicago, IL 60603.

Homemade Money, Barbara Brabec, Betterway Publications, Inc., Box 219, Crozet, VA 22932.

How I Raised Myself from Failure to Success in Selling, Frank Bettger, Cornerstone Library, Simon & Schuster, New York, NY 10020.

How to Keep Score in Business, Robert Follett, Mentor, New American Library, Box 999, Bergenfield, NJ 07621.

How to Write a Winning Business Plan, Joseph R. Mancuso, Prentice-Hall/Simon & Schuster, New York, NY.

Marketing Without Advertising, Michael Phillips & Salli Rasberry, Nolo Press, 950 Parker Street, Berkeley, CA 94710.

MaxiMarketing, Stan Rapp & Tom Collins, McGraw-Hill Book Co., 1221 Avenue of the Americas, New York, NY 10020.

The New Venture Handbook, R.E. Merrill & H.D. Sedgewick, AMACOM, New York, NY.

National Directory of Addresses and Telephone Numbers®. Pacific Bell, Box 8075, Walnut Creek, CA 94596, (800) 848-8000.

Building A Profitable Business, Charles Chickadel & Greg Straughn, Meridian Learning Systems, P.O. Box 21293, El Sobrante, CA 94820-1293, (510) 669-9000, (800) 462-2699.

Running a One-Person Business, Whitmeyer, Rasberry & Phillips, TenSpeed Press, Berkeley, CA.

Secrets of Closing the Sale, Zig Ziglar, Fleming H. Revell Co., Old Tappan, NJ.

The Seven Laws of Money, Michael Phillips, Word Wheel and Random House, Menlo Park, CA and New York, NY.

The Small Business Bible, Paul Resnik, John Wiley & Sons, 605 Third Avenue, New York, NY 10158.

The Small-Business Resource Guide, Joseph R. Mancuso, Prentice-Hall/Simon & Schuster, New York, NY.

Small Business Sourcebook, Gale Research Co., Detroit, MI.

Small-Time Operator, Bernard Kamoroff, Bell Springs Publishing, Box 640, Laytonville, CA 95454.

Successful Direct Marketing Methods, Bob Stone, Crain Books, 740 Rush Street, Chicago, IL 60611.

The Think & Grow Rich Action Pack, Napoleon Hill, E.P. Dutton, 2 Park Avenue, New York, NY 10016.

The Unabashed Self-Promoter's Guide, Jeffrey Lant, Jeffrey Lant Associates, 50 Follen Street, Ste. 507, Cambridge, MA 02138, (617) 547-6372.

U.S. Industrial Outlook, Industry and Trade Administration, U.S. Department of Commerce, Washington, DC.

Working from Home, Paul & Sarah Edwards, Jeremy P. Tarcher, Inc., Los Angeles, CA 90069, (213) 273-3274.

Magazines, Newsletters

Business Week, McGraw-Hill, Inc., 1221 Avenue of the Americas, New York, NY 10020.

Consulting Opportunities Journal, Gapland, MD 21736.

Entrepreneur, 2392 Morse Avenue, Irvine, CA 92714, (800) 352-7449.

Entrepreneurial Woman, 2392 Morse Avenue, Irvine, CA 92714, (714) 261-2325.

Extra Income, Box 21957, Santa Barbara, CA 93120, (805) 569-1363.

Home Business Monthly, 38 Briarcliffe Road, Rochester, NY 14617.

Home Business News, Box 12221 Beaver Pike, Jackson, OH 45640.

Home Office Computing, 730 Broadway, New York, NY 10003.

Homeworking Mothers, Mother's Home Business Network, Box 423, East Meadow, NY 11554.

In Business, JG Press, Box 323, Emmaus, PA 18049.

Inc., 38 Commercial Wharf, Boston, MA 02110, (617) 227-4700.

Independent Business, 875 S. Westlake Blvd. #211, Westlake Village, CA 91361, (805) 496-6156.

National Home Business Report, Box 2137, Naperville, IL 60566.

Opportunity, 73 Spring Street, Ste. 303, New York, NY 10012, (212) 925-3180.

Small Business Success, Pacific Bell Directory, 101 Spear Street, Rm. 429, San Francisco, CA 94105, (800) 237-4769 in CA, or (800) 848-8000.

Success, 342 Madison Avenue, New York, NY 10173, (800) 234-7324.

Booklets, Pamphlets

Basic Facts About Patents (free), Commissioner of Patents and Trademarks, Washington, DC 20231.

Challenges of Managing a Small Business (free), Dun & Bradstreet, Business Credit Services, 1 Diamond Hill Road, Murray Hill, NJ 07974.

Directory of Federal and State Business Assistance: A Guide for New and Growing Companies (order # PB88-101977), U.S. Dept. of Commerce, National Technical Information Service, Springfield, VA 22161.

Various (Request list SBA 115A for free publications and list SBA 115B for publications for sale), Management Assistance Publications, SBA, Box 15434, Ft. Worth, TX 76119.

Various (write for catalog), Superintendent of Documents, U.S. Government Printing Office, Washington, DC 20402.

The Whole Work Catalog (free), The New Careers Center, 1515 23rd Street, Box 297-CT, Boulder, CO 80306, (303) 447-1087.

Software

Express Business Plan, Meridian Learning Systems, P.O. Box 21293, El Sobrante, CA 94820-1293, (510) 669-9000, (800) 462-2699.
A full-featured business planner with word-processor and spreadsheet capabilities built in.

Sales & Marketing Forecasting Toolkit, Tim Berry, Palo Alto Software, 260 Sheridan Avenue, Ste. 219, Palo Alto, CA 94306, (415) 325-3198 (IBM and Mac versions).

Up Your Cash Flow, Harvey Goldstein, Granville Publications Software, 10960 Wilshire Blvd. Ste. 826, Los Angeles, CA 90024, (213) 477-3924 (IBM version only)

INDEX

A

accelerated cost recovery   23-6
accountant   21-2
accounting   21-1
   accrual basis   21-1
   activity calendar   21-8
   alternatives   21-10
   cash basis   21-1
   chart of accounts   21-12
   period   21-2
   records   18-3, 21-8
   software   15-6, 21-10
   systems   21-10
accounts payable   21-3
accounts receivable   21-2
Accounts Receivable Journal with Aging   21-16
accounts receivable turnover,   21-7
accrual basis accounting   21-1, 23-3
acid test   21-7
administrative plan   2-5
advertising   6-5, 9-1, 9-2
   agency   9-3
   copy   9-3
   design   9-21
   graphics   9-3
   media   9-3, 9-8, 9-9
   response rate   9-7
   strategy   9-4
   tactics   9-3
Advertising Design Checklist   9-21
Advertising Media Comparison Guide   9-8, 9-9
Advertising Placement Planner   9-22
advertising plan   9-7
agents, sales   8-7
allowances, freight   10-3
angels (investors)   4-3
answering machine   11-3, 15-1
answering service   11-3
Apple Macintosh   15-4
application programs   15-3
assessment
   business   1-5
   self   1-2
assets   21-5
attitude   B-3
attorney   18-1
automobile tax deductions   23-3
average collection period   21-7

B

balance sheet   21-5
   forecast   25-3
bank
   choosing   22-1
   fees   22-1
   statements   22-4
Bank Account Reconciliation   22-6
Bank Comparison Worksheet   22-5
Basic Marketing Communications Checklist   9-27
benefits, product   7-2, 8-2, 10-1
bids, obtaining   12-2
billable hours   10-5
billing procedures   24-2, 24-3
bonding   16-6
bookkeeper   21-10
bookkeeping services   21-10
bootstrapping   4-2
break-even analysis   10-10
Break-Even Worksheet   10-17
brochures   9-17
broker   8-7
budgeting   25-1, 25-3
business
   agreements   18-2
   checkbook   20-2
   checking account   22-1
   failure   B-1, 4-1, 7-1, 24-1
   franchised   14-3
   identity   9-2, 9-16
   incubators   16-5
   location   16-1. *See also* location
   operations   14-1
   policies   14-1
   success   B-1, 1-1, 6-1, 6-6, 11-1, 19-1
business assessment   1-5
business card   9-17
Business Expense Report   23-11
business mileage   23-3
business name   9-16
   fictitious   3-1
business plan   2-1, 4-1, 4-5, 6-1
Business Plan Guide   2-3
business planning   5-3

Items listed in italics are the forms, worksheets and checklists contained in this manual.

C

calculator 15-2
cash 21-8
   expenditures 21-2
   forecast 25-2
   management 24-1
   receipts 21-2
cash basis accounting 21-1, 23-3
cash flow 15-7, 24-1
   forecasting 24-4
cash flow statement 21-6
Cash Forecast 25-11
cash register 15-2
catalog sales 9-6
Chamber of Commerce 8-9
Chart of Accounts 21-12
chart of accounts 21-2
check register 21-2, 22-3
checklists
   lists of iv
   uses A-1, 14-4
C.O.D. 12-4
collection agencies 24-3
collections 24-2
commission, sales 8-7, 8-8
competition 6-1, 10-3, 10-4, 10-7, 11-3
Competitor Review Worksheet 7-7
competitors 7-3, 8-5, 9-11, 16-2
complaints 11-2
computer 15-2, 15-3
   applications 15-3
   choosing 15-4
   components 15-3
   software 15-5
      accounting 15-6
      database 15-6
      desktop publishing 15-6
      spreadsheet 15-5
      word processing 15-5
consultant contracts 18-4
contests 9-1, 9-10
contingency plan 2-7
Contingency Planner 2-8
contract terms 18-4
contracts 18-2
cooperative mailings 9-10
copy machine 15-2
copyrights 18-5
corporation 3-2, 3-4
   foreign 3-2
   subchapter S 3-2, 3-4
   taxation 23-1
corporations A-5, 22-2, 23-1
cost of goods sold 21-5
coupon books 9-7
coupons 9-10

CPA *See* accountant
CPM 9-4
CPU 15-3
credit
   granting 24-1
   lines 22-2
   reference 22-4
   selling on 21-2
   terms 10-3
   trade 12-4, 24-4
credit cards 10-3, 11-3, 15-1, 16-6, 22-2, 22-3
current ratio 21-6
customer 6-4, 11-7
   complaints 11-2
   confidence 11-3
   contracts 18-2, 18-4
   ordering 11-3
   profile 9-5
   records 15-6, 21-2
   requests 11-2
Customer - Friendliness Worksheet 11-7
Customer Profile Worksheet 7-6
customer service 11-1, 11-7, 15-1
Customer Service Planning Guide 11-5
customers 6-5, 8-1, 10-1, 10-9, 11-1, 14-1,
        16-1, 19-1, 21-1, 24-1
   advertising to 9-1, 9-2
   dissatisfied 11-2
   identifying 7-1, 7-2, 7-3
   satisfied 11-2

D

Daily Sales Journal 21-13
Daily To Do List 5-8
database management 15-6
debt funding 4-2
debt to equity ratio 21-7
deductions 23-4
delinquent accounts 24-2
delivery 11-2
depreciation 21-5, 23-6
direct mail 9-2, 9-6, 9-9
disability taxes 19-6
discounts 6-4, 24-4
discrimination 19-4
disk drive 15-3
distribution 6-4, 7-2
   channels 8-6, 10-3
   retail 8-6
   wholesale 8-7
distributor contracts 18-4
distributors 8-7
diversification 6-3
document retention 20-1

E

Editor/Producer Checklist 9-15
editors 9-15
Effective Hiring Guide 19-15
Effective Networking Checklist 8-14
EIN 19-6
embezzlement 17-2
employee
    attendance records 19-6
    benefits 19-7, 19-13
    compensation 19-7
    discounts 19-8
    hiring 19-5
    manual 19-8
    termination 19-9
    theft 16-6
Employee Attendance History 19-25
Employee Compensation & Benefit Planner 19-13
Employee Information Form 19-16
Employee Payroll Register 19-24
Employee Timecard 19-23
employees 14-4, 16-2, 19-1
    finding 19-1
    hiring A-5
    interviewing 19-3
    training 5-5
employment agencies 19-2
Employment Application 19-17
employment applications 19-3, 19-5
Employment Eligibility Verification, Form I-9
    form 19-19
    information 19-6
equipment 15-1
    office 15-1
    purchase timing 23-6
    rental 15-7
Equipment & Supplies Needed Worksheet 15-9
Equipment List 15-10
equity
    funding 4-3, 4-5
    raising 4-5
evaluation 6-5
executive suites 16-5
expense accounts 19-8
expense forecast 25-2
expense ledger 21-3
expenses 10-5, 10-10

F

Facility Planner 16-3
factoring 4-3
fax machine 11-3, 15-2
feasibility study 7-1
features, product 10-1
Federal Tax Calendar 23-9

federal tax withholding 23-2
FICA (Social Security) 21-3, 23-2, 23-10
fictitious business name A-5, 3-1
fictitious name statement 22-2
FIFO 13-4, 23-3
filing systems 20-3
filing tips 20-4
financial
    forecasts 25-1
    plan 2-5
    planning 4-1
    ratios 21-6
    statements 21-4
fiscal tax year 23-3
fiscal year 21-4
fixed costs 10-10
flaws, business 1-6
flyers 9-7
forecast
    balance sheet 25-3
    cash 25-2
    equipment needs 25-2
    expenses 25-2
    income 25-3
    sales 25-2
    staffing 25-2
Form 1040 23-1
Form 1099 21-9
Form 941 21-3
forms, list of iv
fraud, credit card 22-3
FUTA (Federal Unemployment Tax) 23-2, 23-10

G

general partnership 3-1
goal setting 5-1
Goal Setting Worksheet 5-7
goals 5-1
    long-term 5-3
    short-term 5-3
Going Into Business Checklist A-5
goodwill 8-3
gross margin 21-3
gross profit 21-3

H

habits B-4
hardware, computer 15-3
health insurance 19-7
help-wanted ads 19-2
hiring employees A-5, 19-5
homebased business 16-4, 23-5
hourly rate 10-5

I

IBM 15-4
identity 9-1
  business 9-2, 9-16
income
  business 21-3. *See also* profit
  forecast 25-3
  ledger 21-2
  personal B-1, 1-4
income statement 21-4
income taxes 10-5, 10-6
incorporation 3-2
independent contractors 19-9
Industry Review Worksheet 7-8
inquiries 9-2
insurance 16-4, 17-1
  brokers 17-3
  deductibles 17-4
  disability 17-2
  health 17-2, 19-7
  key person 17-2
  liability 17-1
  premiums 17-4
  property damage 17-1
  replacement value 17-3
Insurance Worksheet 17-5
intellectual property 18-5, 18-6
inventory 12-1, 13-1, 21-8, 24-1, 24-4
  average 13-4
  control 15-2
  cost of 13-1
  excessive 24-3
  FIFO and LIFO accounting 13-4
  management 13-1, 13-2, 15-6
  physical 13-4
  records 13-3
  reorder point 13-1
  shrinkage 10-9
  standard order amount 13-1
  tax valuation 23-3
  turnover 13-2, 13-4, 21-7
  valuing 13-4
Inventory Control Card 13-8
Inventory Control Card (sample) 13-3
investors
  equity 4-3, 4-5
  private 4-5
Invoice 21-14
invoice 21-2
invoicing 24-3
IRS 13-5, 20-2
IRS Publication & Form Request 23-12

J

job description 19-2

K

key code 9-7
Key Tax & Regulatory Requirements 23-8
keystoning 10-8

L

late charge 24-2
lawsuits 18-2, 20-1
lawyer 18-1
leads, sales 8-9
lease
  business space 16-2, 16-3
leasing 4-2, 4-4, 15-7, 24-3, 24-4
ledger books 21-10
legal
  agreements 18-2
  contract terms 18-4
  fees 18-1
legal service plans 18-2
legal structure 3-1
Legal Structure Comparison 3-4
letterhead 9-17
leverage ratio 21-7
liabilities 21-5
liability insurance 17-1
LIFO 13-4, 23-3
limited partnership 3-3
list of forms, worksheets, and checklists iv
list prices 10-2
Loan Package Checklist 4-8
loans 18-3, 22-2
location 16-1
  business 16-1, 16-2
  executive suites 16-5
  Facility Planner 16-3
  home-based business 16-4
  rent 16-4
  retail store 8-6, 16-1
  shared space 16-5
logo 9-1, 9-17

M

MACRS 23-6
magazine
  advertising 9-5, 9-8, 9-9
  publicity 9-12, 9-13
mail order 9-6
management team 2-1
manufacturer's reps 8-8
mark down 10-9
market
  development 6-3
  penetration 6-3
  segments 6-1
market research 6-1, 7-1, 7-3
marketing 7-2
  communications 6-5, 9-1, 9-16
  mix 8-1
  plan 2-4, 6-1
  strategy 6-2, 9-2, 10-7
Marketing Communications Checklist 9-27
Marketing Plan 6-8
markup 10-8
  retail 8-6
maximum/minimum system, inventory 13-1

About the Authors

Charles Chickadel is the founder of Meridian Learning Systems and has been Chairman for six years. Having previously launched other businesses, including Trinity Press, Tomorrow Today Inc., and Fax Communications Inc., he wrote **Building A Profitable Business** so that new business owners could have a business start-up system that would help eliminate the worry, frustration, and wasted effort that he and many other entrepreneurs had to go through.

Charles is also an accomplished author whose publications have sold over three million copies. In addition to his books *Publish It Yourself* and *As You Think*, his *Health Is Wealth* series is used by thousands of corporations across America (including General Motors, AT&T, Johnson & Johnson, and USX) to keep their employees informed and motivated.

A popular speaker on business topics, Charles has a knack for simplifying complex topics so they are accessible to large numbers of people.

An Industrial Design graduate of San Francisco State University, Charles is married and resides in San Francisco.

Greg Straughn is President of Meridian Learning Systems. Prior to joining Meridian in 1989 he was Vice President and Chief Financial Officer of a major equipment leasing company. As one of two founders he planned and guided the growth of the company from start-up to over $10 million in annual revenue.

Greg has brought his knowledge of business systems, planning and finance from the corporate environment and adapted it to serve the needs of smaller organizations. He has used this experience in a variety of businesses he has run or consulted for, as well as during his tenure as Chairman of community organizations.

In his spare time, Greg is an avid scuba diver and pilot. In 1990 he received the Aircraft Owner and Pilot Association's Distinguished Pilot Award for his relief efforts following the 1989 San Francisco earthquake.

An honors graduate of the University of California at Berkeley in Finance, Greg is married, has two sons and a daughter, and lives in El Sobrante, California.

EXPRESS BUSINESS PLAN
The Step-by-Step Approach to Planning Your Business

Let Us Make It Easy For You

Express Business Plan™ will guide you, step-by-step, through the creation of your business plan. And you can do it <u>fast</u> by spending your time thinking about your business, not how to operate multiple software packages.

Everything You Need is Included

Unlike other business planners, with Express Business Plan you don't need any other software to create a professional-looking plan. Express Business Plan **contains** all the word processing power you need. And it **contains** all the spreadsheet power you need. It even has powerful financial tools to build projections based on assumptions you type in plain-English, not confusing formulas. Just install it and start writing.

Express Business Plan includes over 75 "Pop-Up" windows to prompt you about the issues you need to cover to have a complete business plan. No more staring at a blank screen!

Why Express Business Plan?

Whether this is your first plan or your tenth, Express Business Plan simplifies the development of your plan by:

- providing menus to access **all** major functions.
- raising **all** the questions an investor, or you as an astute business owner, will want addressed.
- giving you a simple financial model, and powerful financial tools, to create a full set of projections. The financials are fully-linked, integrated into the text, and do **not** require any other software to operate.
- documenting **all** your financial assumptions and giving you a plain-English report of them. You can easily change assumptions to do "what-if" analysis.
- providing OnLine Help to answer **all** your questions.
- giving you a fully-formatted business plan, including Cover Page, Table of Contents (created automatically), page numbering and full financial appendix.

System Requirements:
IBM PC/XT/AT, PS-2 or 100% compatible, Hard Disk, 640K RAM

Recommended but not required:
Mouse and color monitor.

(Cut here and mail bottom portion)

Name: _____

Business Name: _____

Address: _____

City: _____ State: _____ ZIP: _____ Phone: ( ) _____

Mail completed order form to:

Meridian Learning Systems
P.O. Box 21293
El Sobrante, CA 94820-1293
(510) 669-9000

Quantity	Description	Unit Cost	Price
	Express Business Plan	$99.95	

☐ Enclosed is my check for $ _____

☐ Please charge my: ☐ MasterCard ☐ VISA

Card number: _____

Expiration date: _____

Signature: _____

Sales Tax*

Shipping**

Total Order

* California residents add 8.25% sales tax
** Shipping and handling costs are $4.00 per unit

"This is the best that I have seen and would highly recommend it to all businesspeople I know."

Reginald G. Thompson
Thompson Funeral Homes

". . . especially liked the format; clear, concise, easy to follow and use. An excellent bargain that will do the job for the majority of small business owners."

Janice Durand
Wisconsin Small Business Development Center
Advisory Council

"I've been in business over 15 years, been a guest on 495 radio talk shows, and I still learned over a dozen new tips on marketing. No one should start a business without this at their side."

Joe Sabah, Consultant
Author of "How To Get The Job You Really Want"

". . . well-developed and would serve as a useful tool for those considering starting a new business."

SBDC Connection

"A practical, profound and deeply detailed new publication . . . a big help to those going into business for themselves in helping them not to be a failure, but a success. It's innovative and infinitely resourceful."

Broox Sledge
The Book World

"I see hundreds of books for the start-up business owner. This is by far the best and most comprehensive I have seen. It delivers what the others promise.

Josy Catoggai
University of Southern California

" . . . very complete and well organized. The layout is clear and easy to follow. The forms and worksheets lend much practical support, notably the *Going Into Business Checklist* which is crucial for start-ups, and the *Pricing Mini-Worksheets* will prove especially useful because many new business owners find pricing difficult."

Mark Michelman, Assistant Director
Illinois Institute for Entrepreneurship Education

". . . essential reading . . . a practical guide to starting – and staying – in business."

Jeff Rowe
The Orange County Register

"As a business consultant who deals with more than a thousand entrepreneurial businesses a year, I have long searched for a good business system for my clients. Now I have found it. It covers every question an entrepreneur needs to consider, and presents everything in a way that anyone can follow, which eliminates frustration. I recommend it unequivocally"

Kathi Elster
The Business Strategy Seminar

"I have read a number of publications on starting a business, and I can say that Building A Profitable Business is the most comprehensive I have ever seen. Even though I have had a successful business since 1977, I still found some of the material valuable enough to use in my business."

Scott Hauge, President
Small Business Network